Books are to be returned on or before
the last date below.

0415017610

The Ethnographic Imagination

Social scientists are realizing more and more the extent to which the work of 'scientists' in all disciplines is rhetorical, involving the persuasion of colleagues and students, and depending upon textual conventions. Sociological texts themselves are part of a set of traditions and conventions that are in turn part of our academic culture. *The Ethnographic Imagination* explains how one sociological tradition – the ethnographic – has been reflected and represented in its texts.

Paul Atkinson looks at selected sociological texts in the light of contemporary social theory and analyses how their arguments are constructed and illustrated. His discussion ranges widely, from classic ethnographies of the Chicago School up to contemporary monographs. Using a wealth of illustrations, he explores how ethnographic texts persuade their readers of the authenticity of their accounts; how they portray social actors as 'characters' and 'types'; and how they use narrative to convey social action, and to transmit implicit sociological theory.

Thorough and authoritative, *The Ethnographic Imagination* enables us to read sociological texts with new insight, based on a better understanding of how texts are constructed and how we read them. It will be required reading for all those interested in ethnographic research in sociology, anthropology, education, and the social sciences, and will also appeal to readers with an interest in the literary conventions of realism and factual accounts.

The Author

Paul Atkinson is Reader in Sociology and Head of the School of Social and Administrative Studies, University of Wales College of Cardiff. He is the author of *The Clinical Experience*, *Ethnography: Principles in Practice* (with Martyn Hammersley), and *Language, Structure and Reproduction*.

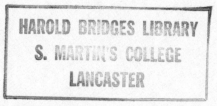

The Ethnographic Imagination
Textual constructions of reality

Paul Atkinson

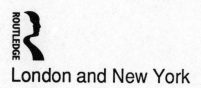

London and New York

First published 1990
by Routledge
11 New Fetter Lane, London EC4P 4EE

Simultaneously published in the USA and Canada
by Routledge
a division of Routledge, Chapman and Hall, Inc.
29 West 35th Street, New York, NY 10001

Reprinted 1991

© 1990 Paul Atkinson

Typeset by LaserScript Limited, Mitcham, Surrey
Printed in Great Britain by Mackays of Chatham PLC, Chatham, Kent

British Library Cataloguing in Publication Data

Atkinson, Paul
  The ethnographic imagination: textual constructions of reality.
  1. Sociology. Methodology
  I. Title
  301'.01'8

Library of Congress Cataloging in Publication Data

Atkinson, Paul.
  The ethnographic imagination: textual constructions of reality/ Paul Atkinson.
  p.   cm.
  Includes bibliographical references.
  1. Ethnology–Authorship.   I. Title.
  GN307.7.A85   1990   89–49330
  305.8–dc20   CIP

ISBN 0-415-05025-1
ISBN 0-415-01761-0 (pbk)

Contents

Preface

This book is an unusual contribution to sociology. It is not a 'methods' book, nor a 'theory' book, nor yet the report of a research project. It bears on all three, but because its subject-matter is relatively unfamiliar, this preface is intended to help the reader come to grips with it. Sociologists are not usually introspective, or self-conscious about what they read and write: they often lack the vocabulary required to reflect on their texts. In an earlier 'methods' book (Hammersley and Atkinson 1983) the argument was put forward that sociologists need to be self-consciously aware of what they are doing throughout the entire research process – from formulating a topic to completing the final report. This volume is a logical extension of that argument, focused on two aspects of sociology: how we read and how we write.

The idea behind this book is that sociologists should be more critically aware of how sociological texts are constructed by their authors. Books and articles do not just appear; they are the result of work undertaken by their authors. They are part of a set of traditions and conventions that are themselves part of our academic culture. This book is a detailed examination of how one sociological tradition – the ethnographic – has been reflected and represented in its texts. Once we understand more about how texts are constructed, and how we make sense of them when we read them, our whole appreciation of those texts is enhanced. We read with new insight. It is also possible that our own sociological writing may become more skilful and more persuasive, although that is not the prime purpose of the approach adopted here.

The reader may benefit from some guidance in approaching this book. For those with little or no acquaintance with the subject or the approach, the Introduction may seem rather dense and irksome. There I try to establish the nature of my self-appointed task. That very first chapter does not, therefore, present any worked examples of sociological texts. The reader who wishes to sample the analysis in action is therefore recommended to dip into one of the subsequent chapters and to return via the Introduction subsequently.

Acknowledgements

The completion of this book has been delayed by a number of circumstances, few of which seemed to be under my control at the time. Along the way, however, it has been helped by a number of people. I had the opportunity to reflect on the subject of the book while holding a visiting appointment at the University of California, Davis. There I taught a graduate seminar on 'The Poetics of Sociology', and I learned a great deal from the seminar members. In particular I wish to thank Bob Bunger, Karen Joe and Marilyn Reynolds: some of the material we worked on together appears from time to time in the course of the book. I am also grateful to all my friends and colleagues at Davis who helped to make my stay there such a productive one. If I single out John and Lyn Lofland, Andy Hiken, Debbie Paterniti and Patty Robinson, then I hope that the many others I remember with affection will not feel slighted.

As always, my work has benefited immeasurably from the support of Sara Delamont. Her sound judgement, sense of humour and critical acumen are indispensable. She should take no blame for the book's shortcomings, however.

The word-processing of various draft chapters has been made possible by the help of Irene Williams.

Chapter one

Introduction: ethnography as method and as genre

This book deals with 'ethnographic' work in sociology. It is not, however, a textbook of research methods. There are already plenty of books of that sort, and I have already contributed to that over-crowded niche of the market myself (Hammersley and Atkinson 1983). My specific concern will be with the *texts* produced from such research ('ethnographies'). Even in this limited sphere, my interest is not in passing on advice and prescriptions. The reader should not expect a manual on how to 'write up' his or her research. Of course, I hope that my colleagues and future students will be encouraged to reflect on what they write and how they write it. But this is not intended to be a book of practical advice. (On the contrary, it has been suggested to me that my own preoccupations make it harder for the aspiring ethnographer, not easier.) The reader is referred elsewhere for more practical advice on the writing of sociological accounts (for example, Becker 1986).

Social scientists are not much given to thinking about writing – except to the extent that students and practitioners often complain that it is hard work. Readers who are not social scientists are occasionally more sensitive; but all too often critiques of social-scientific writing remain at the 'impenetrable jargon' level. Rarely have sociologists or their critics engaged with the serious task of assessing how sociological arguments are constructed or how evidence is assembled in sociological texts. The purpose of this book is to examine how just one variety of sociology is written. I shall argue that there are good reasons for paying serious attention to modes of sociological writing, and that the ethnographic genre is of special interest.

I shall also argue that attention to the 'literary' or 'rhetorical' features of sociological texts in no way undermines their scholarly credibility and status. It would be all too easy for the unsympathetic or careless reader to assume that 'literary' or 'rhetorical' forms and values were incompatible with 'science'. Therefore, it might be assumed, a book of this sort, which emphasizes the parallels between sociology and literature, weakens sociology's case for serious attention. Nothing could be further from my intentions. A recognition of the rhetorical forms that run through *all* scholarly and scientific discourse can only strengthen the awareness and *discipline* of our academic endeavours.

1

Sociologists, like most scholars in human and cultural disciplines, are – in one sense – used to paying close attention to the texts of their subject. The writings of influential forebears are accorded special, almost sacred, status. They are repeatedly subject to detailed reading, re-reading and exegesis. Such doctrinal reverence does not often result in the sort of textual analysis to be advocated in this book, however. When a contemporary sociologist inspects a work by Marx, Weber, Durkheim, or some other luminary, then he or she is normally concerned with the determination of its 'meaning' – by reconstructing its theory, tracing its antecedents, putting it in historical context, assessing its influence. For the most part, however, sociologists have been less interested in *how* sociological texts 'mean' what they do. But sociologists should surely be concerned with how they construct and convey their arguments: not only in relation to historical and theoretical texts, but also in terms of how the 'facts' and 'findings' of sociological research are conveyed in monographs and research papers. For these are not matters of neutral report: the conventions of text and rhetoric are among the ways in which reality is *constructed*.

When we read an ethnographic monograph – say, *Street Corner Society* (Whyte 1981) – we are implicated in complex processes of reality construction and reconstruction. That book, with all its vivid and realistic descriptive writing, is not a literal representation of the social situation of Italian-American street-corner gang members. Whyte's craft resides not just in the conscientious and careful collection of data, and their arrangement into a factual report. The monograph itself is, in the best sense, an artful product. The narratives and descriptions, the examples, the characters and the interpretative commentary are woven together in a highly contrived product. The world we enter into, as readers, is not a direct experience of 'street corner society'; we are engaged in the interpretation of the society-as-reconstructed, and that reconstruction is coded or inscribed in Whyte's text. Moreover, the book does not – cannot – totally determine how we as readers will interpret it. We read, and read into, the text, based on our own background knowledge and assumptions. Those latter include our competence as readers of sociological works. We bring to the work our knowledge and sympathy (or lack of it) for the ethnographic style of writing, as well as a host of barely articulated cultural capacities.

The role of explicit sociological 'theory' is a relatively minor part in the overall act of communication between Whyte and his readers. What is conveyed is dependent upon implicit textual phenomena: the textual formats, the rhetorical figures, the choice of descriptive vocabulary, the selection of illustrative materials. These are all elements within a context of *persuasion*. Over and above any propositional content and the 'conclusions' or 'findings' to be presented, the ethnographic text depends upon the *plausibility* of its account. (This does not detract from its scholarly status or merit. As we shall see, even the most 'scientific' of accounts depends upon rhetorical, persuasive features.)

How, then, could a sociologist fail to find such a topic engaging and challenging? If the scope of sociology includes the understanding of inter-subjective communication and social actors' methods of reality-construction, then surely the methods of textual persuasion fall within that scope. Likewise, if we regard sociology's task as including critical reflection on its own methods, then that will appropriately imply an understanding of our textual, rhetorical methods. By the same token, studying the poetics of sociology extends the scope of textual studies. (By 'poetics' here is meant the study of conventions whereby the texts themselves are constructed and interpreted. There is no implication that the writing is 'poetic' in the everyday sense of the word.) There is no need to confine the study of poetics to domains which are normally thought of as 'artistic': novels, plays, poems. To do so would be an unnecessary restriction on the scope of poetics as a discipline.

The title of this book is, of course, a conceit. It is a direct reference to two classics of modern sociology: *The Sociological Imagination* (Mills 1959) and *The Social Construction of Reality* (Berger and Luckmann 1966). Although it may be hubris to invoke such eminent forebears, it is done with a specific intention. First, it is intended to convey the degree to which the book is about other works of sociology. It does not just use other sociological texts as a resource in reporting or constructing sociological work, as all contributions to the discipline do. Rather, it is about sociological texts: they are both resource and topic. Second, it refers to the theme of Mills' famous work: that is, the *craft* of the sociologist. This book too reflects on one aspect of intellectual craftsmanship. It concentrates on how sociological texts and arguments are constructed. Third, it relates to the argument of Berger and Luckmann. Where they addressed the interpersonal construction of social reality I shall be concerned with the textual construction of social (and sociological) reality.

The scope of the work

There is a modest limitation to this enterprise. This book is about just one genre of sociological texts. No attempt will be made to cover all of sociology. The scope would be vast, and such an exercise could easily founder in diffuse generalizations. Rather, the argument will focus exclusively on the writing and reading of *ethnographies*. The term 'ethnography' refers to a research style, and to the written product of that research activity. This book will be concerned primarily with the latter, although the two are so intimately related that reference to methodology will be inevitable.

Overall, however, this is emphatically not a textbook of sociological research methods. No attempt will be made to prescribe procedures of data collection and analysis. Here I have no interest in recommending ethnographic research methods over other approaches to sociological work. I shall concentrate on how sociologists of a particular persuasion, following a collection of methods and conventions, have written their accounts of society and how they can be read. This is not an exercise in the evaluation of sociological writing. It is proverbial that many sociologists write poorly; and in all conscience a great many do contrive to enshrine their work in execrable prose. As a matter of fact I do not think that the books and papers to be discussed here display the worst characteristics of sociological style. Some of them are, by any criteria, well-crafted products. Few, if any, could lay claim to great 'literary' merit, although I shall argue that they share many features with more literary counterparts. But aesthetic judgements, while not altogether irrelevant, are not the main purpose, and they would be premature if they prevented us examining *how* sociologists present their work and represent aspects of society. It is not the case any more that the novel is the medium through which our society represents itself. We have many media, genres and modes through which we encounter the collective representations of our own cultures. Sociology is one of them, and the ethnographic genre is one of the many ways in which cultural representation has been accomplished throughout this century.

For the purposes of this exercise sociological texts will be the main focus. For the most part, the parallel – and even richer – genre of social (or cultural) anthropology will be discussed only in passing. This decision reflects a number of criteria. The aim of the book is not to explore and contrast a range of genres of social scientific writing. There is a valuable task to the done along those lines in the near future. The various categories which include the anthropological monograph, the community study, the urban ethnography, the social exploration or exposé, the work of 'Mass Observation' – these and their characteristic styles of reportage deserve comparative treatment along the lines to be sketched here. Moreover, social anthropological texts have recently been subjected to scrutiny by a number of scholars. That work will be referred to in due course. Sociological writing, with a few exceptions, remains under-analysed. So a start needs to be made, and for the sake of simplicity I concentrate on just one tradition of work. For all that, the potential field of study is broad. Ethnographies with clear methodological and textual affinities have been conducted for over sixty years, in Britain, North America and elsewhere, on a diverse range of topics from the most mundane to the most exotic or bizarre. In what follows it will be impossible to cover the entire field. The treatment of even so restricted a genre will necessarily be a selective one. In this I have not relied upon specific 'sampling' procedures: the identification of texts in this way is unnecessarily limiting and in any case presupposes that the relevant characteristics of the corpus are known in advance. The study is exploratory, and the salient features of even this one restricted genre are yet to be discerned.

I have therefore adopted a more frankly personal and impressionistic approach. I deal with texts which reflect a diversity of subject-matter, include well-known and firmly established classics together with some less well-known ones, and refer to British and American authors. The texts chosen at least illustrate a range of textual strategies and conventions. No claim may be entered that the treatment is in any sense exhaustive, however. An analysis such as this demands a degree of selectivity. Unless a restricted corpus of texts is considered, then the project becomes unwieldy, and the resulting text itself unreadable. The genre of ethnography is too broad for detailed textual examination; it covers a diverse range of materials, incorporating different disciplinary perspectives. The texts for detailed treatment in the book will therefore be drawn from a rather restricted universe. The criteria for selection have been as follows. The inclusion of sociological texts which deal primarily with topics in urban sociology; this in turn excludes anthropological studies – especially those dealing with 'exotic' other cultures. The tradition of rural 'community studies' (a rich vein in the British ethnographic tradition) has also been relegated. Likewise, ethnographic studies of organizational settings (schools, hospitals and the like) have not been included. Works from British and American authors have been included: there has been considerable influence in both directions across the Atlantic. Work from the earlier decades of this century as well as recent texts have been included. Ethnography is not a static genre, and there have been more or less self-conscious attempts to change and innovate within it. There have also been strong traditions and continuities.

These decisions are necessarily arbitrary: they are imposed in the interest of ensuring a relatively well-bounded and coherent corpus. Even so, they yield a quite sufficient range of styles and subject-matter to suit the analytic purpose. There has, however, been no systematic attempt to 'sample' the literature according to a pre-defined set of criteria. Some attempt has been made to balance well-known, even 'classic', ethnographies with examples which will probably be less well-known, and the criteria listed above have been kept in mind. I have treated this as an exploratory exercise, however, and have felt free to use whatever comes to hand in developing the ideas. No claim is entered for a comprehensive coverage of the field; no formal models or typologies will be derived.

From time to time it may appear that some fairly familiar ground is being covered, and perhaps that some rather hackneyed examples are being trotted out. To some extent that is inevitable. Unlike the writers of many comparable works in literary criticism, one cannot reasonably assume either that one's reader *has* read the relevant materials, or at least *should* have done so. There can be no prior assumption that potential readers of this book will be familiar with the genre to be discussed. For that reason alone, some rather pedestrian observations about the texts in question may sometimes be in order. For the same reason, fairly extensive quotation of passages must be relied on. For the most part the analysis proceeds through a detailed reading of passages from a few works, rather than a sort of survey of a broader – and perhaps more representative – selection.

There is a price for such selectivity. There is clearly a bias inherent in the subject-matter, partly reflecting a more general bias towards the deviant, the marginal, the disreputable. Public settings and relationships are represented rather more than the domestic and the intimate. The worlds that are portrayed tend to be local: the cosmopolitan is missing. These biases are not happenstance. The ways in which sociologists represent social worlds, and the ways in which they study them, are closely related. These biases are thoroughly characteristic of the sociological ethnography as method and as genre.

The significance of texts

Literary and sociological scholars have come to pay increasing attention to the significance of texts and of discourse in the constitution of literary and social domains or realities. The analytic perspectives that are brought to bear differ, but in their various ways they reflect the 'linguistic turn' in the human sciences. This tendency has led to varieties of 'discourse' analysis, structuralism, post-structuralism and deconstructive criticism. On the one hand the critical theorists have become preoccupied with the linguistic foundations of textual semiotics and the critical consequences of such awareness. The emphasis has been on the *text*, conceived as an arrangement of signs and codes, and on *reading* or the reception of the text. While the gaze of the theorist is, in one sense, narrowed to a very close, or slow deconstruction of the literary artefact, the scope of inspiration and sources has been broadened, to incorporate a wide range of philosophical, anthropological, psychoanalytic and linguistic theories. As Culler puts it:

> Whatever their effects on interpretation, works of literary theory are closely and vitally related to other writings within a domain, as yet unnamed but often called 'theory' for short. This domain is not 'literary theory', since many of its most interesting works do not explicitly address literature. It is not 'philosophy' in the current sense of the term, since it includes Saussure, Marx, Freud, Erving Goffman, and Jacques Lacan, as well as Hegel, Nietzsche, and Hans-Georg Gadamer.
>
> (Culler 1983, p.8)

To the outside observer it may sometimes appear that contemporary critical theorists are more concerned with exegesis and doctrinal disputes of these more or less abstruse theories than with the exploration of texts themselves. None the less, critical theorists' interest in textual conventions has led them towards a general view which parallels sociological-cum-anthropological preoccupations with socially shared conventions and codes. Culler's passing reference to Goffman is illustrative of this *rapprochement*.

At the same time sociologists have become increasingly sensitive to the cultural significance of spoken and written accounts, texts, and the nature of 'discourse' in the production and reproduction of social forms. Again, the sources and perspectives are diverse: structuralism, phenomenology, ethnomethodology and their derived schools are among the inspirations. They do not combine to make a single paradigm, much less orthodoxy, but do direct our attention to the conventions whereby our (re)presentations of the world are embodied in practices of speech and writing. Whether their roots lie in Wittgenstein and linguistic philosophy, Saussure and structuralist semiotics or Garfinkel and ethnomethodology these contemporary perspectives urgently demand that sociologists pay close attention to their own textual practices, as well as those of the people they study.

Contemporary critical theory and contemporary sociological perspectives are parallel in a self-conscious awareness of *reflexivity*, with special reference to the work of texts. In principle, the notion of reflexivity recognizes that texts do not simply and transparently report an independent order of reality. Rather, the texts themselves are implicated in the work of reality-construction. This principle applies not only to the spoken and written texts that are produced and interpreted by social actors, but to the texts of social analysts as well. From this point of view, therefore, there is no possibility of a neutral text. The text – the research paper or the monograph, say – is just as much an artefact of convention and contrivance as is any other cultural product. The critical theorist cannot lay bare the conventions of the texts that he or she dissects without simultaneously exposing the conventionality of his or her own textual products. The sociologist who takes seriously the textual production of social reality cannot feign blindness to the conventional character of sociological argument itself.

There is, therefore, a goodly stretch of common ground between the literary theorist and the sociological analyst. No doubt that ground is rough and broken. *Rapprochement* between the two is far from straightforward; and neither side is homogeneous. None the less, there is ample scope for suggesting that the sociologist may learn much about sociological practice by the reflexive application of critical insights to the discipline's texts. Likewise, the scope of critical theory may fruitfully be extended by its application to the domain of sociological writing.

This, then, is the terrain to be explored. No sustained attempt will be made to represent and review all the potentially relevant theoretical perspectives. Here is not the place to seek a comprehensive review of interpretive or hermeneutic sociology, much less of contemporary critical theory. Rather, each will be drawn on eclectically in order to illuminate the main substantive theme: how ethnographies achieve their representations of social/sociological reality. I suspect that the book will thus offend purists of various persuasions. I am aware of the differing, even competing, epistemologies that lie behind contrasting positions in this highly complex intellectual field. I shall try not to gloss over incompatible positions in too cavalier a fashion. On the other hand, I am not convinced that any current paradigm or would-be paradigm can claim sufficiently to cover the field to the exclusion of all others. An unashamedly eclectic approach has therefore been adopted. Further, a good many of the critical perspectives which will be employed and alluded to seem to me to be unduly obscurantist and convoluted. While seeking to avoid an excessively philistine, empiricist or commonsense perspective, I shall try to avoid the more scholastic disputes and epistemological niceties. At the outset I confess a sympathy with the more 'domesticated' versions of contemporary literary theory, often associated with British exponents, than with their more florid versions. To a considerable extent this goes for the sociology too. I have little sympathy for the extremes of theoretical enthusiasm and disputation. This book will be based on a number of general perspectives on sociology, but not tightly bound to any narrow definition of its proper task and conduct.

In various ways, therefore, the book will draw on perspectives normally associated with differing paradigms. The aim will not be to deny the validity of such contrasts altogether, but rather to exploit such differences, by the juxtaposition of contrasting perspectives. In particular, the difference between a 'humanistic' version of sociology, focused or centred on the social actor as 'subject', and the non-subjective theory of textual meaning will be exploited. Indeed, it will be argued that the ethnography itself is a genre which is held, paradoxically suspended, between the humanistic and the sociological, the subjective and the non-subjective. A close reading of the texts will deconstruct them in the revelation of this paradox.

In referring to the ethnographic as a genre I make little claim in relation to the literary theory of mode and genre. The identification of genre and the construction of typologies and genealogies of literary types is by no means straightforward. The criteria whereby genres might be classified are variable and change over time. It would be unwise to assume that any genre, literary or otherwise, can be unequivocally and unambiguously identified for all time and for all purposes. Genres are not identified by unique criteria. It clearly makes practical sense to identify such literary classifications as 'fantasy', 'metafiction', 'science fiction', 'realism', 'romance' and the like. Types may be describable in terms of subject-matter, textual organization, stylistic conventions and so on. For the 'everyday' reader and the critical analyst alike, generic features and marks are sensitizing devices. They permit the reader to establish a framework of expectations, and to read the text in accordance with an available stock of knowledge and conventions. As Fowler (1982) argues, the notion of genre is of little value in a purely classificatory sense, but has a function in 'communication'. The recognition or imputation of genre provides the interpretative 'horizon' (Fowler 1982, p.359) for the construction and reception of a text.

When an 'ethnographic genre' is referred to here, therefore, it should not be taken to imply that there is a unique and homogeneous corpus of sociological texts which share a closed set of common features. On the contrary, it will be readily apparent that ethnographies share conventions with other textual types. Some of those are common with literary modes, such as realist and metafictional novels. Others are shared with other 'factual' genres, such as history, biography and scientific reports. For some purposes it will prove necessary to deny the boundaries of generic difference – or at least to transgress the taken-for-granted thresholds: the distinctions between 'fact' and 'fiction', 'literary' and 'non-literary' modes are certainly part of our interpretative horizons. We should not assume that there are absolute differences in how texts are actually constructed

In other words, for the person who is 'literate' in social-scientific terms it seems to 'make sense' to talk in terms of an ethnographic genre. We should not expect to find that this expectation reflected a hard-and-fast set of topics and treatments. We should reasonably expect, however, to find family resemblances in the organization of ethnographic texts and that there are features of style which relate to schools or tendencies in theory and method.

All scholarly or 'scientific' work must be written and read in accordance with some generic principles. There is no style-less or organization-less writing. The 'facts' of the case do not imprint themselves. Our experience of the world, both physical and cultural, is always mediated by conventions of enquiry, and that experience is equally mediated by conventions of writing. The ethnography is constituted by one collection of conventions, the paper in a scientific journal by another. The products themselves are very different in form and content, but are equally conventional.

We tend to be familiar with a particular range of textual types which are treated as appropriate for the reportage of scholarly and factual work. We need to remind ourselves from time to time that there is a measure of arbitrariness in this array of texts and types. They are not the only ways in which 'facts', 'findings', 'theories', 'speculations' and so on might be written. Indeed, there have at other times been genres which were regarded by their authors and contemporary readers as perfectly proper vehicles for comparable messages. Today, for instance, we are unlikely to think of the 'dialogue' as a proper vehicle for most scholarly writing. Yet at other times, the dialogue form has been employed quite 'naturally' as a mode of instruction.

It is therefore necessary to perform the equivalent of a 'phenomenological reduction'; that is, to step back and bracket or suspend our taken-for-granted assumptions about how 'facts' and 'realities' come to be represented as they are in our monographs and papers. It must be emphasized at the outset that such an exercise is not intended to remedy shortcomings or to propose wholesale changes. An awareness of convention does allow us to consider alternatives and how things might be otherwise. Our allegiance to existing formats may blind us to other possibilities, which may turn out to offer benefits. Certainly, one of the arguments of this book is that some of the generic models and conventions sit uncomfortably with some of the stated assumptions of ethnographers themselves. The prime purpose of this work is interpretative rather than normative, however. That is, I am concerned primarily with the discovery of sociologists' methods for doing sociology rather than trying to prescribe those or other methods.

In the chapters that follow I shall therefore discuss a number of related themes that bear directly on the construction of ethnographic texts. The separate aspects to be covered all contribute to the production and reading of an 'authoritative' text; that is, a text that lays claim to a certain status – it claims authenticity and authority; it claims to be factual and to represent an actual social world, peopled by real social actors. The sociological arguments that such texts convey are largely developed through their construction of plausible social worlds. The next two chapters establish the view that *all* authoritative accounts depend upon rhetorical features in order to persuade the reader of their factual nature and to construct their arguments. The first of those two chapters considers sociological and anthropological texts in general, before the specifically ethnographic genre is explored.

Chapter two

Ethnography and the poetics of sociology

Sociology is a rhetorical activity. That is not an original observation, although the exploration of the poetics of sociology is at an early stage of development. It may be that a relative neglect of such features of sociological argument reflects sociology's recurrent *Angst* concerning its own status. The historical relations between the literary and the sociological have not been unproblematic (Lepenies 1988). Although sociologists agonize over the 'scientific' standing of their activities and products, they may be reluctant to acknowledge any possible affinities with the aesthetic. For everyday commonsense tends to make a radical distinction between two opposed clusters of values: at one extreme, 'facts', 'objectivity', 'science', 'measurement', 'exactitude', and at the other 'art', 'subjectivity', 'discursive', 'aesthetic'. Such a duality may well be taken to imply that the values of reading and writing, of method and evaluation, are diametrically opposed as between the two camps. The scholar who aims at the 'factual' exploration of the social or natural world may thus eschew any reflection which appeals to aesthetic values. Art is extended readily into 'artifice', with all its connotations of spuriousness, misleading appearances, the suspect or straightforwardly bogus.

If anyone were to adopt such a perspective, then they would be guilty of gross over-simplification. Certainly sociologists, of all people, cannot allow themselves to be hoodwinked by uncritical everyday prejudices. 'Science' is itself a rhetorical activity, and the scholarly and the literary share common conventions in the production and reception of their texts. The rhetoric of 'scientific' and other scholarly accounts will be explored in detail in the next chapter. The reflective social scientist, therefore, should be more than willing to explore the textual features of sociology itself – and anthropology, psychology and the other social disciplines for that matter.

Sociology is as inescapably rhetorical a discipline as it is a moral discipline, and for much the same reasons. The texts of sociology – its papers and monographs – are predicated upon the texts of everyday life. The discourse of sociology is not identical to that of everyday life, but it cannot escape the poetics of everyday life. There is no other realm of language to which the sociologists can escape. There is no scholarly nirvana which is untouched by mundane discourse, or our aesthetic or moral appreciation of the texts of the life-world. Unless the sociologist is to lapse into meaningless solipsism and a 'private language' then he or she must engage in communicative acts with hearers or readers. Willy-nilly the lecturer or author will have *effects* upon recipients – of persuading them of the existence of facts and winning them to a point of view (or failing to do so), of surprising or shocking them, or amusing them, annoying, mystifying or puzzling them, boring or exciting them. Readers of sociological texts will find themselves convinced or incredulous, engaged and intrigued or repelled and alienated; they will judge the text and its author correspondingly.

Now the writer of a text and the reader of it do not have to be conscious of such processes for their effects to be real. Nor do they have to be aware of the rhetorical features which contribute to such effects. In attempting to draw attention to them one need not appeal to an intentionalist fallacy by assuming that all the possible literary effects are consciously attended to by the author. By the same token we need not assume that the reader's response is *constrained* by the text. On the other hand, it would be a quite unnecessary excess to abandon the search for rhetorical patterns and devices in texts, or to assume that they have nothing to do with authors' meanings or readers' interpretations.

A consideration of texts is formally equivalent to any disciplined study of language use. We know full well that a hearer's understanding of an utterance is not coterminous with a speaker's intentions; and we know that an utterance's, or sentence's capacity for signification goes beyond a 'speaker's' meaning or any particular 'hearing'. But that does not mean that there is nothing to be learned concerning language and meaning from a consideration of its formal properties (from phonetics to discourse structure). Likewise, a consideration of texts can identify their formal properties without therefore implying that these are always and everywhere interpreted in an identical fashion. A text may have significant properties without always being interpreted in the same way.

When the sociologist produces a text, then he or she is inescapably drawing on a stock of cultural codes and conventions. The text itself will be of a particular type, or for a particular purpose (essay, thesis, journal article, research report, monograph) and will in turn imply an audience (peers in a specialized field, students of the discipline, even 'the general reader'). With varying degrees of conscious control over the process, the sociologist will draw on the appropriate 'literary' conventions to construct a plausible and comprehensible text. (I do not wish to imply that such efforts are always successful. Some sociological texts are, by any criteria, inept and unreadable. For some bizarre reason, some sociologists seem almost to revel in producing repellent texts.)

These considerations apply to all sociologists, but it is especially true of the author who seeks to produce and disseminate qualitative work such as ethnography. For the genre of the ethnographic text is closely implicated in its methodological and epistemological warrants. The ethnography is especially dependent upon discursive formats to inform and persuade the reader. Hence the ethnographer's reliance upon rhetorical formats is especially pertinent. Since the sociologist is enjoined to engage in reflective, self-conscious awareness of his or her own social actions *qua* sociologist, then an explicit awareness of the rhetorical forms and features of sociological writing must be a key element in sociological work.

A reading of qualitative sociology

A particularly telling – if slightly sideways – perspective on the rhetorical and aesthetic features of sociological work is provided by Lofland (1974). Lofland writes with the experience of a journal editor who solicits and evaluates readers' references. This particular process of 'peer review' is especially telling, as the journal's referees are participating in a process whereby their reception of a given text, prior to publication, is rendered explicit (though not public). Lofland's contribution is based on an analysis of referees' comments on papers reporting qualitative research, and his general expertise in the area. While his remarks bear on more than just this issue, it is clear from Lofland's paper that content and style are inextricably intertwined in readers' receptions and reports. The reader of qualitative research cannot proceed 'as if' there were a neutral textual format independently of the scientific message to be conveyed. Lofland himself comments on this, noting that there is a division within sociology when it comes to styles of reporting:

> At one extreme, practitioners of laboratory and experimental work share a highly routinized set of working procedures and schemes for reporting research. Drawing from physical science models of inquiry perhaps facilitates their achieving such consensus. The stylistic and organizational features of their publications reproduce the stylistic and organizational features of physical science journals in particularly striking fashion. While not nearly as shared and codified, demographic and survey practitioners still draw upon a rather consensual pool of research strategies, technical steps, and standardized conceptions of the structure and content of their research reports. Moreover, one even senses a high degree of working agreement among library researchers who employ bodies of historical and substantive materials.
>
> (Lofland 1974, p.101)

In contrast, Lofland suggests a *relative* lack of consensus among those who report qualitative research findings:

> qualitative field research seems distinct in the degree to which its practitioners lack a public, shared, and codified conception of how what they do is done, and how what they report should be formulated.
>
> (Lofland 1974, p.101)

Of course, as Lofland himself acknowledges, the uniformity of the more clearly 'positivistic' styles is itself a textual achievement – a matter of organization and style. As will be argued in a later chapter, even the most 'scientific' of products, the scientific paper, is readable in that way precisely by virtue of certain shared stylistic features. The very uniformity of some scholarly genres reflects and reinforces the presumption of a single, unified scientific method applicable to an invariant world of natural or social facts.

For all that they *are* dependent on rhetorical formats, the more 'scientific' of texts allow the reader to make some distinction between the content and the form of any given text. The consensual reliance on shared conventions may allow rhetoric to be overlooked. As Lofland argues, however, the diversity of ethnographic texts, coupled with their characteristically discursive formats, means that their reception depends very largely on the various interrelationships of content and form – of 'findings' and 'formats'.

Lofland's argument need not detain us in detail here. He suggests a typology of responses that readers make: all are in various ways implied in textual matters. First, there is the criterion involved by readers which reflects the degree to which 'The report was organized by means of a *generic* conceptual framework' (pp.1–2). This refers to the extent to which a particular topic or setting is 'framed' according to more general themes. Such themes are used not simply as explicit sociological theory, but as more general articulating themes, images and devices. Lofland's own examples are ample illustration:

> The on-going daily relationships between milkmen and their customers is framed as an instance of a cultivated relationship.
>
> (Bigus 1972)

> The on-going daily relationship between teachers and children in a nursery school is framed as an instance of guided options management strategy.
>
> (Dixon 1972)

> The activities of a welfare office were framed as an instance of symbolic bureaucracy.
>
> (Jacobs 1969)

> The stages through which the relationship between a visibly handicapped person and a physically normal person may move are framed as an instance of deviance disavowal.
>
> (Davis 1972)

Interestingly, Lofland suggests that referees can predict the presence of a generic frame from the opening sentences of the report. He cites the opening of the Bigus paper as an instance of the successful deployment of such an introductory framing passage:

> America is a service society – so much so that essentially non-service institutions, such as stores, take on service-like characteristics....This emphasis on service has given rise to a preponderance of a particular kind of social activity, which I shall refer to as 'cultivating', and to an associated kind of social relationship which I will refer to as a 'cultivated relationship'.
>
> (Bigus 1972, p.131)

Here, then, Lofland draws attention to – though does not himself elaborate on – some very important features in such texts. The sort of 'framework' is read at the outset of the paper, and provides the reader with an initial attitude from which the significance of the paper is foreshadowed and projected. Openings like this have the function of persuading the sympathetic reader that the report addresses 'real' or 'important' themes *and* that the specific example to be explored is a relevant one.

Lofland goes on to suggest that readers who positively evaluate a 'generic' frame will find unsatisfactory reports which do not use organizational motifs of that sort. He refers, amongst others, to the 'Then they do this' style, whereby a report is organized so that it 'makes evident that participants do many kinds of things over and over, hour to hour, day to day, week to week'. Interestingly, Lofland notes that a text can – as it were – 'get away with' such an organizational format provided that the setting is sufficiently 'exotic': otherwise readers will allege that the text is merely based on 'cute', 'interesting', 'startling', or 'exotic' descriptive content.

Lofland details other types of evaluative criteria invoked by readers of research reports. Readers may seek a 'novel frame'; or when absolute freshness is impossible, then a 'slightly late' frame may be employed – that is, somebody else's recent novelty. As Lofland says:

> In recent years, the frames of Erving Goffman have been applied with particular assiduousness. Researchers report: yes, mental hospitals are total institutions; yes, this or that category of deviant experiences stigma; yes, inmates do use 'making-out' devices. Slightly more novel, look over here, public housing has characteristics of total institutions.
>
> (Lofland 1974, pp.105-6)

Readers, Lofland reports, find such second-hand novelties acceptable up to a point, but beyond that point the 'frame' starts to lose its novelty value, and the readers are likely to condemn the text as a dreary repetition.

At the other end of the spectrum, there is the 'intro text style':

> notions that are 'common knowledge' in American society or that sociologists can find in elementary textbooks will likely be defined as 'obvious'. Few qualitative field reports discover such introductory textbook frames as socialization, norms, deviance, social control, culture or informal organization.
>
> (p.106)

What is at stake here is the degree to which such things may be assumed to be 'common knowledge' on the part of the reader. The successful text, it would appear, is neither so 'novel' as to be *outré*, nor so familiar as to seem hackneyed. Moreover, as Lofland indicates, a successful textual arrangement should be adequately elaborated and enriched. First, the analytic frame should be 'elaborated' – it should be couched in a text which 'specifies consistent elements of the frame, draws out implications, shows major variations, and uses all these as the means by which the qualitative data are organized and presented'. Further, for many readers, it should be 'eventful' – richly endowed with 'concrete interactional events, incidents, occurrences, episodes, scenes and happenings someplace in the real world'. (Lofland's listing here is self-referential.) On the other hand, it should not be over-burdened with the repetitious rehearsal of incidents and illustrations. Otherwise, it may topple over into the failing of being 'hyper-eventful'. A final set of evaluative criteria is closely related: the analytic frame and the qualitative data it comments on should be 'interpenetrated' if the text is to be judged satisfactory.

> taken separately, each is likely to be viewed as having little sociological interest or merit....The frame taken separately is dull because the reader has little conception of the concrete empirical reality to which the frame might refer. The 'data' alone are dull because the reader has no notion of what sort of social structure or process might be involved. But interpenetrated through minute and continual alternation between data and frame-elements the whole is more than the parts.
>
> (Lofland 1974, pp.108–9)

These by no means exhaust Lofland's observations, and his are not exhaustive of the textual arrangements of qualitative sociology: if they were this book would stop here, or run the risk of having absolutely no novelty. They are not reproduced here in order to build a prescriptive set of recipes to aid novice sociologists to organize material and publish their work (useful through Lofland is for such purposes). Rather, my interest in them derives from the insight provided into readers' *receptions* of sociological texts, and hence into the significant features of those texts.

The importance of textual arrangements

The most general issue to emerge from Lofland's informal content-analysis is the importance of textual arrangements themselves. The text has a given force or effect which is not based simply on some evaluation of whether it is 'correct' or not. Indeed, it is difficult to think how *any* written or spoken text could convey 'facts' or 'findings', let alone analyses, hypotheses, conjectures, criticisms and refutations without recourse to conventionally appropriate textual formats. In the reader's evaluative readings, then, form and content are inextricably linked. The text cannot simply transcribe or report, but it must also persuade. The reader must be drawn into its own frame of reference, and come to share the perspectives of the text; it must be found plausible and engaging, arresting or novel; it must establish relations of identity and difference with other equivalent texts; it must establish relations of similarity and difference with the social world it reports. It needs to reproduce a recognizable world of concrete detail, but not appear to be a mere recapitulation of it.

15

In all these ways – and others – the sociological text deploys rhetorical or textual devices. Indeed, sociological texts in general are inescapably rhetorical. Whether they adopt an explicitly exhortatory tone, or purport merely to report neutral 'facts', they rely upon devices of persuasion to construct plausible accounts, striking contrasts, historical inevitabilities; to link data into convincing sequences of cause and effect; to embed theory into data and vice versa.

So far, Lofland's analysis of readers' receptions is indicative of a general orientation – the importance of textual organization – but does little to illuminate the fine grain of sociology's rhetorical organizations. Yet the text is organized at many levels – from the general strategy of overall arrangements down to the most detailed minutiae of language use. It is at this latter level that much of the argument of sociological texts is conveyed. We need to be aware that there are 'analyses' conveyed in the text in *implicit* as well as explicit ways; and often the two interact in complex ways. Anderson (1978) has drawn attention to some features relevant to the 'production of a plausible text':

> If sociological reasoning shares the characteristics of commonsense reasoning, then it may be that sociologists also use conversational sequence, commonsense collections and interactional and presentational resources to go about their business of understanding each other and judging each other's work. Some of these resources are displayed in sociological texts. Our work suggests that the sociological reader produces at least some of whatever order and plausibility he finds through his use of presented and situated features such as pairs, lists, titles and heading so that a consideration of the accomplishment of plausibility should take the literary context of that accomplishment very seriously both in practice and in principle.
>
> (Anderson 1978, p.116)

Anderson's full analysis is based on the sampling of sociological works, and the published paper on a detailed reading of just one of them (Hamblin 1974), a study which Anderson himself refers to as 'anthropological' in character. The paper is substantially devoted to a close reading of the opening passages of this paper. Anderson suggests that from the very outset, with the title ('The Counsellor and Alienated Youth') and the abstract, the paper establishes a framework of expectations for the reader: implicit directions as to how the paper is to be read are suggested to the competent reader.

For instance, basing his argument on ethnomethodological commentaries on reading, Anderson speculates on how readers can read into the title alone much more than is stated in so many words:

> In the title in question the two substantives 'Counsellor' and 'Youth' repair each other in a way totally unprovided for by the grammatical understanding of conjunction. In one sense 'Alienated' modifies 'Counsellor' more than 'Youth'. Alienation is a problem and a trouble as we all know: counsellors are in the problem business in that people with problems do and should go to

counsellors. Youth can also be troublesome but is not so necessarily or totally. Further, counsellors are routinely accredited people for deciding that others are alienated but not for aging them. The juxtaposition of 'alienation' and 'counsellor' produces an orientation to the diagnosis and/or solution of alienation as the preferred matter at hand. The youth of the people is not *brought* into question. Titles such as the above title are not sentences and may make no grammatical sense. Yet they abound. Readers do make sense of them by finding the conjunctive link; they then use that link as a topic guide.

(Anderson 1978, p.121)

Here, then, Anderson suggests that the paper's title functions like a newspaper headline, an abbreviated juxtaposition of lexical items, the import of which depends upon the reader 'filling in' a projected story on the basis of commonsense attributes and activities. On the basis of such an initial interpretation, therefore, readers can find themselves under implicit instructions to expect and search out a collection of topics, types and orientations. In an academic paper, of the sort described by Anderson, this work is continued in the 'Abstract' (if there is one). Again, it orients the reader, providing guidelines for a 'reasonable' way of reading the paper – of 'framing' it – and hence contributing to the overall plausibility of the paper itself.

Anderson also suggests that the plausibility of the paper he analyses depends on the work done by the reader in evaluating the 'authority' of the author – and by the text in documenting such authority. In the Hamblin paper, for example, Anderson identifies the following self-displays by the author as someone with the authority of knowledge about the matters in hand:

(a) Through explicit claims, for example, 'The individuals I have been privileged to work with during the last four years....

(b) Through repeatedly doing classifications of materials that 'could' only be done by someone who had extra knowledge (unless we are to attribute characteristics out of keeping with trust) for example 'Such individuals....'

(c) Through grammatical classification of self into 'external' states like counsellor rather than incidental activities 'some conversations I remember'.

(d) Through privileged access to 'person' states both of others...but more crucially here to self.

(Anderson 1978, pp.130–1)

In ways such as these, Anderson argues, the text presents itself as the work of an author 'with extra knowledge in the subcategories of knowledge of more instances, more occasions, more depth, more regularity and more theoreticity' (p.131).

Furthermore, the plausibility of the text, in Anderson's treatment, is provided by displays of coherence and homogeneity. The text collects contexts under the auspices of categories. If the reader is to find the plausibility of the work sustained, then, the author must establish that the various elements of the work are 'about the same thing':

> If we are to see him as having deep and regular access into a series, he must display seriality. He must present the studied population as a discriminated one and not *some* people. He must display the events as containing the same ingredient, in this case, the same problem (alienation).
>
> (Anderson 1978, p.131)

Finally, Anderson discusses how a text is 'invested with purpose' – that is, the construction of order in the text; as an 'analysis' of the sociological problem, by displays of the purposeful and reasonable motivation of actors even (or especially) when action might appear senseless, chaotic or idiosyncratic in the absence of the account. In the Hamblin text, for example, the attributes of 'alienated' youths are projected as those of 'intelligent' persons, and as consistent with their intelligence.

Anderson's is by no means an exhaustive treatment of all the themes and issues. His detailed analysis of just one brief sociological text (though it reflects his own work on a larger collection of examples on 'youth') shows how fruitful such fine-grained analysis can be. He argues convincingly that the paper persuades the reader into a frame of reference whereby the reader may sympathetically 'fill in' the things which render it coherent. The authoritative text establishes its status and its relationship with an audience through textual or rhetorical devices. It establishes a privileged stance towards the 'facts' or evidence presented by its imposition of a textual order – through the selection of elements and their arrangement into lists of similar or contrasting elements; into projections of cause-and-effect, or rational ends-and-means. The text itself is 'packaged' and prefaced by such items as a title and an abstract which alert the reader to more than just the text's referential contents and functions: they sensitize readers and provide instructions for the act of reading itself. For the most part, Anderson draws attention to rhetorical, but 'literal' uses of language. That is, he concentrates primarily on devices of *ordering* in the text (contrasts and collections, for instance). Sociology is, however, replete with more rhetorical tropes, or figures of speech, through which the import and effect of its arguments are conveyed.

The aesthetics and the rhetoric of sociology

Hitherto we have had two monograph-length treatments of the rhetoric or poetics of sociology. Brown (1977) and Edmondson (1984) have each made substantial contributions to this field of enquiry. Their approaches are complementary. Brown pays relatively little explicit attention to modern critical or rhetorical theory in developing a very broad appreciation of sociological texts. Edmondson, on the other hand, uses the technical apparatus of classical rhetoric to examine selected sociological texts in greater detail.

Brown's general thesis is that an appreciation of the aesthetic dimension of sociological knowledge is an important way of understanding that knowledge. He argues for a 'cognitive aesthetics' as a way of reconciling the 'artistic' and the 'scientific'. From Brown's perspective, the aesthetic is not opposed to the rational: 'For cognitive aesthetics, both science *and* art are rational in that they both presuppose various criteria of economy, congruence and consistency, elegance, originality, and scope' (p.3). His ambition is considerable. Whereas others – myself included – are content to map the textual conventions of works and genres, Brown wants to propose an aesthetic approach that will provide a metatheoretical framework for assessing *all* approaches. The recurrent problems and antinomies of sociological epistemology are thus to be recast and reconciled under the rubric of cognitive aesthetics.

The argument rests on the exploration of a number of major tropes and textual devices over a wide range of sociological works. He begins with 'point of view', an elementary critical concept which, as Brown himself remarks, is so general as to have 'no necessary relation to any particular genre, or even to what is conventionally known as art' (p.52). He follows through the classic formulations of Simmel, Park and Stonequist the perspective of the 'outsider' or 'stranger' and the 'marginal man' in characterizing the point of view of the sociologist as the observer poised between intimacy and distance: 'The participant side of participant-observation thus affords nearness, while the observer side lends farness. The two combine through aesthetic distance in a relationship between intimate sociological strangers' (p.55). That 'distance' between observer and observed is elaborated by Brown in commentary on Garfinkel, Goffman and others, including Malinowski. Brown also examines how the relative position of the sociologist *vis-à-vis* the 'observed' is represented, and how sociological texts represent the 'points of view' of the actors reported there. Brown suggests that this is particularly demanding for the sociological author:

> The chief materials for this structuring activity are the relationships between the observer's point of view and those of the people on whom he reports. In a novel, for example, the author's command of his characters' thoughts and actions allows him to create material suitable to the manner in which he desires to report it. The characters can be shaped to fit the author's style and genre. But for the sociologist, the characters have much more of a life of their own and, hence, a greater tension exists between what is observed and the manner in which it will be conveyed.
>
> (Brown 1977, p.58)

To begin with, Brown refers us to Oscar Lewis, not simply for his self-consciously literary style, but also for Lewis's use of a 'multiple perspective' technique. He reports the experiences of his informants as a series of 'autobiographical' accounts in texts like *Five Families* (Lewis 1959). Here, Brown proposes, the voice of the anthropologist and the voice of the informant blend:

19

Because the style is indirect, the reader and author have it both ways. If the reader is sympathetic with the implicit ideology, he will ease himself into the author's chair and impute a 'rightness' to the mixture of author's comments and characters' thoughts. But if the reader is unsympathetic, he will accuse the anthropologist of lacking 'objectivity', of mixing commentary and text.

(Brown 1977, p.60)

While Brown mentions this specifically in relation to Lewis's particular style, the same or similar remarks and reader responses may reasonably be made about all ethnographic writing.

Brown develops his analysis of 'point of view' by considering the authorial stance of the sociologist-as-author. He shows how authorial omniscience is adopted as the 'basic stance', but then the author may invoke any of several representational modes, which allow for the development of different perspectives. Drawing on Macauley and Lanning (1964) Brown outlines several strategies that are open to the author of the sociological monograph:

1 He can make selective use of a number of individual points of view, borrowing a specific character's angle of vision when it suits his purpose.

2 He can use the theatre of 'showing not telling', for the moment presenting a quite objective look at things.

3 He can analyze anything about the story by use of critical comment and generalization....

4 He can take a panoramic view of events, giving an account of simultaneous happenings or disassociated scenes that a narrator-agent could cover only by the use of most improbable devices.

5 He can discover multiple traits and facets of characters (or cultures) under study readily and plausibly without having to work things around to bring any single point of view within discovery range.

(Macauley and Lanning 1964, pp.111–12 in Brown 1977, pp.61-2)

Brown suggests that as sociologists have developed their various strategies in reporting their work, they have differentially distanced themselves from their subject-matter. Early Chicago sociologists like Anderson or Zorbaugh are described as 'under-distanced', becoming too closely involved with their topics. Brown cites the following passages from Anderson, Zorbaugh and Hayner – all representatives of the Chicago School of the 1920s:

Jungle populations are ever changing....Here is one place where every man's past is his own secret....The hobo is his own housewife. He not only cooks...but has invented dishes that are peculiar to jungle life. Chief among these is 'mulligan stew'. Moreover the art of telling a story is diligently cultivated by the 'bos' in the assemblies about the fire.

(Anderson 1923, pp.18-20)

The rooming house which has replaced the boarding house is a very different sort of place to live. One comes and goes as one wishes, does very much as one pleases, and as long as one disturbs no one else, no questions are asked.... It was at the 'Y' that I had my first acquaintance with that most pitiful figure of the rooming house – the old and unmarried woman who works. They were conspicuous in either the cafeteria or the upstairs sittingroom, because of their loneliness – eating lunch at the solitary table, sitting by themselves knitting, with shabby and unbecoming clothes, care-worn faces, and toil-worn hands. I was to learn later some of the tragedies their mute lips harbored.

(Zorbaugh 1929, pp.73,75,77)

One may be ill and die without producing a ripple on the surface of the common life.

(Hayner 1929, p.113)

Attention is drawn to the writers' focus on the here-and-now; the local situation; the first-person 'shock of recognition'; the use of 'member speech'; the 'graphic, sentimental images'; the 'placing of the reader in the midst of the action'. All these textual elements, Brown contends, create no distance between what is observed and the reader's response to it. The texts may be highly successful in persuading the reader to adopt a particular perspective, identifying with the observer and the observed, vicariously entering into the 'social world' of the hobo, the rooming house or the hotel. However, Brown is not concerned with such matters, being more preoccupied with criticizing the writers for their 'over-rapport' (cf. Miller 1952). He contrasts this point of view with the over-distanced perspective of a Talcott Parsons.

Brown goes on to examine how the relative 'superiority', 'equality' or 'inferiority' of the author is represented by the reportage of speech in the texts. In general terms, he suggests:

Generally, the more authoritative the stance of the author, the less the leeway between truth and falsehood, between good and bad, will remain in the reported speech. The 'what' of speech will be separated from its qualifying 'why' and 'how' – at least as they might be understood by the speaker. Equivocality of the speaker's context will be prohibited from the text, and the author's context will have been purged of ambiguity before the reported speech is placed in it.

(Brown 1977, p.66)

He suggests that the 'superior' style of reportage will be favoured by positivists. It generates a 'one-dimensional' and depersonalized text. At the opposite extreme is what Brown calls a 'pictorial' or 'humanistic' style, as exemplified in the work of Oscar Lewis. Here the text incorporates the subjects' speech and the author's commentary to interpenetrate in complex ways. Brown thus concludes that there is a direct relationship between modes of textual representation and the 'distance' between sociologists and their subjects. There is, therefore, an intimate connection between the author's style and the mode of 'authority' implicitly claimed on behalf of the reported research.

Brown also explores the role of metaphor. He reminds us that the social sciences are permeated with metaphorical usages. Brown is interested in defending and advocating metaphor in the context of 'cognitive aesthetics', arguing that the search for 'literal' uses of language, implied by at least some versions of positivism, is unrealistic and misleading. The failure to recognize the metaphorical character of 'scientific' language leads one to mistake the proper nature of theories, models and representations. Not all sociological metaphors are equally apt or equally successful. Brown goes so far as to propose that great theorists have been 'great' precisely 'because he saw how material that he researched directly could be metaphoric of a larger, more important domain' (p.102). The translation from the local or specific to the larger, theoretical or ideological domain is a metaphorical operation. As Brown himself suggests, the relationship between 'Middletown' or 'Yankee City' (a British author might have instanced Banbury or Bethnal Green) and general social processes is that of a microcosmic icon or emblem.

Indeed, he argues that most sociological metaphors are iconic in nature: 'They picture what things are, rather than compare how things are alike' (p.115). The entire range of 'systems' models in sociology consists of descriptive devices of this sort. In a similar vein, sociological enquiry based on classical forms of research design and analysis are essentially based on analogical reasoning – again a metaphorical operation in Brown's view: 'Analytic induction, controlled comparison, hypothesis testing, and inference can thus be seen as unselfconscious names for what may be understood as aspects of metaphoric thinking' (p.125).

There are, he suggests, 'root metaphors' that characterize major conceptual frameworks of sociological thought. The metaphors of society as 'organism' or as 'mechanism' are recurrent motifs of this degree of generality. Brown suggests too that the dramaturgical metaphor, and the view that social action or social structure are 'like language' are also of this kind and scope. Brown is good at sensitizing the reader to the extent to which sociological thought is predicated on metaphor and analogy. As with the rest of his treatment of the poetics of sociology, however, he does not try to examine any particular genre of sociology in great detail. Nor does he subject any texts or textual fragments to a close reading. He is content to treat the whole scope of sociological writing, and to describe its works in a very general fashion. The same can be said of his discussion of irony, the third of his main themes. He shows how many theories and theorists have developed their sociological insights through the trope of dialectical irony. There is the revelatory function of irony whereby the social world is 'unmasked':

Wherever sociological analysis is interesting, its basic concepts have this ironic edge. Unexpected similarities are revealed, as are unnoticed differences; opposites are seen to require each other or even to converge; sincerity is seen as bad faith, therapy as manipulation, law as opposed to order, evil as containing hidden good.

(Brown 1977, p.185)

In a similar vein is the ironic demonstration that opposites imply one another, that purposive action may have unanticipated consequences. The perspective may result in a reversal of conventional morality: the categories of normality and deviance are shown to be mutually defining and interdependent.

Brown's analyses are illuminating, but limited. As I have suggested, the reader lacks sufficient textual detail. It is impossible to see *how* the various tropes are deployed, how they interrelate. Brown refers to the textual devices whereby sociologists construct and convey their arguments and insights. He alludes to them, that is. He does not examine individual works and authors in detail, however. He leaves unfulfilled the desire to examine texts in terms of their various textual devices, or to examine particular schools and genres for their shared discursive features.

A complementary approach has more recently been provided by Edmondson (1984). This is an exercise very different from Brown's on two counts. First, it is grounded in a close reading of a small number of sociological texts. Second, the analysis is couched almost exclusively in terms of classical rhetoric. Edmondson thus contributes to the recent 'rediscovery' of rhetoric in the human and social sciences. In common with other authors in this vein, her work shows that 'rhetorical' form is no mere ornament or epiphenomenon: the form of the argument, its style and imagery are constitutive of its substance. Edmondson focuses attention on how the text *persuades* its readers.

Edmondson restricts analysis to a small number of key texts, taken to represent major styles of sociological research. Qualitative sociology is examined through *Race, Community and Conflict* (Rex and Moore 1967) and *Learning to Labour* (Willis 1977). More 'positivist' work is represented by *The American Occupational Structure* (Blau and Duncan 1967) and *Industrial Organization: Theory and Practice* (Woodward 1965). This explicit sampling and contrast of styles is especially useful, as it readily disposes of any implication that positivist or quantitative research is not dependent on rhetorical forms and that such issues are of relevance *only* to explicitly hermeneutic, qualitative exercises. Other texts drawn into the argument include the *Affluent Worker* volumes (Goldthorpe *et al.* 1968a, 1968b, 1969) and Dore's *British Factory–Japanese Factory* (Dore 1973).

Edmondson shows how the power of these various sociological monographs rests on the deployment of several recurrent rhetorical figures. The 'affluent worker', for example, is constructed and conveyed through the figure of the *epitome*. This device is derived from several procedures which

contribute to the image of a single figure whose textual function is to demonstrate what can be expected from members of the group in question. An epitome of this sort can more usefully be judged in terms of the coherence of the characteristics it assembles, and its effectiveness in presenting them to the reader, than according to more easily quantifiable criteria.

(Edmondson 1984, p.95)

This is analogous to the use of the 'actual type' as a persuasive device, especially in texts derived from qualitative research: that is, the use of 'examples' to encapsulate states of affairs and alert the reader to a particular interpretative framework. Those actual types may be held to be 'typical' in that they seem to sum up cultural forms, processes or types; they are not necessarily 'typical' in the sense of statistical representation. These 'types' or illustrations have a number of common features, Edmondson suggests:

First, they are details or quotations from real cases; this fact alone would distinguish them from 'ideal types', whose components are not intended to represent real events....Second, they need not be statistically typical of the situations in which they occur in the sense of having been chosen from many similar items, just because they are similar. Instead, they are related as symptoms or signs to more general states of affairs.

(Edmondson 1984, p.55)

On the basis of this and similar rhetorical devices, Edmondson refers to 'rhetorical induction', which

is a guide to expectations in which an author goes from a limited number of observations to a statement about what can reasonably be anticipated in general. It is characteristically sociological not only in being subject to the limitations intrinsic to information about social situations, but also in its strengths. It has the strength of enabling the reader to interpret situations which are not exactly like those described; it does not involve the artificial modesty of pretending that the author can *only* talk about what he or she has actually observed; nor does it imply the excessive claim that the author can infer from the observations made to *all* possible cases of a comparable type.... A rhetorical induction is not a matter of *mere* expectations but is modulated to the way in which anticipation functions in social situations; and it is *interactive*, relying on the reader to decide what new situations to classify as comparable with those with which the author deals.

(Edmondson 1984, p.106)

Edmondson's last point there is important. She stresses throughout her account that the communication between the sociological text and its reader depends upon the active interpretative work brought to bear by the latter. The work of the author lies in addressing the expectations and understandings of the implied or hypothetical reader. These communicative acts between texts and their readers are frequently accomplished through the figure of *enthymeme*, or 'rhetorical deduction'. In sociological texts, Edmondson identifies the 'ordinary person' and the 'reasonable person' enthymeme: 'These accounts make what people do intelligible by situating it in relation to standard anticipations and habits of response which the reader is assumed to use in negotiating social life; they answer questions relevant to the reader's interaction with other people' (p.144).

Edmondson's work is a valuable, if limited, contribution to the understanding of sociological texts. It has the advantage over an enterprise like Brown's in that it is *precise*: it clearly identifies and documents a specific range of textual devices, and displays their use in a clearly defined corpus of texts. It is limited, however, in so far as Edmondson concentrates almost exclusively on the descriptions of rhetoric. No attention is paid to alternative methods of textual analysis. A restricted number of rhetorical figures is identified in the chosen texts, but a much wider domain of literary and cultural studies is untouched. Edmondson's rigorously defined 'classical' approach is, ultimately, too austere. The entire scope of contemporary criticism is excluded.

The anthropological field

It is, perhaps, surprising that there has not been more explicit attention to the forms of sociological argument in published texts. In recent years there has been increasing emphasis on 'reflexiveness' and the constitutive work of sociologists' accounts. But it has really been left to the anthropologists to explore their own canon from such a perspective; see Spencer (1989) for a recent review. American anthropologists in particular have now developed a flourishing sub-field in which the object of scrutiny is the anthropological text itself. The classic texts and the founders of the discipline are now subjected to multiple readings, and more modern works are also subjected to critical scrutiny.

The anthropological interest frequently revolves round the representations of 'authority' on the part of the anthropologist–narrator, and the implied relationship between the author and the 'other' of his or her subject-matter. The range of analytic issues is summarized by Clifford in an introductory essay to a major collection of papers in this genre, pertinently titled *Writing Culture* (Clifford and Marcus 1986):

> Ethnographic writing is determined in at least six ways: (1) contextually (it draws from and creates meaningful social milieux); (2) rhetorically (it uses and is used by expressive conventions); (3) institutionally (one writes within, and against, specific traditions, disciplines, audiences); (4) generically (an ethnography is usually distinguishable from a novel or a travel account); (5) politically (the authority to represent cultural realities is unequally shared and at times contested); (6) historically (all the above conventions and constraints are changing). These determinations govern the inscription of coherent ethnographic fictions.
>
> (Clifford 1986, p.6)

Clifford's reference to 'ethnographic fictions' here alerts the reader to the view – now widely acknowledged in anthropological circles – that the work of ethnography is made or produced. It is something that is crafted by the anthropologist. As Clifford says in the same context, 'The making of ethnography is artisanal, tied to the worldly work of writing' (1986, p.6). A number of distinguished commentators have established the view that ethnographies are 'persuasive fictions' (for example, Geertz 1973; Strathern 1987).

Pratt (1986a) provides useful pointers concerning the affinities and conventions of the anthropological monograph. She notes the characteristic interweaving of 'personal narrative' and 'objectified description'. The style has a long tradition – precisely in that genre from which anthropology emerged, but from which it sought to differentiate itself. The tradition of travel writing combines the two modes of discourse in distinctive ways:

> In its various guises the narration–description duality has remained remarkably stable in travel writing right down to the present, as has the conventional ordering – narration first, description second; or narration superordinate, description subordinate. By the late nineteenth century, however, the two modes often had about equal weight in travel books, and it was common for a trip to result in two separate volumes....
>
> Modern ethnography obviously lies in direct continuity with this tradition, despite the disciplinary boundary by which it separates itself off from travel writing. Ethnographic writing as a rule subordinates narrative to description, but personal narrative is still conventionally found, either in the separate personal volumes or in vestigial form at the beginning of the book, setting the stage for what follows.
>
> (Pratt 1986a, p.35)

Pratt's observations on the continuities between travel writing and the ethnographic monograph have been developed in another essay (Pratt 1986b), where she emphasizes the textual conventions of 'manners-and-customs' accounts by nineteenth-century travel writers. She shows there how European writers 'fixed' the people they encountered into a homogenized, anonymous 'they' and then transformed them into the iconic 'he', as archetypal representative of the 'Other'.

In modern ethnographic writing the use of personal narrative and 'objective' description, Pratt suggests, is crucial 'because it mediates a contradiction within the discipline between personal and scientific authority' (1986a, p.32). Indeed, the nature of anthropological 'authority' is a recurrent preoccupation for contemporary commentators. Clifford (1988, p.25) summarizes the analytic and moral issues involved:

> If ethnography produces cultural interpretations through intense research experiences, how is unruly experience transformed into an authoritative written account? How, precisely, is a garrulous, overdetermined cross-cultural encounter shot through with power relations and personal cross-purposes circumscribed as an adequate version of a more or less discrete 'other world' composed by an individual author?

Clifford describes how the development of 'professional' anthropology, post-Malinowski, marked by claims for special expertise and practices, was accompanied by textual representations of anthropological authority. The new monographs introduced a 'sharp image' of the outsider encountering and penetrating a new culture, 'undergoing a kind of initiation leading to "rapport" (minimally acceptance and empathy, but usually implying something akin to friendship)' (p.34).

The 'classic' monographs of authors such as Firth or Evans-Pritchard display the authority of the fieldworker-as-author in the 'peculiar amalgam of intense personal experience and scientific analysis' (Clifford 1988, p.34). Evans-Pritchard has indeed exerted a particular fascination for contemporary anthropological commentators. Rosaldo (1986), for instance, uses Evans-Pritchard's *The Nuer* (1940) to examine the rhetoric of ethnographic authority. Rosaldo shows how Evans-Pritchard establishes his authority through the narrative account of his own acquaintance with the Nuer, under the most trying of circumstances and despite numerous hardships. He writes about himself with an ironic detachment and humour: 'a version of the heroic cast in a low mimetic mode rather than in the grander epic mode of great deeds' (Rosaldo 1986, p.89). Yet, for all its understatement (American readers probably find it intriguingly British), the author claims authoritative credentials for his text, based on his uniquely intimate knowledge of the Nuer. Rosaldo suggests that the author's self-revelations are devices for establishing his honesty: 'In the end, far from undermining his account, the narrator's often contradictory confessions enhance his credibility as a fieldworker' (p.92). Rosaldo employs a somewhat disturbing juxtaposition in comparing the 'authority' of Evans-Pritchard with that of the inquisitor whose investigations furnish the materials for Ladurie's *Montaillou* (Ladurie 1978).

Geertz (1988) has also paid close attention to Evans-Pritchard's style. Like Rosaldo, Geertz remarks on the assurance and clarity of Evans-Pritchard's expositions. He invokes terms such as 'assured', 'limpid', 'effortless'. Perversely, perhaps, Geertz chooses to analyse in detail an obscure publication rather than any of Evans-Pritchard's major monographs. The style is, however, pervasive throughout much classic anthropology – not just that of Evans-Pritchard himself. Geertz comments in particular on the intensely *visual* representations of cultural phenomena: what Geertz refers to as his 'anthropological transparencies' (1988, p.64). The written texts thus have a particularly vivid quality and constitute the textual equivalent of a magic lantern presentation. The anthropologist constructs himself as a credible *witness*, using graphic description to convey the credibility and authenticity of his account.

The various commentators use authors like Evans-Pritchard to epitomize the textual inscription of a particular style of anthropology. It is an anthropology in which there is a clear difference between the author and the objects of scrutiny. As Rosaldo puts it, the ethnography reports acts of surveillance from 'the door of the anthropologist's tent'. The classic monographs also embody, implicitly in their very organization, the *functionalist* approach to understanding culture and social structure (cf. Hammersley and Atkinson 1983). Boon also summarizes the point: 'Functionalist monographs portrayed cultures as functionalists assumed them to be: islandlike, space-time isolates of interlocking, reinforcing systems of relationships' (Boon 1982, p.14).

The monographs' arrangement of chapters and themes reflected the standard view of anthropological understanding. The functionalist format was therefore a faithful representation of the functionalist paradigm. It was probably more influential than any explicit statement of theoretical principles in establishing the taken-for-granted image of anthropology and its subject-matter. It was, as Boon suggests, buttressed by its omissions: no discussion of the culture's relations with others; no exploration of the culture's own sense of others; a lack of self-awareness concerning the anthropologist's work in achieving the ethnographic account.

The ethnographic genre in sociology

The genre of the sociological ethnography was heavily influenced by early classics from the Chicago School of sociology. In that historical period, the relationship between 'literary' forms and the sociological genre is discernible. The influence of Robert Park at the University of Chicago was largely instrumental in encouraging an ethnographic approach to sociology. Park himself came relatively late in life to the Department of Sociology at Chicago, and prior to that his career had included lengthy periods of work as a journalist and as a publicist. He brought to sociology in Chicago and the sociology *of* Chicago the characteristic perspectives of an experienced journalist – a journalist, moreover, who was accustomed to a good deal of 'leg work' in searching out his stories and his informants. This work depended upon, and produced, detailed, first-hand knowledge of the city. As Park himself remarked:

> I expect that I have actually covered more ground, tramping about in cities in different parts of the world, than any other living man. Out of all this I gained, among other things, a conception of the city, the community, and the region, not as a geographical phenomenon merely but as a kind of social organism.
>
> (Faris 1970, p.29)

Throughout the development of sociology at Chicago, under the influence of Park, W. I. Thomas, their colleagues and students, the ethnographic study of aspects of urban life – rather in the manner of Park the journalist – was a major preoccupation (though, contrary to some current misconceptions, quantitative methods were equally important to the Chicago School). Whereas in the early decades of this century anthropological fieldworkers were turning outwards to the study of 'exotic' peoples, including Native Americans for anthropologists in the United States, the Chicago ethnographers found equally remarkable forms of social organization and culture in their own backyard – or at least in the ethnically and economically variegated setting of a rapidly growing and changing environment. Admittedly, like the anthropologists, the sociologists often focused on the more exotic settings of the Chicago urban scene – the *demi-monde*, the deviant and so on. As Faris tells us:

> Hobo areas of Chicago were among the least-visited parts of the city, and many readers outside the profession of sociology found the descriptions almost romantically interesting. While ordinary tourists coming to Chicago normally visited parks and museums (and sometimes even the vast stockyards for contrast), it was the University which provided tours for visiting students to such places as Hobohemia, and for a time slumming visits were a fashion among young Chicago intellectuals.
>
> (Faris 1970, p.65)

To a considerable extent this preoccupation with 'underlife' in the city, the 'underdog' and the 'deviant' has remained a characteristic preoccupation of ethnographic enquiry, though by no means so to the exclusion of all else.

The ethnographic tradition was soon characterized by theses, papers and books which contained vividly and thoroughly documented accounts of 'social worlds'. It has rarely been characterized by a pure reliance on 'participant observation', but that has often been taken to be the type-case of ethnographic procedure. It was not originated in Chicago; it did not spring fully-armed from the head of a Park or a Thomas. The sociologists were influenced by the work of social anthropologists, such as Malinowski, Boas and Redfield.

The early ethnographies of the American school were based explicitly on the combination of 'anthropological' inspirations and the preoccupation with the first-hand exploration of urban types and settings. Park encouraged his students and colleagues to adopt the same methods and approaches to their research in the 'natural areas' of Chicago as were being used by anthropologists in their studies of Native American cultures.

The *demi-monde* of Chicago city life which made the subject-matter of much sociology was also the haunt of many literary figures of the same period. Indeed, the sociological and literary circles overlapped socially, and their members shared common interests. Carey quotes the following extract from an interview with Herbert Blumer, one of the major figures in Chicago sociology, and one of the foremost expositors of symbolic interactionism as a distinct theory:

> [Some of us] had the opportunity of moving in certain of the literary circles in Chicago that were, so to speak, on the fringe of the 'underworld'. For example, some of our eminent American figures...Anderson, Bodenheim, Carl Sandburg – they were all there in Chicago in the early twenties. Some of them were clustered down there at the end of 57th Street and the Park. There was a literary colony down there of writers and artists and what not....And

there was also the lower North Side, where there was a similar literary gathering. Some of us, I know I was one of them, got into those groups.

(Carey 1975, p.181)

The sociologists and their contemporaries in literature shared very similar backgrounds and preoccupations. Cowley (quoted by Carey) remarks of the literary men:

These new men, who would be the first American naturalists were all in some way disadvantaged when judged by the social and literary standards then prevailing. They were not of the Atlantic seaboard, or not of the old stock, or not educated at the right schools...or not sufficiently respectable in their persons or in their family backgrounds. They were in rebellion against the genteel tradition because, like writers from the beginning of time, they had an urgent need for telling the truth about themselves and there was no existing medium in which they were privileged.

(Cowley 1950, pp.301-2)

The sociologists themselves were also relatively unelevated socially. The relative newness of the Department of Sociology, and of the city of Chicago, allowed them some degree of freedom from constraints of tradition and good breeding. For novelists and sociologists alike the city provided endless fascination and 'data':

From the beginning they [the novelists] have exulted in the wealth and ugliness of American cities, the splendour of the mansions and the squalor of the tenements. They compared Pittsburgh to Paris and New York to Imperial Rome. Frank Norris thought that his own San Francisco was the ideal city for storytellers; 'Things happen in San Francisco', he said. Dreiser remarked of Chicago, 'It is given to some cities, as to some lands, to suggest romance, and to me Chicago did that hourly....Florence in its best days must have been something like this to young Florentines, or Venice to the young Venetian.

(Cowley 1950, p.330)

As Carey and other historians of Chicago sociology have pointed out, there were explicit affinities and parallels between naturalist fiction and the sociological work. It has been pointed out that the students in Chicago were encouraged to read naturalist novels, both to provide them with ideas and insights into social worlds, and to inform their written accounts. Bulmer (1984, p.96) notes that for the early sociologists there was a lack of 'an adequate American literature on urban phenomena' and goes on:

To some extent this gap was filled by literature. Just as students were encouraged to write their own life histories, so they were encouraged to read novels and autobiographies. Burgess, for example, encouraged his students in the 1920s to read Dreiser and Anderson. At the Summer Institute of the Society for Social Research in 1924, one session was devoted to the sociological use of literary materials. Whether naturalistic writers influenced sociologists to a greater extent is harder to determine. The Chicago novelist James T. Farrell studied sociology at the university during the 1920s and was influenced by the experience, though he retained a sense of irony. In one of the Lonigan novels a character studying at the university recounts for fellow students how he went to a brothel and discussed sociology with one of the prostitutes. His friends describe his adventures as a 'sociological experiment' and suggest that he put it all down on 3 x 5 index cards as field work for his sociology course.

(Bulmer 1984, p.96)

Farrell himself was to display his acquaintance with Chicago sociology in an essay, 'Some Observations on Literature and Sociology':

University of Chicago sociologists were among the pioneers in shifting the course of American Sociology from the plane of theory to that of empiricism. They embarked on a search for facts, and they sought these in many social areas, most of them marginal. Various sociologists, such as Frederick Thrasher, Nels Anderson, Paul Cressey, and others studied the 'interstitial' area, the rooming-house districts of Chicago, the taxi dance halls, the boys' gangs of various neighbourhoods, the West Madison or Bowery section of Chicago, and so on. They attempted to develop the technique of the interview and to rely rather heavily on case histories. Also, they went to newspapers for data. Along with this search for facts, the sociologists attempted to utilize statistics, especially co-relation equations. For instance, Dr Walter C. Reckless, a University of Chicago sociologist, in his book *Vice in Chicago*, attempted to establish a co-relation figure between the number of brothels and the number of roadhouses and taverns or saloons in a chosen 'interstitial' area in the city of Chicago.

(Farrell 1954, p.184)

Bulmer, however, goes on to say that 'There were marked affinities between journalism, naturalistic writing, and Chicago sociology, but they should not be exaggerated' (1984, p.96). He is quite right to caution against the over-simplified view of mutual influences between the different forms of writing. As he goes on to remark,

Just as the work of Park and Burgess's students was not journalism, neither was it mere naturalistic description. The research procedures used resulted in a much more systematic attack on social reality than that of the novelists. Chicago sociologists conceived of themselves as scientists.

(Bulmer 1984, pp.96–7)

Bulmer's caveat is in order, but is based perhaps on too narrow a view of what is relevant in this context. The interest in the historical parallels between the sociology and the literature is a heuristic one. In the first place, it alerts us to the elementary fact that ethnographic writing was – and is – a genre which has elective affinities with other modes of writing.

We need make no assumptions as to equivalence, to presume that ethnography is a debased literature. The literary parallels reflect a number of common stylistic features between naturalistic fiction and ethnographic reportage. Carey notes, for instance:

> Characteristically, as in the naturalist novel, the reader is introduced to the topic by the writer's looking at, or walking around and observing, the phenomenon as it might appear to a newcomer. This is what Cressey does in 'a Night in a Taxi Dance Hall', what Wirth does as he guides his reader along Maxwell Street, Thrasher as he takes his audience through gangland, and Zorbaugh in his description of the lower North Side 'In the Shadow of the Skyscraper'.
>
> (Carey 1975, p.178)

Here, by way of illustration, is the last mentioned 'In the Shadow of the Skyscraper'. It is extracted from a longer 'guidebook' introduction to the contrast between the fashionable areas and the slums which are in close proximity in the city of Chicago:

> For a few blocks back of 'the Drive' – on Bellview Place, East Division Street, Stone, Astor, Banks and North State Parkway, streets less pretentious but equally aristocratic – live more than a third of the people in Chicago's social register, 'of good family and not employed'. Here are families that lived on the once fashionable Prairie Avenue and later Ashland Boulevard, on the South and West sides. These streets with the Lake Shore Drive, constitute Chicago's much vaunted Gold Coast, a little world to itself, which the city, failing to dislodge, has grown around and passed by.
>
> At the back door of the Gold Coast, on Dearborn, Clark, and La Salle streets, and on the side streets extending south to the business and industrial area, is a strange world, painfully plain in contrast, a world that lives in houses with neatly lettered cards in the window: 'Furnished Rooms'. In these houses, from midnight to dawn, sleep some twenty-five thousand people. But by day houses and streets are practically deserted. For early in the morning this population hurries from its houses and down its streets, boarding cars and buses, to work in the Loop. It is a childless area, an area of young men and young women, most of whom are single, though some are married, and others are living together unmarried. It is a world of constant comings and goings, of dull routine and little romance, a world of unsatisfied longings.
>
> (Zorbaugh 1929, pp.8–9)

These descriptive passages are in the classic 'realist' mode such as Carey refers to. The reader is introduced, as if a stranger or outsider, in the fashion of a guidebook. The *setting* is portrayed in concrete terms, its features catalogued and some social types sketched in.

Bulmer is quite right in his caveat, referred to earlier. It is unwise and unhelpful to attempt to conflate the different modes of writing – the ethnographic and the literary. On the other hand, the invocation of 'systematic' work and 'science' should not blind us to a more general and fundamental concern. Scientists they may have been, but the sociologists still had to embody their scholarship in textual formats and styles. The relationship with contemporary American realist or naturalist fiction highlights the fact that the sociologists were grappling with the task of writing persuasive and plausible descriptions of social reality. This was not their sole task, but it was the bedrock on which their 'scientific', scholarly reasoning and synthetic generalization rested.

Since its early history in the Chicago School, the ethnography in sociological discourse has, of course, undergone changes. The models of literary texts have changed, while various sub-genres have developed. To some extent this book will necessarily do violence to the varieties and differences within the genre at large. A fuller and more systematic review remains to be written. We need more detailed explications of the textual characteristics of the 'community study', of 'Mass Observation', the life-history, the autobiographical research confessional, feminist ethnography, and so on. There has undoubtedly been a process of change, development and diversification within the domain of 'the ethnography'. But we have yet to define it coherently. There have been complex relations between the anthropological monograph, with all its antecedents and varieties, the sociological text, literary texts, and other varieties of writing (such as the 'new journalism'). The 'realism' of earlier literary and non-fictional texts can no longer be taken entirely for granted. While many authors continue to write in older and more 'conventional' formats, there are increasing numbers within the social sciences who attempt more self-conscious modes of representation.

Van Maanen (1988) is the only author of whom I am aware who has attempted to delineate even the grossest varieties of ethnographic writing by sociologists in a sustained fashion. His analysis does not derive from any very sophisticated perspective, but is more than a useful starting point. He identifies three types of 'tale' in which the ethnography is couched: 'realist', 'confessional' and 'impressionist'. The realist mode is the most common, sharing as it does conventions with many other types of reportage. Van Maanen outlines a number of salient characteristics for the style. It is typically written as an impersonal narrative, the author absent from the tale:

> Basically, the narrator of realist tales poses as an impersonal conduit who, unlike missionaries, administrators, journalists, or unabashed members of the culture themselves, passes on more-or-less objective data in a measured intellectual style that is uncontaminated by personal bias, political goals, or moral judgements. A studied neutrality characterizes the realist tale.
>
> (Van Maanen 1988, p.47)

The realism is, Van Maanen suggests, conveyed through textual representations of the concrete, the local, the detailed. Such details 'accumulate systematically and redundantly to demonstrate some point the fieldworker feels is important. Details are in a sense precoded in a realist ethnography to serve as instances of something important' (p.48). The author of the realist account claims the 'final word' on matters of interpretation, while allowing the 'native's point of view' to be glimpsed and reconstructed via extensive quotations and excerpts.

Van Maanen contrasts this 'conventional' realist mode with the 'confessional' tale. This is often employed in self-conscious opposition to realist representations. In contrast to the traditional genre, the confessional – Van Maanen maintains – celebrates a personalized author, and does not rely on impersonal authority. Hence, the fieldworker's own point of view – his or her personal experiences and conversions – are foregrounded and embedded in realist accounts: 'The attitude conveyed is one of tacking back and forth between an insider's passionate perspective and an outsider's dispassionate one' (p.77). In this way, the realist and the confessional accounts may prove mutually supportive in the *oeuvre* of any given ethnographer. Together they vouch for the ethnographer's personal, first-hand experience of the culture in question *and* for the detached 'scientific' status of the main body of published work.

Lastly, Van Maanen refers to the 'impressionist' style of ethnographic writing. This term he employs for vivid accounts of events witnessed and participated in:

> The form of an impressionist tale is dramatic recall. Events are recounted roughly in the order in which they are said to have occurred and carry with them all the odds and ends that are associated with the remembered events. The idea is to draw an audience into an unfamiliar story world and allow it, as far as possible, to see, hear and feel as the fieldworker saw, heard and felt. Such tales seek to imaginatively place the audience in the fieldwork situation – seated ringside as witness to a tribal ceremony of consequence, tasting the low life with the Hell's Angels in some sleazy bar, or shooting the falls in a barrel at Niagara.
>
> (Van Maanen 1988, p.103)

Although Van Maanen provides some references to published work under his three types, his approach is too general, and too constrained by limitations of space to allow a precise appraisal of the typology's value. In practice it seems difficult to make hard-and-fast distinctions, and the types certainly do not characterize entire texts. Ethnographies are not homogeneous. We frequently find 'impressionist' writing embedded in more 'realist' accounts, which are in turn contrasted with 'confessional' passages or chapters, all within the same monograph. Indeed, it is really more illuminating to see how the different styles of representation are interwoven in the completed texts.

In this book no attempt has been made to separate out different types of ethnography. Rather, as the reader will discover in subsequent chapters, a more thematic approach has been adopted. While this may at times obscure the diversity of emphases and changes over time within the genre, it seems to allow for a more detailed examination of the texts themselves.

Chapter three

Ethnography and the poetics of authoritative accounts

This book is concerned with ethnographic texts and their rhetorical forms. It is argued that their sociological messages are conveyed through a variety of textual devices and that they can be understood in ways analogous to those applied to 'literary' texts. There are, as already implied, close affinities between the ethnographic and the more overtly literary. There is, however, no implication that ethnographies alone among 'factual' genres exhibit such textual qualities. All scholarly or 'scientific' writing must rely on textual conventions and rhetorical methods. As Culler (1988) reminds us, critical theory has increasingly encompassed 'the relation between the literary and the non-literary' (p.22). None the less, the detailed analysis of texts by literary theorists has normally been undertaken on works of 'literature' – on poetry, novels and dramatic works. For such commentators, factual accounts are often treated as a background or yardstick. In principle, it is often argued, the 'poetics' of text can be applied to texts of any type or genre. In practice, however this is not developed within the 'literary' context. Consider, for instance, how Lodge characterizes 'realist' fiction:

> A working definition of realism in literature might be: the representation of experience in a manner which approximates closely to descriptions of similar experience in non-literary texts of the same culture. Realistic fiction, being concerned with the action of individuals in time, approximates to history: 'history is a novel which happened' as the Goncourt brothers put it. Thus the realistic novel, from its beginning in the eighteenth century modelled its language on historical writing of various kinds, formal and informal: biography, autobiography, travelogue, letters, diaries, journalism and historiography.
>
> (Lodge 1977, p.25)

There is clearly a problem in the view enunciated by Lodge. The identification of 'realist' fiction in terms of non-literary texts leaves untouched the stylistics of 'factual' accounts themselves. The danger lies in treating the 'non-literary' writing as if it were unproblematic – a privileged representation of a given 'reality'. Although Lodge himself is certainly not guilty of such over-simplification, his remarks could be taken to imply that the 'realism' of journalism, travel books, diaries or scientific monographs is self-evident, and that the 'realism' of fiction alone deserves attention.

That view would be quite misleading, however. 'Factual' accounts by biographers, naturalists, historians, journalists or scientists must themselves depend upon textual conventions in order to achieve their status as 'factual' accounts. That is, readers interpret texts as being 'factual' in so far as they encounter appropriate textual conventions which can be read in the appropriate way. In other words, *all* texts, 'literary' or otherwise, must depend upon their conventional forms. The rhetorical construction of texts in the natural and human sciences is coming under increasingly close scrutiny from their practitioners and commentators.

The argument is not that there are particular devices appropriate to factual texts and a completely different set of devices that pertain to literary works. On the contrary, there are undoubtedly features of accounts which can be found among works of literature and works of a non-literary character. It would be strange if different genres deployed totally different and incommensurable textual arrangements and devices. Lodge's remarks on parallels between realist fiction and non-literary texts indicate that such shared features may be very important in defining a genre or style.

Constructing 'factual' accounts

The factual account, like any other, has to *persuade* the reader of the 'facts' it purports to describe and comment on. That is, the argument has to be sustained by a text which is congruent with its stated purposes. The mere declaration on the part of the author that an account is 'true' is no guarantee that a text will be read in that way. This elementary fact can be demonstrated from both sides of the problem: fictional accounts which lay claim to actuality, and vice versa.

It is, after all, a common and well-established convention for works of pure invention to include explicit claims for their status as true and faithful accounts – discovered and presented to the public, or transcribed, by a narrator or implied author who vouches for authenticity, claims no credit and accepts no blame. A recent, highly self-conscious example is to be found at the beginning of Eco's *The Name of the Rose* (1983). It begins:

On August 16, 1968, I was handed a book written by a certain Abbé Vallet, *Le Manuscrit de Dom Adson de Melk, traduit en français d'après l'édition de Dom J. Habillo* (Aux Presses de l'Abbaye de la Source, Paris 1842). Supplemented by historical information that was actually quite scant, the book claimed to reproduce faithfully a fourteenth-century manuscript that, in its turn, had been found in the monastery of Melk by the great eighteenth-century man of learning, to whom we owe so much information about the history of the Benedictine order. The scholarly discovery (I mean mine, third in chronological order) entertained me while I was in Prague, waiting for a dear friend. Six days later Soviet troops invaded that unhappy city. I managed, not without adventure, to reach the Austrian border at Linz, and from there I journeyed to Vienna, where I met my beloved, and together we sailed up the Danube.

This introduction goes on to describe in more detail the narrator's search for Adso's manuscript and the pursuit of clues through libraries and sources; this is followed by an erudite discussion of the appropriate style in which to publish this 'Italian version of an obscure, neo-Gothic French version of a seventeenth-century Latin edition of a work written in Latin by a German monk toward the end of the fourteenth century' (p. 4). Hence Eco's highly and elaborately contrived fiction is introduced as a 'discovery', in which the narrator/author has intervened only through the determination of translation and style.

Contrast such an example with the following, which illustrates an alternative possibility:

The following account is based on a period of participant observation undertaken over a period of several months. It formed part of an ethnographic study of the everyday life of young children in contemporary culture. In this paper I shall seek to provide a preliminary account of a normal feature of children's experience of their lives in a world which they incompletely understand and over which they have only very partial control: that is, frustration....

This one, and the one I am now beginning describing is Martha Hersland, and this is a little story of the acting in her of her being in her very young living, this one was a very little one then and she was running and she was running and she was in the street and it was a muddy one and she had an umbrella that she was dragging and she was crying. 'I will throw the umbrella in the mud', she said and no one was near her and she was dragging the umbrella and bitterness possessed her, 'I will throw the umbrella in the mud', and there was desperate anger in her.

Of course, this is not an extract from a research report on childhood. The first paragraph is entirely my own fabrication. The second is taken from Gertrude Stein. While it might be possible to sustain a link between the two fragments, a little tenuously perhaps, in terms of topic, the style of the Stein paragraph does not conform to the realistic, documentary or 'factual' style of the first paragraph. In fact, the reader just might be able to 'naturalize' the hypothetical hybrid example – as almost any text can be naturalized, or recuperated. At the very least a strange and confusing text may be naturalized as a representation of disordered thought or chaotic events. As Culler (1975, p.138) notes: 'If all else failed, we could read a sequence of words with no apparent order as signifying absurdity or chaos and then, by giving it an allegorical relation to the world, take it as a statement, about the incoherence and absurdity of one's own language.' If one were not familiar with Gertrude Stein's distinctive style, then one might be able to recuperate my hypothetical example in a number of ways. One might suspect that it was intended as a 'literary' representation of a young child's thought and internal dialogue; one might think that it might have been used to force upon the reader a sort of 'phenomenological reduction', so as to disrupt his or her 'natural attitude'; it might develop such a phenomenological approach to intend a literary representation of Bergsonian *durée*. No doubt there are many ways in which my hypothetical text could be recuperated and naturalized. On the other hand, I think that most readers of a 'factual' account would find such naturalization hard to sustain were it to continue in that vein. We should expect such a style to be abandoned, and to give way to a style more suited (conventionally) to realistic and factual texts: the more 'literary' mode should be at most a temporary and self-conscious departure from the 'normal' state of affairs. Otherwise, the 'literary' style would undermine the introductory paragraph's explicit claims for a factual warrant.

These examples – real and hypothetical – suggest two things: first, 'factual' accounts are conventionally expected to conform to certain sets of textual devices; second, that there are clear similarities between 'realistic' fictional accounts and factual accounts. A number of things follow. First, there may be ambiguity in recognizing 'factual' or 'literary' accounts. Take the following example:

Everybody had a good time on Christmas Day at Mr Ben's. Fanny May went to church. The old folks began a whist game in the morning that ran continuously until midnight, with visitors dropping in to take a hand, eat a turkey sandwich, and drink from Mr Ben's sideboard. The janitor sat in his rocking chair like a king holding court, as the tenants streamed in and out and Baby Chile bustled about making him comfortable. Baby Chile was 'high' enough to be lively, but was careful not to get drunk. No one mentioned the tragedy of the night before. Only Slick was uncomfortable.

(Drake and Cayton 1945, p.570)

Quite apart from value judgements of literary merit, a reader would, I suggest, be hard pressed to decide whether the above passage – devoid of other context – derives from a work of fact or a work of fiction. It is 'in fact' taken from a sociological monograph, *Black Metropolis: A Study of Negro Life in a Northern City*. The joint authorship and the title are surer guides to its 'factual' claims than the style of the passage.

Second, of course, no text can unequivocally establish its actuality, whatever the auspices of its production. This is highlighted by those instances where a purportedly 'factual' account of first-hand experience is found implausible by readers. The texts of Carlos Castaneda provide a useful reminder of that here. For all that Castaneda's books are presented under the auspices of anthropological field research, and include anthropological commentary, many readers have confessed to finding the accounts implausible, and doubting the veracity of Castaneda's claims.

There is nothing inherent, then, in any text which marks it off as 'factual' or 'fictional'. There are, however, *conventions* which contribute to a text being read as realistic and plausible. To that extent, therefore, factual and fictional accounts are equivalent. There is not one set of conventions for literature and one set for science or scholarship: there may be differences, but they are by no means absolute. On the contrary, science and literature inhabit the same common discourse of textual conventions. There are differences of genre within the non-literary domain, just as there are within the literary. Some 'factual' accounts are close to some varieties of literature (for example, history, biography and the *Bildungsroman*); one can also think of other varieties of text which are very different (such as a report of a scientific experiment and a lyric poem). The recognition of such similarities and contrasts is itself part of the 'literary' competence of members of our society.

Verisimilitude

The plausibility of a text – of whatever genre – is referred to as its *vraisemblance*. This is a complex matter, relating at it does to genre and to everyday life. Todorov (1968) offers some indication of the various layers of *vraisemblance*. First, there is the relation between the given text and 'public opinion'; second, there is the text's degree of correspondence to the expectations or conventions of a given genre; third, there is the extent to which the text masks its own textual conventions, appearing to conform to a 'reality'. There are, therefore, two very general perspectives which can be drawn on in reading the text. There is the perspective of everyday discourse on the natural or social world, and there is the perspective which draws upon the literary discourse of other texts.

Culler (1975, p.140) expands these elementary relations into a five-fold classification of *vraisemblance*:

> First there is the socially given text, that which is taken as the 'real world'. Second, but in some cases difficult to distinguish from the first, is a general cultural text; shared knowledge which would be recognised by participants as part of culture and hence subject to correction or modification but which none the less serves as a kind of 'nature'. Third, there are the texts or conventions of a genre, a specifically literary and artificial vraisemblance of specific intertextualities, where one work takes another as its basis or point of departure and must be assimilated in relation to it.

When literary critics write of the first of these levels as the text of the 'natural attitude' or some such designation, there is a temptation apparently to gloss over it – perhaps born of a desire to hurry on to the more heady complexities of 'intertextuality'. By the same token, it might be thought that the factual text is analysable only in terms of the first two or three levels: that the factual text is merely a text of the natural attitude. Such views, if taken together, would imply little analytic interest in a consideration of factual accounts. Both views, however, are unnecessarily restricted, and individually or jointly may beg or gloss over important questions.

The 'factual' reportage or narration of events is never entirely devoid of textual conventions. In the first place, there is no neutral language of observation available to authors. The discourse of everyday life is itself a matter of convention. Mundane experience is itself socially constructed through discursive practices. It is the world in which we place our trust: a bedrock of taken-for-granted faith. We should not be misled by the natural attitude of everyday understanding into thinking that this discourse of the natural attitude is itself given 'naturally'.

Neither the factual account nor the realist literary text depends upon a correspondence between the everyday world and the text of its representation. No text can 'picture' the world; nor can there be a complete, literal description of the world. Our use of natural language – whether spoken or written – necessarily reflects the fact that it is inescapably *indexical*. The indexical property of language use means that its meaning is in principle dependent upon context of its use, and that language conveys more than might be said 'in so many words'. Hence the text can in no way furnish a literal description or transcription of people, places or events. By the same token, no such description can be exhaustive. Indeed, any attempt at a literal and complete description is doomed to appear absurd rather than realistic or 'scientific'. It would resemble an exercise in literary experimentation: rather than having a mimetic quality, such texts will seem to be quite the reverse – artificial rather than natural. A classic literary exemplification of such an approach would be Robbe-Grillet's writing, which includes the 'immensely detailed, scientifically exact and metaphor-free description of objects' (Lodge 1977, p.237). The effect of such exactitude and detail is quite the reverse of clarity. It results in a concatenation of particulars which ultimately defy recognition. It produces what Lodge goes on to describe as 'metonymic overkill'. Such descriptions parallel the intolerable cognitive and existential situation of the person who remembers everything and forgets nothing. There is certainly nothing 'natural' or 'realistic' about such accounts, and they do nothing to approximate to the natural attitude of everyday experience.

Moreover, David Lodge's reference to 'scientific' exactitude in relation to Robbe-Grillet's texts is ironic. At least, if we take 'scientific' to refer to the accounts produced by scientists, then it is clear that they are themselves highly conventional in ways different from Robbe-Grillet's contrivances. They rely for their referential exactitude upon features other than 'literal' detailed accounting. Neither the objects they describe nor the procedures and findings they report are couched in that fashion.

There is, therefore, a close relationship between the text of everyday 'reality', in all its concrete detail and mundane action, and the level of verisimilitude of cultural knowledge. When we read an account – literary or factual – we bring to bear our stocks of knowledge about our own or similar cultures and environments. Culler summarizes this *vraisemblance*:

Citing this general social discourse is a way of grounding a work in reality, of establishing a relationship between words and world which serves as guarantee of intelligibility; but more important are the interpretive operations which it permits. When a character in a novel performs an action, the reader can give it a meaning by drawing upon funds of human knowledge which establishes connections between action and motive, behaviour and personality. Naturalization proceeds on the assumption that action is intelligible, and cultural codes specify the forms of intelligibility.

(Culler 1975, pp.142–3)

Explicit citations of cultural knowledge blend almost imperceptibly with implicit interpretative reliance on everyday knowledge of a diffuse sort. Consider, for instance, Liebow's description of his sponsor and key informant, Tally, the eponymous protagonist of an ethnography of black poor in Washington, DC:

Tally is a brown-skinned man, thirty-one years old. He is six feet tall and weighs just under two hundred pounds. His size and carriage lend credibility to the general belief that he was once a professional heavyweight fighter. When asked to affirm or deny this status, Tally merely grins, assumes the classic stance of the boxer, and invites the questioner 'to come on'. No one does.

(Liebow 1967, p.23)

This is a fairly sparse introduction to a major character, which is followed by another three short paragraphs of biography. We might ask for more detail about Tally, perhaps, but certainly not for an inch-by-inch, feature-by-feature, exhaustive account. We do not need a full anthropometric survey of him: his physique is adequately conveyed by the description. Note that this description relies on two sorts of information. The first is the selective description of his height and weight – the bare representation of attributes – and the second is the cultural knowledge of the sort of 'size and carriage' which might be characteristic of a heavyweight boxer. Likewise, the reader may use his or her stock of tacit knowledge to envisage the 'classic stance of the boxer'. The reader may or may not bring to bear other cultural knowledge in fleshing out this description: that boxing is part of the cultural milieu of urban black males in North America, perhaps. The reader may also extrapolate to make other interpretations too, of course: that Tally's response suggests a reluctance to disclose personal information, and also hints of a streak of (ritualized?) aggression in face-to-face relationships. (The point is not whether such inferences would be 'correct', but how they could be used to construct a plausible and 'informative' description.) In so far as Liebow's description 'works', then, it rests upon its *evocation* of familiar cultural forms.

The description of Tally also evolves other types of descriptions of persons. The 'bare facts' of colour, height, weight and age might evoke the sort of descriptions to be found in newspaper accounts – where the numerology of age is an almost universal descriptive identifier; likewise one might also think of

41

police or military or penal descriptions. Whether or not one was aware of them, then, there are culturally available ways of doing and recognizing such descriptions. The description of Tally is a telling one in that it resonates with such cultural conventions and prototypes.

Considerations such as these bring us to the next levels of *vraisemblance*: the text gains verisimilitude in so far as it bears resemblance to other texts and formats. First, the text is a 'proper' representative of the appropriate type or genre. Second, it partakes of paradigmatic relations with other texts within and beyond the genre. The 'scientific' paper should thus display the conventional textual format if it is to be read as an authentic and authoritative representation of the natural world. Likewise, the discursive formats of social-scientific accounts conform to conventional aspects of genre.

This is readily apparent in relation to the tradition of social anthropology. As has already been mentioned, the anthropological monograph is a well-established textual format for the 'proper' reporting of 'other cultures'. Boon (1983) notes this tradition, founded by Malinowski:

> As with any revolutionary leader Malinowksi's freshness, so 'lively and stimulating' to Richards and others, withered in the routinizations of his followers. A stylistic taboo on authorial viewpoint helped rigidify the monograph format. Its orders of contents – physical surroundings firmly first, religion vaguely last, kinship and social organization determiningly at the core – became so unquestioned that any departure from the convention, such as Bateson's *Naven* was instantly conspicuous. Because the proper fieldwork method was presumed equal to solving any problems, the genre provoked little self-consciousness....[I]ncreasingly methodology was formulated for fieldwork alone, with writing left to occur, one supposes, commonsensically – that is in accordance with the implicit monograph conventions....Radically differing cultures were paradoxically inscribed in disarmingly similar books.
>
> (Boon 1983, pp.138–9)

In other words, as Boon makes clear, the textual format itself becomes taken-for-granted, but exercises a normative constraint on the construction and interpretation of factual reports.

The transformation of diverse cultures into 'standard' monograph formats is the textual analogue of the subordination of particularity and variety to a uniform epistemology. Likewise, the anthropological genre, composed of self-contained monographs of similar formats, thus underlines the twin themes of the functionalist anthropological project: the unique character of each culture, coupled with the goal of a comparative science of social structure. Arguably, the anthropological monograph, by virtue of its textual arrangement and its relations with other texts of the same genre, squares the epistemological circle: it reconciles the idiographic description of a unique cultural configuration (frozen in time and space) with the nomothetic imperative of a comparative and generalizing discipline.

The rhetoric of science

In precisely the same way (though by means of different conventions and formats) the 'standardized' presentations of scientific papers re-present the natural world under the auspices of a uniform method. It might be thought that the scientific paper would display an *absence* of rhetorical devices. 'Scientific facts' might be thought to display objective facts and reality quite independently of any such artifice. Such texts would correspond to what Roland Barthes (1967) calls 'degree zero' of writing. (Of course, Barthes himself does not subscribe to a belief in the existence of a residuum of neutral language: quite the reverse, he argues that all writing is 'style', and 'white writing' cannot exist.) Conventionally, the scientific paper is self-effacing, in that its style and organization are not foregrounded. As Gusfield (1976) puts it, such a commonly held view would imply that 'The style of non-style is itself the style of science', and as Yearley (1981) notes, 'Until fairly recently these formal papers have been accepted as straightforwardly representing the arena in which knowledge-claims are scrutinized.'

By contrast, more recent approaches have addressed the *textual* arrangements of scientific products. It has been pointed out that the 'standard' style and format does not literally *report* the process of discovery, but imposes a reconstructed logic. The emphasis is upon an inductivist discovery of the facts, while the role of personal interests, or circumstances is elided (cf. Gilbert and Mulkay 1980). Moreover, the scientific paper does not simply report: it *persuades*. Since there is no single, neutral and objectively given medium which directly corresponds to 'the facts of the case', there are many possible ways in which the scientific paper might be constructed. Law and Williams (1982) provide a fascinating insight into the process whereby relevant decisions are made in the production of a paper. They are able to show how a group of researchers collaboratively work at 'packaging' a paper so as to render it as attractive as possible. Law and Williams suggest that in performing such work, the authors

> *are trying to array people, events, findings and facts in such a way that this array is interpretable by readers as true, useful, good work, and the rest.* We may say that they are organizing bits and pieces. That is, they are attempting to structure and juxtapose elements in such a way that any interested reader will find himself compelled to interpret them in the manner desired by the authors. [emphasis in original]
>
> (Law and Williams 1982, p.537)

They go on to note in passing that no such text can actually 'compel' or determine reception on the part of the reader, though the authors' intentions may be oriented to such an outcome. The text can thus be seen in the process of creation, and some insight is gained into the 'packaging'. Relevant considerations include the selection of a title and the form of the opening paragraph. They help orient the reader, providing a frame of reference for the paper's reception. That is, such textual elements furnish the reader with resources for the construction of 'networks' or frameworks of relevance. Law and Williams document how texts have three functions: 'They tie together objects and facts. They tie together people. And they tie them together in a manner that is stylistically and grammatically acceptable.'

The net result is that 'scientific' papers construct accounts which are plausible and persuasive. This is a perspective adopted by Yearley (1981), who explicitly argues that 'formal scientific papers should be regarded primarily as contributions to scientific debates. They take the form of arguments, aimed at persuading the reader of the correctness of a specific point of view.' Yearley's contention is developed through a detailed examination of just one text. In a 'rereading' of the text he disentangles some of its 'argumentative strategies' and 'modes of accounting' which constitute the persuasive force of the argument. The author's scientific purpose is to refute the theory advanced by another scientist and to propose an alternative version of 'reality'. Yearley shows how the author seeks to undermine his opponent and carry the day by means of a range of discrediting implications. The author's own preferred position is not subject to the same devices. The persuasive function of the paper is sustained by an asymmetrical application of these modes of accounting. The paper is shown to be 'rhetorical' through and through.

The scientific paper is persuasive in so far as it creates and sustains a framework of expectations and relevancies. The use of citations has an important part to play here. Their function in the text is not simply referential, but also persuasive (Gilbert 1977; Small 1978). Citations 'tie together people', as Law and Williams put it, by providing the reader with a sort of 'reference group'. Inspection of the citation of authors permits the reader to 'place' the text and its argument. Authors may be cited in order to demonstrate the existence of the phenomenon under discussion, to point to other positions which are then shown to be inadequate, to establish partial accounts to be built on and developed, parallel cases and so forth. Of course, citations have a referential value which is faithful to the reconstructed logic of scientific discovery. The deployment of citations also has a more diffuse persuasive function. Without necessarily adding specific information, references may show the author to have paid his or her dues. The reader can find in the text evidence for locating it within certain sorts of traditions or genealogies. Indeed, without such guidelines, many types of scientific or scholarly texts would become much more difficult to read. The citations help the reader to impute certain sorts of claim on behalf of the text and its author(s). The competent reader who is a member of or acquainted with an 'invisible college' can use the citations as evidence for 'completeness', 'relevance', 'topicality' and so on. The overall shape of approving or disapproving references can help the reader to trace alignments, affiliations, and distances. The 'network' of expectations and relevancies may be constructed through a 'filling in' of networks in the more conventional sense of that term. (Note that such networks should be thought of as readers' achievements and not necessarily literal representations of actual social networks – if social networks can even be said 'actually' to exist in such a sense.) The apparatus of citations and similar sorts of reference thus help to establish the credentials and the credibility of a given text.

By the same token, it is constitutive of the competence of a reader that he or she can perform interpretative work on citations. The reader who is thoroughly versed in a particular area of scholarship may be able to infer a great deal about a text on the basis of its title and its references – almost to the extent of merely reading the substance of it to confirm initial expectations. By contrast the reader lacking background resources will not be able to read 'beyond' the text to construct the available frameworks of debate and refutation, alliance and opposition. In the interpretation of a scholarly text, the identification of 'faction' is as significant as the recognition of 'fact'.

One of the most salient aspects of the text, illustrated by Law and Williams (1982) is the 'introduction' established between the text and the reader (whether or not explicitly marked as 'preface' or 'introduction' in the textual format). Together with such apparatus as a title, citations and a preface or abstract (or perhaps the 'blurb' on a book jacket) the opening sections of a text are crucial elements in the production or inhibition of rapport between text and reader. Bazerman (1981) demonstrates some functions of opening sections. In particular he shows how a paper on DNA by Watson and Crick in *Nature* assumes a community of competent readers:

> The audience is assumed to share the same criteria of closeness of fit, discreteness, robustness, and reproducibility for acceptance of claims (or symbolic formulations) about phenomena; therefore, the audience can be relied on to have much the same assessment of the literature as the author does, and persuasion may proceed by maintaining apparent focus on the object of study.
>
> (Bazerman 1981, p.365)

Bazerman contrasts this with a sociological text (by Merton) and a work of literary criticism (by Hartman). He summarizes the comparison thus:

> The biological and biochemical audiences share an acceptance of much knowledge, evidence gathering techniques, and criteria of judgement against which to measure Watson and Crick's claims and to suggest how the claims might be applied; therefore, the authors do not urge, but rather leave the audience to judge and act according to the dictates of science. The sociological audience, sharing no uniform framework of thought or criteria of proof, must be urged, persuaded, and directed along the lines of the author's thoughts. The literary audience, concerned with private aesthetic experience, must find the critic's comments plausible, but more important must find the comments enriching the experience of reading; evocation of the richest experience is persuasion.
>
> (Bazerman 1981, p.378)

45

While he does not claim that his examples are 'typical', Bazerman's paper is suggestive of important differences between the scientific paper and the literary commentary, with the sociological text somewhere between them. The 'scientific' text assumes that it reports 'facts' which have been discovered and which occupy a world of perceptions shared with the audience. The sociological and literary text must be more overtly persuasive – even to the point that they need to persuade readers of the existence or possibility of their subject-matter.

The archetypal 'scientific' text – in common with some other types of factual accounts – approximates (but does not reach) the 'degree zero' of writing in that the presence of the author in the text is minimized. Or rather, the presence of the author is managed in such a way as to emphasize the facticity of the reality reported in the text. As Latour and Woolgar (1979) put it:

> The production of a paper depends critically on various processes of writing and reading which can be summarized as literary inscription. The function of literary inscription is the successful persuasion of readers, but the readers are only fully convinced when all sources of persuasion seem to have disappeared. In other words, the various operations of writing and reading which sustain an argument are seen by participants to be largely irrelevant to 'facts'....A text or statement can thus be read as 'containing' or 'being about a fact' when readers are sufficiently convinced that there is no debate about it and the process of literary inscription processes are forgotten.
>
> (Latour and Woolgar 1979, p.76)

The elimination of the author's voice is not absolute, however. Bazerman (1981) draws attention to the presence of first-person subjects in the DNA paper by Watson and Crick. Such usage as is revealed there is based upon a *contrastive* device which emphasizes the facticity of the facts reported. The correspondence of the text with the natural world is left inviolate (in appearance), even when the paper begins with 'We wish to suggest a structure for the sale of deoxyribose nucleic acid':

> all the uses of the first person are to indicate intellectual activities: statement making...making assumptions...criticizing statements...and placing know-ledge claims within other intellectual frameworks....None of the first person uses imply inconstancy in the object studied, but only changes or development of the authors' beliefs of what the appropriate claims about the object should be. The object is taken as given, independent of perception and knowing; all the human action is only in the process of coming to know the object – that is, in constructing, criticizing, and manipulating.
>
> (Bazerman 1981, p.367)

The general implication of 'writing degree zero' is thus sustained in the scientific paper, by the textual maintenance of a distinction between subject and object. Although the author is present or implied, he or she is not allowed to impinge on the facticity of the natural world.

The important issue is, therefore, that the elision of 'modalities' and the approximation of 'degree zero' writing is itself an *accomplishment*, grounded in the conventions of textual performance. It is itself *persuasive* in warranting the facticity of its contents (as opposed to, say, matters of 'belief' or 'opinion').

While no claim is made as to the direct parallels between literary and non-literary texts, it is surely clear that the verisimilitude they achieve is, in principle, as complex as that outlined by Barthes, Todorov, Benveniste or Culler for the literary. It may well be that the non-literary genre is more restricted in its exploration of alternative textual codes and conventions; the use of parody is rare, for instance. None the less, it would be quite misleading to assume that any factual account 'simply' described or reported the world, or that the text stood beyond the influence of genre and other texts. The world (natural and social) appears to be 'real' and 'natural' precisely in so far as the many levels and layers of convention allow the reader to naturalize the text.

Some texts or genres may embody literary or mythical forms, so that their relations of 'intertextuality' are contracted with both 'factual' and 'non-factual' texts. The texts which constitute a genre may naturalize transformation of the same cultural motifs and codes. This is well illustrated by Landau's analysis of a collection of anthropological texts which narrate the evolution of human beings (Landau 1984). She shows how the accounts offered by the texts differ, but do so as variations on an underlying set of constituent elements. Landau uses Propp's analysis of the morphology of the folk-tale to perform this formal analysis (Propp 1958). Propp's work on the folk-story was one of the earliest exercises in the formalist approach to narratives, and a major precursor of modern structuralist thought. The enormous diversity of fairy-stories and the like can be represented in terms of a restricted number of primitive elements. These comprise 'functions' which are distributed among performers and their spheres of action. Functions and performers are limited and finite in number (thirty-one and seven respectively). They make up the elementary structures of the genre. Landau is able to show that competing accounts of the evolution of *Homo sapiens* all deploy the same narrative elements, which are directly comparable to those identified by Propp. The contrasting theories are constructed out of different *sequences* of the same narrative units. Landau (1987) has subsequently developed the argument through an analysis of imagery in theories of human origins. She examines how the emergence of humans is treated figuratively in metaphors of 'expulsion' and 'escape' that are redolent of yet more general archetypes of 'the fall' or 'salvation'.

Of course, it might be argued that Propp's 'functions' are so general that any account which had some chronicling or unfolding of events, and which had sufficient non-trivial ordering to render it a history or narrative of some sort would necessarily display at least some of Propp's devices. In one sense that is true, and we gain little by engaging in purely reductionist arguments, whereby literally everything is rendered down to its elementary particles. On the other hand, the value of analyses like Landau's is the demonstration that scholarly, factual books and arguments can fruitfully be explored in terms of such narrative formats. What becomes interesting about these anthropological exegeses is the manner in which each creates a distinctive contribution while re-creating the patterns of the genre. Each text thus affirms its difference from the others, while relying on shared textual arrangements.

We thus move from the appearance of 'degree zero' writing of the purely factual account – with all its textual devices as accounting methods – to the more overtly 'literary' presentation of the narrative account. At this end of the spectrum, genres such as narrative history quite clearly depend upon stylistic devices for their persuasive function. The selection of 'facts' and their arrangement into a plausibly coherent framework is more obviously a matter of rhetoric. Here the parallels with literary models may become more apparent. Indeed, in narrative formats of a more discursive nature, there may be a two-way flow of influence between fiction and science.

It is, after all, well known that the general field of evolutionary writing is one where literary styles have interpenetrated, as well as other genres. Beer (1983) has provided a detailed treatment of Darwin's account of evolution, which explicitly relates his approach to writing with novelists' treatment of evolutionary themes (George Eliot in particular). Beer makes clear the common elements in the literary and the scientific – in the management of *narrative*:

> Evolutionary theory is first a form of imaginative history. It cannot be experimentally demonstrated sufficiently in any present moment. So it is closer to narrative than to drama. Indeed in the then current state of knowledge many of the processes of inheritance were beyond explanation.... Evolutionary ideas proved crucial to the novel during that century not only at the level of theme but at the level of organisation. At first evolutionism tended to offer a new authority to orderings of narrative which emphasized cause and effect, then, descent and kin. Later again, its eschewing of fore-ordained design (its dysteleology) allowed chance to figure as the only sure determinant. On the other side, the organisation of *The Origin of Species* seems to owe a good deal to the example of one of Darwin's most frequently read authors, Charles Dickens, with its apparently unruly superfluity of material gradually and retrospectively revealing itself as order, its superfecundity of instance serving an argument which can reveal itself only *through* instance and relation.
>
> (Beer 1983, p.8)

Beer goes on to display – among other things – the role of analogy, metaphor and narrative in *The Origin of Species*. Her thorough and detailed treatment provides ample exemplification of the interpenetration of rhetorical devices with the reporting of observations and presentation of inferences. Indeed, it is impossible to separate out the 'factual' and the 'rhetorical', as if the latter were an optional extra or a 'mere' embellishment.

Indeed, Darwin's account has attracted several analysts of rhetoric and narrative. Campbell (1987) shows how Darwin succeeded in *persuading* readers (not all readers, obviously), most notably through his use of Everyday English. The theory is advanced by various commonplaces (cf. Gillespie 1960) and appeals to common sense. Likewise, Young (1985) draws attention to some of the grand tropes of Darwin's thought. Of course, there was far less distance between nineteenth-century 'sciences' and the 'arts', in terms of their modes of writing: the highly specific registers and formats of contemporary scholarship reflect a progressive differentiation of rhetorics.

The rhetoric of the cultural disciplines

Historical discourse is an arena where narrative and metaphorical features have been examined. Hexter (1968) argues for a rhetorical understanding of the writing of history, while White (1973) provides a major commentary on the subject. White insists that the written style of history reflects profound commitments on the part of the historian. The historiographical trope is part of what White refers to as the 'deep structure' of the historical imagination. The historian and the ethnographer share very similar commitments and resources. Each is committed to a systematic and thorough account of cultural phenomena, yet neither can reproduce all the 'evidence' and detail available. There is an element of *bricolage* in both types of writing. The historian will find him or herself using 'telling' examples, quotations and instances in order to convey to the reader more general or diffuse phenomena. So too will the ethnographer. They will both employ appropriate metaphors or models in order to impose order, coherence and meaning on their materials.

As several commentators have suggested, 'many historians remain unconsciously wedded to the historiographical equivalent of mainstream nineteenth-century narrative fiction' (Megill and McCloskey 1987, p.226). The narrative style itself produces coherence and unity from diverse and fragmentary sources. The unifying voice of the narrator produces the effect of authority and certainty on the part of the historian. But with a few exceptions (for example, Danto 1985; Ankersmit 1983) students of historiography have not engaged in detailed analyses of history's texts and its narrative forms. Megill and McCloskey (1987) provide some brief indications of the relevance of classical rhetoric to such a task, while claiming that for the most part historians themselves remain unaware of their own narrative conventions.

Ethnography and history may appear to be 'rhetorical' in contrast to the more self-evidently 'quantitative' or 'scientific' among the human sciences. While their conventions differ, however, the quantitative, mathematically oriented discipline of economics and the experimentally oriented discipline of psychology are equally dependent on rhetorical tropes and textual formulae. Donald McCloskey is in an excellent position to explore the former, as a distinguished economist and as a leading figure in the contemporary application of rhetoric to the human and social sciences. In his monograph treatment of economics (McCloskey 1985) and a series of related papers (for instance, McCloskey 1983) he outlines the essentially figurative nature of economic argument. At root he suggests that the economist has two alternative modes of expression: the economist can either use a metaphor ('a model') or can tell a story. The two modes thus correspond to the metaphorical and metonymic poles respectively. Even the 'hardest' of cliometricians or econometricians, McCloskey shows, is as much dependent on textual devices as any other practitioner. Likewise, Klamer (1987) argues that one of the central themes of neo-classical economics – the assumption of 'rationality' on the part of agents – is a key example of the metaphorical foundations of economics.

From psychology, the textual codification of epistemology is very well illustrated by Bazerman's commentary on the *Publication Manual* of the American Psychological Association (Bazerman 1987). Tracing its historical development, he shows how a set of behaviourist assumptions have become increasingly taken for granted and inscribed in the required formats of APA style. The increasingly voluminous prescriptions of the style manual progressively impose a uniform style on what may be reported and how it shall be presented. They define discourse in ways more fundamental than mere 'house style' might seem to imply. The APA style has been adopted well beyond its national and disciplinary origins: it is one of the restricted range of acceptable styles that place constraints – in some cases quite severe – on what is to count as a well-formed scholarly representation.

The presence of metaphor and similar tropes in scholarly and factual accounts again underlines the extent to which such texts may achieve their coherence and plausibility from such rhetorical features. Donald Schön's classic account of the role of metaphor in scientific discovery and discourse is one of many which strongly suggest that metaphorical thought is an intrinsic component of discovery and argumentation (Schön 1963). From this perspective, such 'literary' turns are not artificial contrivances to be contrasted with the unvarnished presentation of the truth. Art and artifice they may be, but are not therefore 'artificial' in opposition to the 'natural' world. Literary and scientific or technological metaphors continually interpenetrate, as well as entering into the discourse of mundane, everyday knowledge.

Metaphor and metonymy

The contrast between metaphoric and metonymic uses of language is an important one in the analysis of realism in literature. It provides an apparent means for distinguishing realistic or factual writing from more obviously 'literary' aspects. The underlying opposition is derived from Jakobson and posits two polar types of language use. In terms of classic semiotic theory, they exploit different possibilities of selection and combination (namely, paradigmatic and syntagmatic relations) which inhere in the system of language itself:

The development of a discourse may take place along two different semantic lines: one topic may lead to another either through their similarity or their contiguity. The metaphorical way would be the more appropriate term for the first case and the metonymic for the second, since they find their most condensed expression in metaphor and metonymy respectively.

(Jakobson 1956, p.63)

It is argued that prose tends towards the metonymic pole, while poetry tends towards the metaphoric. 'Realist' literature is perhaps the most extreme case of metonymic writing.

Now it might be thought that the production of authentic 'factual' accounts would result in a most purely metonymic type of text. And if that were the case, would it not defy any 'literary' analysis, such as the attempt to identify the 'poetics' of the factual report? It is the case that the metaphor/metonymy polarity helps us to identify the contours of realism in writing, if only through the implied contrast with its opposite.

David Lodge's commentary on metaphor and metonymy proceeds by way of example (Lodge 1977, pp.93–108). These focus upon types of description. At one extreme there is the case of 'pragmatic prose' with, supposedly, no 'poetic' or literary aspect: Lodge cites an encyclopaedia entry which simply lists a number of facts about the city of Birmingham. When he turns to a journalist's account of the same city he finds more obvious markers of 'literary' style – more self-conscious rhetorical devices and oppositions contribute to the coherence of the style. The encyclopaedia entry merely lists features, while the journalistic account gives shape and purpose to the description, and implies an explorer of the setting. Lodge goes on to arrange descriptions of 'similar' events – executions – on a continuum, from a predominantly metonymic treatment (an account of a hanging in the *Guardian*) through to the metaphoric treatment ('The Ballad of Reading Gaol').

The realist account may rely primarily on the metonymic use of language – relying on the principle of 'contiguity' – but that certainly does not absolve it from rhetorical features. In contrast to the figure of metaphor, metonymy relies more on the figure of synecdoche. The type-case of synecdoche is the substitution of the part for the whole. The figure is metonymic in that it rests on a relation of cause-and-effect, class membership, and so on, but not on the metaphorical relationship of similar but unrelated phenomena. The type of description favoured by the metonymic voice thus depends upon the part-for-whole selection from among the many possible describable features of a scene or situation. The metaphorical description posits a relationship of similarity in difference, but need not refer to any particular detail or facet of the object to be described. Metonymy implies selection from multiple elements, while metaphor implies a more holistic perspective.

The poetics of the factual are typically (but not exclusively) based on those of metonymy, therefore, and the figure of synecdoche may be employed, as Lodge describes, generated by *deletion*:

> The sentence, 'Keels crossed the deep' (a non-metaphorical but still figurative utterance) is a transformation of a notional sentence, 'The keels of the ships crossed the deep sea' (itself a combination of simpler kernel sentences) by means of deletions. A rhetorical figure, rather than a précis, results because the items deleted are not those which seem logically the most dispensable. As the word *ship* includes the idea of keels, *keels* is logically redundant and would be the obvious candidate for omission in a more concise statement of the event, and the same applies to *deep*. Metonymy and synecdoche, in short, are produced by deleting one or more items from a natural combination, but not the items it would be most natural to omit: this illogicality is equivalent to the coexistence of similarity and dissimilarity in metaphor.
>
> (Lodge 1977, p.76)

Such a principle of deletion accounts for the device for the *production* of synecdoche: the maxim for reading such a text would seem to be the reverse procedure – 'filling in' the deletions in order to recover the whole which is implied or referred to.

When we turn to the use of synecdoche in factual accounts, the same general principles apply. But here the intended or imputed relationship is one of *logical* selection or deletion, and hence of reasonable, rational inference. In both varieties the 'part' (or example, or appearance) may stand for the whole. In the factual account, the relationship may be treated as equivalent to that of evidence or justified inference. The realist account may approximate to either the more literary or the more factual mode. The part-for-whole substitution may, for instance, be read as a 'symptom' or to imply a logical sequential organization (so that cause or motive is inferred). This is evident in the following description of 'the slum' in a classic of Chicago sociology, *The Gold Coast and the Slum* (Zorbaugh 1929):

> The slum harbors many sorts of people; the criminal, the radical, the bohemian, the migratory worker, the immigrant, the unsuccessful, the queer and unadjusted. The migratory worker is attracted by the cheap hotels on State, Clark, Wells, and the streets along the river. The criminal and underworld find anonymity in the transient life of the cheaper rooming-houses such as exist on North La Salle Street. The bohemian and the unsuccessful are attracted by cheap attic or basement rooms. The radical is sure of a sympathetic audience in Washington Square. The foreign colony, on the other hand, is found in the slum, not because the immigrant seeks the slum, nor because he makes a slum of the area in which he settles, but merely because he finds there cheap quarters in which to live, and relatively little opposition to his coming. From Sedgwick Street West to the river is a colony of some fifteen thousand Italians, familiarly known as 'Little Hell'. Here the immigrant has settled blocks by villages, bringing with him his language, his customs, and his traditions, many of which persist.
>
> (Zorbaugh 1929, p.11)

This paragraph is only part of a longer description of parts of the city of Chicago relevant to Zorbaugh's general sociology, but the more extended treatments all take the same general form. The description of 'the slum' is in no sense an exhaustive one. A somewhat restricted set of features is selected in order to exemplify salient aspects which the reader may treat as symptomatic of a recognizable or plausible state of affairs. The slum area itself is represented synecdochically: streets such as State, Clark and Wells are mentioned, linked with 'cheap hotels', to stand for a larger area and for a generic characteristic of the slum quarter. The listing of the people 'harboured' by the slum is characteristic too of metonymic style. It is an association by contiguity, but is almost certainly not an exhaustive listing. In 'describing' the slum the list – itself metonymic – functions as a synecdoche. The description of the slum Zorbaugh offers here is a plausible and 'convincing' one. The reader does not need a detailed knowledge of the slum, Chicago, or even American cities to be able to construct some sense of the place (though the actual competence brought to bear, the resources used to interpret the text, and the descriptive detail 'filled in' will vary from reader to reader).

In practice, the majority of texts draw on both metaphorical and metonymic aspects. The attempt to classify texts in terms of one or other pure type is unlikely to be fruitful. Even the most extremely 'literal' account, apparently devoid of any 'literary' aspects, may nevertheless have functions within a literary context. Lodge (1977, p.96) cites the opening of Kingsley Amis's *The Green Man*, which begins with a pastiche entry in the *Good Food Guide* and comments, 'but such a novel could not possibly continue for long in the same mode: the encyclopaedia article could only serve as a prelude or foil to the main narrative'. Likewise, in scholarly or scientific accounts the most strictly metonymic passages may be played off against more overtly persuasive and figurative features in the overall organization of the larger text.

From this point of view, therefore, even the least 'literary' text may partake of the mode of *vraisemblance* based on 'intertextuality'. Indeed, in several – perhaps rather mundane – senses many 'factual' accounts are the most explicitly intertextual of productions. Their assimilation may well depend upon their explicit or implicit relations with other equivalent texts. At the most elementary level, the factual account may, as we have seen, incorporate specific references to other texts through citations. Such features are of considerable importance. They are not simply persuasive in the sense that they provide additional support for and so 'bolster' any given fact or argument. That is certainly one important function which may be fulfilled, and the selection of citations can convey the 'weight of evidence' inclining the reader to accept or reject findings and positions. (Note that the weight of 'evidence' is a matter of social construction, as in any such context, and that the accumulation of evidence through citations is never constraining on the reader's reception of the text.)

The explicit intertextuality of, say, a scientific paper also provides for its location within a network or framework of meaning. Indeed, in this guise one might think of the text itself as a 'sign', partaking of systemic relations of similarity and contrast with other signs within a complex field. Again, it would be wrong to think of such systemic relations as 'given' or as inherent features of the texts themselves. There is a large domain in the social studies of science which uses such a resource to *construct* systems of relationships (through studies of co-citation, for example). From my point of view, however, it would be more appropriate to say that work equivalent or analogous to that analyst's construction may be done (practically and implicitly) by the reader. The complexity or otherwise of such a construction will be informed by that reader's stock of knowledge.

That reading does not only rest on devices such as citations and footnotes. The language of the text may itself furnish the reader with implicit links with other texts. The text's selection of terminology, imagery or metaphor can – without need for explicit citation – provide 'intertextual' paradigmatic relations with styles, traditions and authors. The textual construction of scholarly reality rests upon the shared linguistic resources of an epistemic collectivity or network. These need not be matters of arcane 'jargon' (though such restricted vocabularies are a case in point), but can also be related to the use of relatively ordinary language, which gains pointed relevance in context and in relation to other linguistic usages. Such shared languages are more than mere 'optional extras' in the writer's or reader's expressive repertoire. The use of language constitutes the text's mode of representation – its reality or *vraisemblance*, that is. Such echoes and resonances may be pointed up through conscious reprises of previous formulations in a manner analogous to the element of 'parody' or 'pastiche' in more overtly 'literary' contexts.

Hence, when the author of an ethnographic text employs the rhetoric of 'self-presentation', 'negotiation', 'stigma', 'status passage', 'strategic interaction', 'face work', 'information games', 'moral career' and so on, there may be little need to invoke a vast collection of citations. The terms themselves evoke a network of associations which cross-refer to other authors, other social settings so described, and a dense tradition of taken-for-granted concepts. Such a shared vocabulary of concepts and assumptions does not merely provide the writer and reader with a range of descriptive or explanatory possibilities: it is deeply implicated in the process whereby the text constructs its 'reality' and so invites the reader to participate in its own processes of 'reality-construction'. The intertextuality of the ethnography is thus a fundamental aspect of its *vraisemblance*. Texts may be organized through themes which are more or less explicit echoes of other texts in the genre. The text thus lays claim to the rhetorical legitimacy of its predecessors in the field. The language is persuasive through such paradigmatic relations, over and above its referential functions.

At various points in this chapter I have referred to the poetics of 'factual' accounts, and documentary constructions of reality which approach the degree zero style of modality-less writing. It is apparent, however, that ethnographic writing does not actually correspond to the extremely 'factual' and metonymic pole. It is a genre or collection of genres which reports (claims to report) social worlds and social realities in an authentic manner. It is rare for extremely self-conscious literary modes to be accepted, although Krieger claims to have based her ethnographic style on a 'multiple person stream of consciousness' (Krieger 1984, p. 278; cf. Krieger 1979a and 1979b) and refers to Virginia Woolf as one literary influence on her writing.

Rather than referring simply to 'factual' accounts as if there were only a Manichean universe composed of fact and fiction, we should allow the world of texts, their readers and writers, to be more finely tuned. In the context of ethnography it is more fruitful – and more faithful to the phenomena – to talk of 'authoritative' texts. That designation recognizes that whether or not it is consistently inscribed in the text, the ethnography is not a naïvely naturalistic account. Rather, it explicitly or implicitly lays claim to a particular status and a particular sort of attitude on the part of the reader. It is to be read as an account of 'actual' or 'historical' events rather than fiction or invention. In common with texts of biography, history, journalism and the like, the ethnography claims factual status, but not by eliminating the voice of the author or approximating 'degree zero'. Rather, the ethnographic text is permeated by stylistic and rhetorical devices whereby the reader is persuaded to enter into a shared framework of facts and interpretations, observations and reflections.

The 'author' is present or implied in the authoritative text. The reader can usually find grounds for imputing or withholding authority: qualifications, knowledge (indexed by citations and allusions), experience, methodical procedure – these may all be 'read into' the text. The reader's evaluations of the status of the text – its credibility and scholarly value – will rest upon such imputations and interpretations. Moreover, the overall credibility of the text will imply much more than the sheer facticity of the objects and events it reports. Its *vraisemblance* – to extend the connotations of the term further – depends on the internal coherence and plausibility of the overall product.

This is not confined to factual or authoritative accounts, but is a particularly crucial feature of them. The verisimilitude of the text thus rests not only upon congruence with a given type of genre. Rather, the text should be found to be 'true to itself'. The reader who approaches the text as a factual as well as a realistic one will normally bring to it a natural attitude which expects a certain coherence. It presupposes no sudden – still less unexplained – changes in style, or shifts in perspective. The surface of the text is by no means uniform, but the reader will expect a relatively restricted repertoire of forms: the conventions of factual accounting normally rule out the vertiginous excesses of self-consciously 'literary' works. Even texts which claim a certain affinity with literary models provide fairly penny-plain versions, and a modest array of textual devices. The 'factual' text is thus internally fairly homogeneous.

In general terms, therefore, we can examine authoritative texts, such as ethnographies, in terms of the various layers of verisimilitude. Such an exercise is not to be embarked on as if we could thus identify and pin down specific, distinctive criteria of what is 'factual' as opposed to what is 'fictional'; or to separate what is 'real' from what is merely 'realistic'. There are no *differentia specifica* which uniquely guarantee authenticity. On the contrary, there are many textual devices which are common between scholarly and literary accounts. That comes as no great surprise: they are written and read by social actors who share stocks of knowledge and assumptions about how written texts 'represent' the world. It would be strange if different emphases and uses relied upon totally different sets of cultural resources.

In the next chapter I shall examine some textual elements of ethnographic monographs and papers whereby plausible scenes and settings are established. The argument will be that the ethnographic text invites the reader sympathetically to endorse its verisimilitude and authenticity. The use of descriptive writing is a means to convey implicit sociological commentary. Finally, even the *title* of the ethnography is imbued with textual significance.

Chapter four

Ethnography and the representation of reality

In this chapter I shall deal with various key features whereby the ethnographer constructs versions of social reality, and persuades his or her reader of the authenticity, plausibility and significance of representations of social scenes or settings. To begin with one should note that the ethnographic text conveys the authority of its account very largely through its persuasive force. The socio-logical message is conveyed through the use of descriptive writing, in which implicit analysis and 'point of view' are inscribed. Second, the 'data' – from which the published text is constructed – themselves frequently (not exclusively) consist of authored representations of social scenes. In other words, there is a process of translation and transcription that goes through several stages. The first stage of conventional, textual representation is the construction of 'field notes'. The ethnographer records the scenes and settings that have been observed and engaged with.

The fieldworker must therefore operate as a day-to-day chronicler of the transactions and reflections of field experience. Nearly all fieldworkers create such narratives. The reader frequently gains glimpses of them, since many authors use fragments of their own accounts as 'data' and illustrations in their published works. (The rhetorical force of such exemplars is explored in greater detail in the following chapter.) To a considerable extent, however, field notes remain private documents, and we do not have major data-bases to subject to analysis. In the long term it remains a major task to examine the stylistic features of field notes from particular authors or sociological schools. To a considerable extent they remain an unexamined resource. We do, however, have some examples reproduced in textbooks – most notably in Junker's account of Chicago fieldwork (Junker 1960). There he reproduces several lengthy field-note extracts which allow us to inspect some aspects of the inscription of social reality and sociological enquiry.

The first example quoted here is by Everett Hughes, a leading Chicago-trained sociologist, and is quoted by Junker (1960, pp.22ff.). The research was reported in Hughes' monograph *French Canada in Transition* (1943):

Saturday, July 11, 1936 (first trip to Cantonville) Emma drove us to Can-tonville. St Bernard we merely passed through. It is an old-looking town with well-kept houses and gardens along the river, and many religious establishments, some of red brick and others, newer, of stone, without much care to make the architecture match. Even from the outskirts Cantonville looks quite different. There are more lots for sale and more cheap new houses. Going through the town up toward the XYZ Plant, one can see a small new stone United Church. The whole end of town near the XYZ Plant and south along the river is new. Save for a couple of streets of 'Staff Houses' owned by the company, nothing is planned or ordered. These two streets have good brick houses, trees and shrubbery, and there is a company recreation house and tennis courts. A sign at the end of the street says 'Private Property – Staff Houses' and threatens trespassers with a fine of ten dollars. I learned from Norton, an engineer, that the company has agreed with the town to build no more houses of its own. Also that the company property is, by agreement, free of taxes until next year. The other streets are built up with houses and tenements of all sorts. Near the river and in some of the adjoining streets are rather nice houses in which members of the staff live. But nearby and sometimes in the same streets are three-story tenements of concrete blocks, brick, or wood and houses of wood, square as boxes.

Some lots even have an extra house in the back yard. There are apparently no building restrictions. Houses seem to be scarce and rents high, relatively.

There are many of these new cheap tenements between the plant and the older part of town, and new work is being done on sidewalks and streets. Water, electricity, and sewers have been extended to the newer districts only recently. On the main street near the river, leading down into town are many beauty shops, etc., of a cheap sort. On one house was a sign, 'Tireuse heureuse des cartes,' and 'Horoscopes à la main.' It would be interesting to know the origin of the people who run these new small businesses, evidently established for the mill-worker trade, and their relation to the older business people of the town.

At the brow of the hill below which lies the old business district, stands the old Protestant Church with a graveyard full of old-fashioned stones. The names are all English – Perkins was prominent, also Stuart. These were probably the original settlers' families (the town was founded by the English about 1812.) The fate of the old families ought to be looked into; they are not much in evidence now.

The business district lies below the little hill and seems small for a town of the size. The buildings do not look particularly old. One of them is a three-story building with flats on the upper floors, dated 1928.

At the barber shop I inquired for the mayor. He is M. Millet, who runs a hardware store. Since it was Saturday, he was rather busy, but he talked to me for a little while. He figures that there are 17,000 people in the district – including Cantonville and suburban parishes. The latter are adjoining villages, one at least having been only recently formed. I understood that each of these was a new Catholic parish. There are, he said, too many people coming to look for work. The city and district are now larger than St Bernard. Before the mill came, there were but two hardware stores; one run by him and another in the upper town run by his cousin. Now there are seven: too many. There is, as before, but one movie.

There are practically no English farmers in the district; some about ten miles south in another community. The old English names in the town were Burns, Perkins, Stuart, etc. The city engineer is Lussier.

The secretary is Tremblay, a lawyer, who is running for the legislative on the Union Nationale ticket. He would have all the information licenses for business, the number of building permits, etc.

The curé is M. Lachance. He makes an annual house-to-house census of the town and can therefore give the best information about the population.

In looking for a camp, we visited the police station and saw the Chief, who is a champion weight lifter. He was said to own a summer camp, but he had got rid of it. We went to it anyway, on the river about two miles south of the town. It was a colony of cottages in the woods, rented to the French people of the town by the week or the month. There was none available for the week end. The man in charge said he had a son working the XYZ Plant; he made no progress and, after four years, was earning $18 a week for work and $22 in the weeks when he worked nights. The girls, he said, get the better pay, from $20 to $30 a week. The whole town depends on XYZ now, as the other factories are not working much. People are coming in from all over to look for work, so that there are now 4,000 unemployed. Families come in trucks with their furniture, from the U.S. and from all over Quebec.

We camped on the other side of the river north of the town on the land of M. Beauchamp, who owns a hotel, the biggest garage, and this camp. His daughter runs a florist's shop. The camp is a wooded strip along the river with cottages for rent. They were all full, but M. Beauchamp gave us permission to camp under the pines at the lower end of his land. The Beauchamp family live, apparently for the summer only, in a very nice cottage with screened porch, fireplace, etc. M. Beauchamp is a well-dressed businessman with a gracious manner (a hotel keeper) and speaks English. His wife speaks scarcely any English. She is a well-bred French lady. There were a number of young people about the house.

Beauchamp is apparently one of the leading businessmen of the town.

(Cited in Junker 1960, pp.22–4)

In this first extract we can see Hughes constructing an account of an initial encounter with Cantonville. He weaves together a 'guide-book' annotation of its physical characteristics and introduces some key characters. The physical description is developed into various social observations. The presence of the 'XYZ' Plant, its ownership of staff houses, the absence of planning restrictions and so on are observed by the stranger/ethnographer and recorded as potentially relevant issues. Hughes notes the contrast between St Bernard (older houses, well-kept, solid building materials) and Cantonville (new, more cheap building). Hughes speculates on social origins and social change, as he reads off evidence about language. He notes the French in contemporary public settings, contrasting it with former English. He reads the dates on buildings. He contrasts the Protestant Church with the Catholic parish and the curé. He sprinkles English names (of the dead, from the graveyard) and French names (living inhabitants of the present town). He notes business ownership and reports conversations concerning the town's social structure and social change.

In general, then, Hughes writes down the physical and cultural traces or signs. He hears and 'reads' these signs of life and transcribes them into his notes. The notes themselves are fairly polished. Hughes has worked up his observations and reflections into a narrative format. The extract reads like the account of a professional traveller describing the encounter with a new place. It is the 'gaze' of the traveller analogous to that described by Pratt (1986a), who writes of the antecedents of anthropology in travellers' accounts of 'people and customs'. The style Hughes adopts is a topographical one: the encounter of an observant stranger who embarks upon a cultural exploration, recording points of local colour and traces of local history. Hughes also enters into the beginning of a dialogue with himself, in foreshadowing future lines of development and further enquiry.

The following extracts, also reproduced from Junker, further display how the narrator 'reads' and writes signs in the field. Here the narrator is not constructing the description of a social setting. The genre owes less to the topographical and is focused on the discovery of 'character'. The character under consideration is revealed through the signs of personal belongings (books, furnishings). These are treated as codings of character and values. Likewise, the informant's own words are partially recorded in order to assemble what the writer of the notes finds a coherent and plausible account of motive and social action.

Looking at the built-in bookcases, which contained a number of well-thumbed books, I had a better chance to 'size her up.' In the book case were volumes on the topics of philosophy, world problems, art, and several recent novels. On the coffee table were books more appropriate for younger children, such as *Winnie the Pooh*. From these books a thought immediately came to me. It may be far off the track were I to investigate the family more intensely. The family seemed to be well informed about and quite aware of what is going on around them. Unlike the books of many of their contemporaries, who use the bookshelf to impress the guests with the 'first editions' or the '100 great books,' these books indicated fairly clearly that the family did not buy them to impress others, but rather to really read them and obtain some useful information from them....The books indicated that the family takes an interest in their children's school work.

The furnishings of the room, and the other rooms which could be seen, showed good taste. Although it is not ultra-conservative, it indicated that Mrs

Lemontree might be a rather reserved person. The atmosphere of the whole house seemed to supply the necessary words to a missing sign – if such a one were to be hung – 'Quiet.' One can spot this over-protective attitude which she has over her children. She rationalizes into saying that 'they need me'.

I would assume that from her rather tenderly and over-exaggerated description of the good points of her children, she spoils them quite a bit. Needless to say, the big disappointment of not having her children accepted into the ———— School made her turn against all private schools. But how did she justify sending her son to ———— [another private school]? 'He's too brilliant for the ———— [local public] School' was the answer – as if, 'in desperation', she had to turn to a private school to bring out all of the boy's above-average intelligence. Mrs Arnold's constant watching-out of her children's work has made her well-informed about the teachers of the schools, and she seemed to take great pride in telling me that she was not the usual kind of parent who did not know much about the schools to which their children go. Knowing her teachers 'well', Mrs Arnold's [justification for denouncing the teachers is strong indeed]. If we took her statement as is, we could feel that her children are above reproach in character – 'perfect saints and halos.' However, Mrs Arnold's over eagerness in telling the interviewer all about the 'goodness' of her children betrayed her genuineness.

(Junker 1960, p.113)

Here again, then, one sees the ethnographer moving from 'appearance' (signifier) to what is signified. Sometimes the observer writes as if the appearance is to be taken at face value; sometimes the overt message seems to betoken a *different* underlying reality. Throughout, however, the author is engaged in a complex set of 'readings' – of observations and inferences. These are transformed into the personal narrative of the ethnographer, who constructs this textual 'reality' from the shreds and patches of appearances and verbal testimony. Even though the informants speak, their authenticity is warranted by the ethnographer's incorporation of them into the definitive record.

The conduct of an ethnographic project will result in the accumulation, over months or even years, of voluminous notes of this sort (together with other data). The second major act of textual construction involves what is usually (and revealingly) called 'writing up'. Indeed, the traditional folk terminology of the craft is indicative of how the two processes are conceptualized. In the first mode, the ethnographer is engaged in 'writing down' what goes on: the imagery is that of transcription uninterrupted by self-conscious intervention or reflection. The second phase of 'writing up' carries stronger connotations of a constructive side to the writing. In this phase what was written 'down' is treated as data in the writing 'up'. As we have seen, however, *both* phases of the work involve the creation of textual materials; both are equally matters of textual construction.

The text that is constructed out of the field notes and whatever other data are to hand (such as interview transcripts, documents and so on) constructs and describes a social world. It conveys to the reader a sense of place and of persons. The physical space of the social world is peopled with actors who go about their daily lives and whose culture is portrayed. It is, therefore, part of the rhetorical work of the ethnography to persuade the reader of the existence of the world so represented and of the reasonableness of the account itself. Here therefore I shall deal with some aspects whereby ethnographers can construct 'descriptions' which warrant the plausible, factual nature of their accounts, and which artfully foreshadow important thematic elements in the sociology itself. In other words, my argument is that we are dealing not with mere descriptive writing (whatever 'mere' description might connote). It contains within it the *analytic* message of the sociology itself. In other words, when we talk of the role of 'understanding' or 'interpretation' in interpretative, qualitative studies, we are often dealing with something other than or additional to explicitly stated propositions. Often, the argument is conveyed at a more implicit level, through the very textual organization of accounts: in the way we select and write descriptions, narratives and so on; how we organize texts in thematic elements; how we draw upon metaphorical and metonymic uses of language; how, if at all, we shift point of view, and so on.

This descriptive work is accomplished throughout the ethnographic text, but it is especially important towards the beginning. Together with other bits of the textual apparatus, such as the title, it is crucial in establishing a framework of expectations and trust between the text and its reader. We often find that ethnographies begin with passages that 'set the scene' by way of introduction to the entire work. One of the most important functions performed by introductory or prefatory passages is the provision of certain sorts of warrant for the account it precedes. A term widely used in structuralist and post-structuralist literary theory, *vraisemblance*, captures part of this function particularly well. That is, the production of 'reality-like' effects – the ways in which an account's 'authenticity', grounded in an everyday shared reality, is guaranteed. In general terms, it is not usually sufficient for a text/author simply to announce that a given account is to be read as a 'factual' one. For a text to 'come off' in that way then it normally has to conform to what we (conventionally) take to be realistic and factual texts.

What I have said so far applies equally well to what we normally think of as 'literary' rather than scholarly or scientific products. This is certainly the case for varieties of 'realistic' fiction. Indeed, this is one particular focus for a good deal of attention on the part of literary theorists. In theorizing about the textual conventions and codes of the novel and the short story, critical theorists have sought to uncover some of the ways in which texts achieve their reality-like effects, and can be read as plausible accounts of the everyday world of shared mundane experience. This is how Todorov (1968) puts it:

> one can speak of the *vraisemblance* of a work in so far as it attempts to make
> us believe that it conforms to reality and not to its own laws. In other words,

the *vraisemblance* is the mask which conceals the text's own laws and which we are supposed to take for a relation with reality.

(Todorov 1968, pp.2–3)

This is not a simple relation. As Todorov also remarks, 'there are as many versions of *vraisemblance* as there are genres'. There is, therefore, another facet to such verisimilitude: the extent to which texts recognizably conform to the canons of an appropriate mode of organization for a given genre.

As I have remarked at much greater length elsewhere (Atkinson 1983), there is a long, but often ambivalent, relationship between the literary and the ethnographic. It is abundantly clear that while they differ in many respects, such texts share many similar stylistic devices, used to achieve parallel effects. In the rest of this chapter I intended both to illustrate and to exploit such parallelism. For obvious reasons, the great majority of critical studies have been undertaken on works of 'literature'. It is, therefore, a handy heuristic device – at bare minimum – to take comparable extracts from literary and sociological texts, and to see what mileage may be gained from the use of 'literary' insights towards an understanding of the ethnographic.

I intend, therefore, to take comparable extracts from the *openings* of texts, with particular emphasis on how the text creates an 'introduction' to a 'spirit of place'. This is by no means the only sort of opening which is conventionally available, and as we shall see, it has sub-types. It is, however, a style of opening which is common in many realist novels and stories; it is also used by authors of ethnographic texts.

Literary and sociological accounts

Rather than pre-empting much of the later discussion by offering general propositions about such textual elements, let me now continue by presenting some specific examples. I have chosen two opening paragraphs from published works. They comprise a 'literary' and a 'sociological' exemplar. The choices are far from random. They have surface similarities in the subject-matter and treatment. Furthermore, the 'literary' example has already been considered by critical theorists. Hence my own approach here is somewhat artful. It will no doubt tend to exaggerate similarities between the literary and the sociological but, initially at any rate, I would seek to justify it on heuristic grounds. In defence of the strategy, furthermore, I add that the pairing was in no sense hard to find. I did not have to spend a great deal of time and effort rummaging through the literature in order to come up with relevant examples.

The pair of extracts has been selected because the two extracts apparently describe similar scenes and settings – the first a lunch-room and the second a cocktail bar – and both describe similar social activities of 'ordering'. Moreover, as will become apparent, both do a great deal more than that. Furthermore, as I have already said, both extracts have the textual function of opening or introducing a longer written account: in one case a short story, and in the other an ethnographic account.

The first of the extracts is taken from a short story by Hemingway ('The Killers'); the second is the opening of the ethnography *The Cocktail Waitress* by Spradley and Mann (1975). The opening of the Hemingway is chosen primarily because it has already received critical consideration from a number of authors, including Fowler (1977). For ease of reference I have adopted the convention of numbering the separate sentences in each of the passages. First, then, the Hemingway extract, 'Henry's Lunch-Room':

1   The door of Henry's lunch-room opened and two men came in.

2   They sat down at the counter.

3   'What's yours?' George asked them.

4   'I don't know,' one of the men said.

5   'What do you want to eat, Al?'

6   'I don't know,' said Al.

7   'I don't know what I want to eat.'

8   Outside it was getting dark.

9   The street-light came on outside the window.

10   The two men at the counter read the menu.

11   From the other end of the counter Nick Adams watched them.

12   He had been talking to George when they came in.

13   'I'll have a roast pork tenderloin with apple sauce and mashed potatoes,' the first man said.

14   'It isn't ready yet.'

15   'What the hell do you put it on the card for?'

16   'That's the dinner,' George explained.

17   'You can get that at six o'clock.'

18   George looked at the clock on the wall behind the counter.

19   'It's five o'clock.'

20   'The clock says twenty minutes past five', the second man said.

21   'It's twenty minutes fast.'

22   'Oh, to hell with the clock,' the first man said.

23 'What have you got to eat?'

24 'I can give you any kind of sandwiches,' George said.

25 'You can have ham and eggs, bacon and eggs, liver and bacon, or a steak.'

26 'Give me chicken croquettes with green peas and cream sauce and mashed potatoes.'

27 'That's the dinner.'

28 'Everything we want's the dinner, eh?'

29 'That's the way you work it.'

30 'I can give you ham and eggs, bacon and eggs, liver –.'

31 'I'll take the ham and eggs,' the man called Al said.

32 He wore a derby hat and a black overcoat buttoned across the chest.

33 His face was small and white and he had tight lips.

34 He wore a silk muffler and gloves.

(Hemingway, quoted in Fowler 1977, pp.48–9)

In order to establish at least a preliminary framework, I shall rely heavily on Fowler's commentary on this extract. First, Fowler (1977) shows how the organization of the text achieves certain kinds of *effect*. The text is highly ordered and stylistically coherent, while the repetitive style, he suggests, contributes to a sense that the main 'action' of the narrative is being postponed. This is achieved in large measure by the arrangement of nouns and pronouns. This, Fowler argues, 'simultaneously holds the text together, and holds it up'. In other words, it contributes to an overall effect of 'suspense'. This tight, repetitive ordering is evident, for instance, with respect to the thematic content of 'food'. As Fowler himself puts it:

'What's yours' in sentence 3 implies a deleted object naming a choice of food; in 4 the deletion is sustained; the food-choice is named by the referentially opaque 'what', echoing George's 'what' in 3; 6 and 7 repeat the refusal-to-name of 3–5 (note that 7 is an echoic syntactic transformation of the sum of 4 and 5). 13 implies a proverb 'have' to 'eat' in 5 and 7 and fills in the previously unspecified object-position 'a roast pork tenderloin'; this object is then pronominalized as 'it' and 'that' in 14 and 15, 16 and 17. A new routine figuring the same topic begins with 'what' in 23 (recalling 3, 3, 7) which is replaced by fully lexicalised noun phrases specifying items of food in 24, 25, 26, 30 and 31, and pronominalized in 27 and 28.

(Fowler 1977, p.50)

The fragment of text also reveals a general stylistic feature of Hemingway's writing; that is, a tendency to write as an 'impersonal' author who neither discloses himself, nor claims privileged insight or knowledge concerning the characters. Certainly the extract from the story is marked by a minimal degree of overt 'interpretation' on the part of the author/narrator. As Fowler points out, there are

> no verbs such as 'feel' which would suggest an inner view, or 'seem' which would draw attention to a narrator tentatively judging from outside a character ('He felt nervous' or 'he seemed nervous' are taboo here); no sentence-adverbs indicating degree of commitment ('probably', 'definitely'); no evaluative adjectives.
>
> (Fowler 1977, p.53)

As Fowler also remarks, this general stylistic feature is paralleled by the minimal use of verbs introducing the dialogue (almost entirely 'asked' and 'said'). The only hints we get of the author/narrator's knowledge and allegiance are these:

> the very first phrase, 'The door of Henry's lunch-room', which, because it is definite, refers to an institution we assume to be already familiar to the narrator; sentence 12 which relates information about the Nick–George group's behaviour anterior to the entry of the gangsters, and so suggests the narrator's membership of the group; and 31, 'the man called Al', by which the narrator disclaims knowledge of 'Al's' real identity.
>
> (Fowler 1977, p.53)

> Overall, then, this brief and rather spare opening of 'The Killers' achieves a good deal, in terms of style and narrative. The textual organization, coupled with the narrator's apparent lack of knowledge about 'Al' and his companion, suggest an element of suspense. The two newcomers are not simply that – they are 'outsiders': not known to the narrator and the other 'insiders', they themselves do not 'know the ropes' (hence the wrangle over what food is available). As the actors are introduced to the reader, so they are separated into the two opposed groups. Fowler concludes his brief analysis:

> The action and the characters begin to receive some more specific, and at the same time mythological, symbolic, semantic content. I have already spoken of 'intrusion', 'aggression'; there is an opposition between the familiar and the alien, the inside or domestic and the outside or foreign, a stock thematic opposition expressed here by the polarization of the characters.
>
> (Fowler 1977, p.54)

Even without further detailed analysis one can glimpse here how the various elements of the text combine to produce the coherence and effect that they do by way of introducing the story.

When we turn to the second fragment, from *The Cocktail Waitress* (1975), we find that we are dealing with a not dissimilar text. Although I am not for one moment claiming that they are 'the same' in content, style or author's intentions, there are certainly instructive similarities.

Brady's bar

1 It is an ordinary evening.

2 Outside a light spring rain gives softness to the night air of the city.

3 Inside Brady's the dim lights behind the bar balance the glow from the low-burning candles on each table.

4 A relaxed attitude pervades the atmosphere.

5 Three young men boisterously call across the room to the waitress and order another round of beer.

6 For one of them, recently come of age, tonight marks his legal entry into this sacred place of adult drinking.

7 A couple sits at a secluded corner table, slowly sipping their rum and Cokes, whispering to one another.

8 An old man enters alone and ambles unsteadily toward the bar, joining the circle of men gathered there.

9 The bartender nods to the newcomer and takes his order as he listens patiently to a regular customer who talks loudly of his problems at home.

10 Four men pick up their drinks and move away from the commotion at the bar to an empty table nearby.

11 The cocktail waitress brushes against a shoulder as she places clean ashtrays and napkins in front of them.

12 'Would you care to order another drink here?'

13 Her smile is pleasant, yet detached.

14 Her miniskirt and knee-high boots add silently to the image that her smile conveys.

15 'Scotch and water.'

16 'Same.'

17 'Manhattan.'

18 'Gin and tonic.'

19 She remembers the orders easily and on her way back to the bar stops to empty dirty ashtrays and retrieve the used glasses and bottles.

20 Two customers at the next table are on their third round, and as the waitress passes their table, one reaches out, touching her waist.

21 'What are you doin' after work, honey?'

22 The other man at the table laughs, she steps out of reach, ignoring the question, and continues on her way.

23 Seconds later, she gives the bartender her order, bantering with him about the customers.

24 In a few minutes she is back, effortlessly balancing a tray of drinks, collecting money, making change and always smiling.

(Spradley and Mann 1975, pp.1–2)

Without for a moment suggesting that the authors of the sociological monograph were deliberately modelling themselves on Hemingway or any other specific author of fiction, one can immediately note some similarities in the respective treatments of similar social settings. There are differences too, of course. One immediate difference is that the narrator is willing to commit him- or herself to greater freedom in describing the action: 'a relaxed attitude'; 'boisterously call'; 'listens patiently'; 'her smile is pleasant yet detached' and so on. Nevertheless, the overall impression conveyed in the passage is that of the observer. Although the narrator remarks on the participants, he or she does so from the point of view of an interpreter of observable actions and attributes – the waitress's clothing, 'effortlessly balancing drinks' and so forth. Apart from the readily observable work of the bartender and the waitress, the narrator offers only two pieces of information which may not be observable directly: one young man has recently come of age, and one customer is identified as a 'regular'. Either we must assume that the narrator is claiming privileged prior knowledge, or that these were directly inferred from their behaviour at the bar.

These two titbits of information about the people in the bar serve only to highlight how little we are told about a relatively large number of customers. By and large they are identified for us by means of the most general and anonymous of categories: 'three young men'; 'one of them'; 'a couple'; 'an old man'; 'the circle of men'; 'the newcomer'; 'a regular customer'; 'four men'. Similarly, 'the bartender' and 'the waitress' are not identified any further. The only name which is mentioned is Brady's, the name of the bar itself.

The repetitious nature of this fragment lies in the series of more or less anonymous characters about whom little more is learned. The only thematic coherence which is used to link them together as a series of 'attributes' lies in the drinks which at least some of them are described as having or are heard ordering. In large measure this stylistic feature parallels the thematic coherence of the Hemingway passage, generated through the ordering (or not ordering) of food. Here we find the separate, minimally identified characters with: 'another round of beer' (5): 'their rum and Cokes' (7); 'four men pick up their drinks' (10); 'Scotch and water' (15); 'Same' (16); 'Manhattan' (17); 'gin and tonic' (18); 'on their third round' (20). In the stretch of dialogue in 15 to 18 ('an order') the naming of drinks is all that is done; and, apart from Brady's, drink names are the only names which appear.

Presumably, the ethnographer/narrator, having completed the research to be reported, knows more than is given away here. There is, one assumes, a good deal which could be divulged at the outset. For example, the bartender, the waitress and the regular should be known, at least by name. More 'privileged', 'inside' information could be vouchsafed the reader. In fact, in refraining from mentioning such things, this introduction is quite artfully managed, in much the same way that the Hemingway extract is constructed.

Neither extract is explicitly labelled as a 'preface' or 'introduction', or 'setting the scene'; but quite clearly each of these extracts can be read as an opening passage. Both have a certain economy of style and within a relatively brief span each accomplishes basic and important prefatory work. As already suggested, the Hemingway extract achieves a degree of 'suspense'. In a rather similar fashion, the opening of the *The Cocktail Waitress* deftly sets the scene by simultaneously establishing significant themes *and* holding back potentially available information.

Although clearly trading off accumulated knowledge (by virtue of the research to be reported in the monograph) the narrator in *The Cocktail Waitress* introduces the reader to the setting as if both were relative strangers, observing the scene from the outside, as it were. Hence the work is introduced with the expectation that there will be further exploration and discovery of 'inside' knowledge. At the same time, as I have hinted already, themes are introduced and foreshadowed implicitly. Briefly, we might characterize them thus: Brady's is a relatively anonymous place, where customers have in common only their shared pursuit of drinking. It is characteristic of such a setting, then, that the only episode of social interaction which is reported here – apart from the ordering of drinks – is the waitress's *refusal* of an invitation and avoidance of social engagement. The way in which the waitress coolly disengages from this advance thus pinpoints the anonymity and lack of overall cohesion among the various parties. Similarly, the *variety* of the customers in Brady's bar is hinted at – again by virtue of the way in which they are introduced as a series, with no overt linkage, with only a bare amount of information. Other than the bar itself, the reader has no further framework in which to locate this collection of, apparently, randomly selected customers.

At this stage in the reading, an inspection of the text does not guarantee that such thematic strands will be confirmed. For all we know, the author/narrator will overturn our expectations. It is however, instructive to note the paragraph which immediately follows this introductory scene-setting. Here the style shifts abruptly, from a 'literary', descriptive mode to a discussion which is more clearly and recognizably 'sociological':

Ritually, this scene is repeated millions of times each night in bars and cocktail lounges throughout the country. Here one finds a wide range of behavior to observe: lonely individuals seeking human companionship for a few hours, people hustling for a little action, business men conducting interviews and closing deals, others gambling, dancing, holding wedding celebrations, and even attending birthday parties – those individual rites of passage by which our culture marks off the transition from child to adult. From corporation executive to college student, to skid-row bum, nearly every kind of person can be found in one or another type of bar.

(Spradley and Mann 1975, p.2)

Here, then, at least one of the themes which has been presented implicitly in the first-hand 'observational' account is now generalized into an explicitly sociological observation and related to recognizably sociological or anthropological concepts, such as 'rites of passage'. The *local* in Brady's bar is thus transformed into the *archetypal*, a thoroughly familiar and pervasive aspect of contemporary American culture.

What, then, of the relationship between these two paragraphs from *The Cocktail Waitress*? Arguably, perhaps, the first is redundant. The authors state their sociological themes explicitly and succinctly enough in the second section. But such a view would mistake the textual function of the introductory passage. It serves to warrant the subsequent sociological discourse by establishing its *vraisemblance*. It furnishes the 'guarantee' of an eyewitness report, couched in terms of the dispassionate observer, using the conventional style of the realist writer of fiction, or documentary reporter.

The Cocktail Waitress and 'The Killers' share one further specific feature relevant to their *vraisemblance*. Each contains a passing reference to conditions 'outside'. In the Hemingway: 'Outside it was getting dark. The street-light came on outside the window' (8 and 9). In the Spradley and Mann: 'It is an ordinary evening. Outside a light spring rain gives softness to the night air of the city' (1 and 2). Again, one might at first glance think that such remarks were gratuitous, but in the context of the two descriptions these two fleeting observations are far from insignificant.

In the first place they both have a function in helping to establish the contrast between 'inside' and 'outside' – a basic theme in both narratives, where the arrival of unknown outsiders to a place of familiarity and 'regulars' is of some significance. Further, these references are all that link the enclosed settings to the world beyond their confines. They have an important function in these texts quite disproportionate to their length or complexity. Indeed, it is their very 'mundane' or 'matter-of-fact' expression which contributes to their force.

Roland Barthes (1968) indicates for us the function of these two very similar passages, in identifying the importance of the 'reality effect' (*l'effet de réel*). Such descriptive elements function to establish the 'narrative contract' whereby the reader is, at least provisionally, guaranteed that the narrative refers to a recognizable world of shared everyday reality: 'Elements of this kind confirm the mimetic contract and assure the reader that he can interpret the text as about a real world' (Culler 1975, p.193). Appositely enough for the particular examples considered here, Culler cites a counter-instance from Robbe-Grillet, in which mutually contradictory statements about conditions 'outside' are made, so that the mimetic contract of the natural attitude is rendered problematic: 'Outside it is raining...outside it is cold...outside it is sunny...'. There, in the opening paragraph of *Dans le labyrinthe*, it is the arrangement – the symmetry and development – of the text itself which is of prime importance. A realistic referential function is subordinated and disrupted here. As Heath (1972) remarks in this context:

> The vraisemblance of traditional narrative is 'brought to the surface', the expectations of the novel, so much a part of our Real, are demonstrated in the forms on which they depend; the 'subject' of the novels is their composition, the structuration of the *text* itself which is present(ed) as such, strictly 'un roman qui se pense lui-même'.

This contrast, then, helps throw into relief the conventional character of the sort of *vraisemblance* and reality-effect achieved by the short passages referred to from 'The Killers' and *The Cocktail Waitress*. They are by no means arbitrary or insignificant.

In general terms, therefore, a preliminary inspection of our first pair of examples helps to illuminate some features of ethnographic writing as exemplified in *The Cocktail Waitress*. We have seen how stylistic elements are used to 'set the scene', to foreshadow sociological themes and arguments, and to establish a mimetic contract with the reader. The introductory passage provides the warrant of first-hand, authentic and 'realistic' reportage, whereby the reader is introduced to a convincingly plausible reality.

Establishing the narrative contract

One of the important devices whereby the narrative contract is invited in the text is via the rhetorical device known as *hypotyposis*; that is, the use of a highly graphic passage of descriptive writing, which portrays a scene or action in a vivid and arresting manner. It is used to conjure up the setting and its actors, and to 'place' the implied reader as a first-hand witness. The opening section of *The Cocktail Waitress* exemplifies it.

Crapanzano (1986) has discussed the role of ethnographic hypotyposis in relation to the writing of George Catlin's early descriptions of North American Indian scenes: 'His aim is to impress his experience of what he has *seen* so strongly, so vividly, on his readers that they cannot doubt its veracity. It is the visual that gives authority' (p.57). Likewise, Edmondson (1984, p.38) remarks on the use of vivid visual imagery in Rex's introduction to Rex and Moore (1967), where 'the immigrant' is presented to the reader in vivid terms and visual imagery. Edmondson also notes how Willis uses varieties of hypotyposis to enable the reader to 'visualize' individual 'lads'.

The figure of hypotyposis is not used throughout the ethnographic monograph in equal measure. It is frequently deployed at key junctures. It is used to establish and reaffirm the relationship of co-presence of reader and author 'at the scene'. The narrative contract is thus maintained through these vivid representations. The figure is used, as we have seen already, to introduce settings and social actors, or to establish key transitions in the text. The reader enters into a sympathetic engagement with the social scene and its characters.

The use of this figure is especially well exemplified in Gouldner's *Patterns of Industrial Bureaucracy* (1954), at a point where the text establishes a new social and physical location, and seems to invite a particular response from the reader. The scenic transition represents a crucial analytic point in Gouldner's sociological analysis. Readers familiar with Gouldner's book will recall that its subject-matter concerns rule-use and social control in a gypsum plant. Among other themes and contrasts is the distinction between miners working underground and surface workers in the factory above. Gouldner wishes to argue that social relationships, groups and uses of social rules differ in the two contrasting locations. At one point in the text Gouldner takes the reader underground. The relevant chapter starts with a passage which is remarkable for its use of graphic imagery. It stands out even against the background of a vigorously written and memorably argued book. It has perhaps elements of the 'purple passage', but it functions very clearly as a transition: the reader is transported into the new physical setting.

> The two production spheres, mine and surface, were sharply contrasting parts of the total work system at the Oscar Center plant. The workers themselves saw these two divisions as vitally different in many ways. Miners and surface men, workers and supervisors, all viewed the mine as being 'in another world'.
>
> Access to the mine could be secured by either of two routes: One way was to take a battered, gate-enclosed elevator at the surface, down to the mine's 'foot'. Another, was to walk down (what to a sedentary researcher appears to be) an interminable length of rough, wooden staircases, under a low roof which necessitated frequent bending and careful footwork. A vault-like spiral of rock entombed the staircase as it crisscrossed downward. While descending the air grows moister, and trickles of water seemingly ooze out of nowhere.
>
> At the bottom, or 'foot' of the mine, the rough offices of the mine supervisor were hewn into rock, and here, too, were the miners' locker rooms and the maintenance men's machines and equipment. The rooms were separated from each other by unfinished walls, adorned by an occasional pin-up girl and desultory office-notices. Dominating the scene with its roaring noises was the rock crusher. Into the rock crusher railroad cars dumped large lumps of gypsum which came from the mine....
>
> At the 'face', in these mining rooms, the men worked in near darkness, while moving beams of light from the lamps in their helmets formed ever-changing patterns against the darkness. Generally, the light was focused on objects, gyp rock and machines, while the men peered out of the darkness which enveloped them. A low ceiling, three and one-half to five feet high,

often forced the miners to work bent over, and sometimes on their knees. The noise created by the machinery in operation, which was most of the time, made communication among the men at the face difficult. The roar of the crusher at the foot was matched by the clang of the joy-loader at the face as it scooped up the gyp set free by the miners' blasts. It was frequently necessary to shout in order to be heard, and even this occasionally proved inadequate.

(Gouldner 1954, pp.105–7)

At this point Gouldner himself notes that this description of the mine was deliberately written in what he calls a 'subjective' way. In that footnote Gouldner raises the analytically important issue: that he and his research team felt that, unlike the surface, 'the mine was not, and could not be, bureaucratised'. The sociological observation was initially tied to the researchers' personal response to the mine itself. Their 'hunches', theories and responses are mutually interdependent, and Gouldner attempts to convey them in the writing which introduces the underground mine as a physical and social environment. Gouldner draws on sensory imagery – tactile emphasis on the texture of the surfaces; the play of light and dark; the enveloping noise from the machinery. Noticeably, the miners themselves remain obscure and shadowy figures in comparison with the physical scene.

The use of hypotyposis here, therefore, serves several functions in the development of Gouldner's argument. It forcefully introduces the new setting, and marks the transition between above-ground and below-ground. The arrangement of the passage and its style 'take' the reader beneath the surface, recapitulating the journey of the miners, and of course of the researchers. Again, therefore, we find this rhetorical figure being used to align the reader empathetically with a particular perspective on the social setting, the actors and the action within it. It draws reader and narrator together into a complicity of shared viewpoints.

There is a close relationship between the 'authenticity' of these vivid accounts and the authority of the account – and hence of the author. Authenticity is warranted by virtue of the ethnographer's own first-hand attendance and participation. It is therefore mirrored in the 'presence' of the reader in the action that is reproduced through the text. The ethnographer is a virtuoso – a witness of character and credibility. It is therefore important that 'eye-witness' evidence be presented which recapitulates that experience.

The graphic representation of physical or social scenes is but one important textual element that exemplifies the significance of metaphorical writing. As Crapanzano says in relation to the Catlin reportage of the O-Kee-Pa ceremony: 'he is in fact no objectivist, no Robbe-Grillet, describing the ceremony laboriously, metonymous step by metonymous step' (Crapanzano 1986, p.56). Indeed, none of the texts of sociological or anthropological ethnography essays non-metaphorical descriptions; and certainly the graphic descriptive passages that 'place' the work are often highly metaphorical. The 'realism' of such textual elements is not achieved by their purely metonymic features.

The figure of hypotyposis may be coupled with a major metaphor which simultaneously establishes the setting to be explored and the proposed way of understanding that setting. An early example from the Chicago School can be taken from the opening sequence of Thrasher's *The Gang* (1927).

The characteristic habitat of Chicago's numerous gangs is that broad twilight zone of railroads and factories, of deteriorating neighborhoods and shifting populations, which borders the city's central business district on the north, on the west, and on the south. The gangs dwell among the shadows of the slum. Yet, dreary and repellent as their external environment must seem to the casual observer, their life is to the initiated at once vivid and fascinating. They live in a world distinctly their own – far removed from the humdrum existence of the average citizen.

It is in such regions as the gang inhabits that we find much of the romance and mystery of a great city. Here are comedy and tragedy. Here is melodrama which excels the recurrent 'thrillers' at the downtown theaters. Here are unvarnished emotions. Here also is a primitive democracy that cuts through all the conventional social and racial discriminations. The gang, in short, is *life*, often rough and untamed, yet rich in elemental social processes significant to the student of society and human nature.

The gang touches in a vital way almost every problem in the life of the community. Delinquencies among its members all the way from truancy to serious crimes, disturbances of the peace from street brawls to race riots, and close alliance with beer running, labor slugging, and corrupt politics – all are attributed to the gang, whose treatment presents a puzzle to almost every public or private agency in the city, which deals with boys and young men.

Gangs, like most other social groups, originate under conditions that are typical for all groups of the same species; they develop in definite and predictable ways, in accordance with a form of entelechy that is predetermined by characteristic internal processes and mechanisms, and have, in short, a nature and natural history.

(Thrasher 1927, pp.3–4)

Thrasher's monograph here begins with a highly coloured introductory passage. (The text reproduced above is the entire 'Introduction'.) It establishes a special physical setting for the account, and foreshadows a particular stance towards it. The style presages a romantic and naturalistic tone that will be repeated throughout the monograph. It is especially noticeable how the author implies authoritative knowledge which is provisionally withheld from the reader. There is a constant interplay between the familiar and the strange, the mundane and the exotic, the drab, everyday surroundings and the exotic action they contain. Here, then, the descriptive scene-setting is mingled with metaphorical writing which foreshadows much of the sociological treatment: the images of the 'primitive' and 'elemental' are significant. Thrasher begins to weave together the urban landscape with a parallel set of images – that of the 'jungle'. The 'introduction' thus contains an implied contract. The text will display the unknown and the exotic, and will render it comprehensible. At the outset the taken-for-granted order of experience has been questioned: what to the casual observer is repellent will be shown to be exciting and vibrant, while the life of the 'average' reader will be shown to be humdrum by comparison. The reader's attention is thus solicited in this titillating introduction. Moreover, as the last paragraph of the four makes clear, this alien reality will be naturalized once more into the domain of natural entities, of species and forms and mechanisms. The reader may embark on the journey of discovery safe in the knowledge that for all its strangeness, this social world will ultimately be revealed with all the reassuring certainty of natural history.

The initial 'scene-setting' of ethnographic description is just one of several introductory and prefatory elements in the text that help to establish its authenticity and foreshadow an appropriate frame of reference for its implied reader. These elements all contribute to the potential persuasiveness of the text and its sociological arguments. The rhetorical devices already alluded to combine with what we might normally think of as the more straightforwardly 'scientific'. The sociological reader is unlikely to be engaged and swayed by a text merely by a 'factual' account of its methodology, a careful review of the literature, and so on, if the rest of the text is found severely wanting.

Ethnographic entitlement

One of the many textual elements which contribute to the 'self-presentation' of the text is the *title*. Together with elements such as an abstract (in the case of some journal articles) they establish a framework, and a set of reader's expectations. The title does not simply name or identify the monograph or paper; nor should it necessarily be thought of as a 'mere' preliminary. Even something like the title may be an important constituent of the 'meaning' of the text.

It would be quite wrong to imply that there is a unique set or style of ethnographic titles. One cannot scan a list of sociological works and tell simply from the titles what methodological or theoretical approach is inscribed in each. On the other hand, there are tendencies which are observable within the discipline. One suspects that the reader who is moderately well versed in the genres of sociology will read at least some titles as indicating the probability of one or other approach.

It is hard to pin down in any definitive way, but the ethnography is more likely to be topped off with a 'literary' title, with an apparently self-conscious use of rhetorical devices and allusions. Again, these devices are by no means unique to ethnographic texts, but are highly characteristic of them. There is a marked tendency for descriptive titles to be avoided, or relegated to sub-titles, while main titles (especially in monographs) are more likely to draw on allusive and figurative uses of language.

Titles do more than merely announce the subject-matter and contents of what is to follow. Indeed, some titles seem to invite closer inspection of the text precisely in so far as they do not explicitly reveal their subject-matter to the uninitiated. The organization and contents of titles thus reflect the rhetorical or literary features of the ethnographic text in general. Moreover, the construction of ethnographic titles may often reflect more general features of the rhetoric of ethnographic argument.

One of the most noticeable of such parallels between titles and styles of argument is the use of paired clauses which indicate a specific, concrete, local topic and a general sociological theme. This reflects the sort of approach to problem formulation and analysis based on a distinction between 'topical' and 'generic' issues. 'Topical' issues – which could also be referred to as 'local' – refer to specific social settings or locales; 'generic' issues are trans-situational analytic concepts which refer to general, formal categories. Whereas the former are more concrete, the latter have a more abstract quality.

Many titles, then, are constructed out of pairs of phrases – either Topical: Generic or Generic:Topical. The following exemplify the Topical:Generic ordering:

The World from Brown's Lounge: An Ethnography of Black Middle-Class Play

'Parole Interviews of Sex Offenders: The Role of Impression Management'

'Conducting Presentencing Investigations: From Discourse to Textual Summaries'

'Chicano Used Car Dealers: A Social World in Microcosm'

The second alternative – a Generic:Topical ordering – seems to be rather more common. The following are of this form:

From Obscurity to Oblivion: Running in the Congressional Primary

Predicting Dangerousness: The Social Construction of Psychiatric Reality

'Occupational Aesthetics: How Trade School Students Learn to Cook'

'Collective Matters as Individual Concerns: Peer Culture Among Graduate Students'

'Meanwhile Backstage: Public Bathrooms and the Interaction Order'

The two orderings of topical and generic concerns seem to me to have no difference in rhetorical force. What they share is a very succinct manner of announcing the strategy (or at least *a* strategy) for finding significance in the book or paper. The reader may there find grounds or search strategies for linking the concrete detail and description derived from the fieldwork with analytic frameworks. The title itself thus demonstrates a number of things. The first is that it is about something 'more than', 'beyond', or of 'wider significance than' the boundaries of the author's own local study. Second, the reader may be led to fill in links with other texts which relate to 'the same' generic framework. Indeed, a reader may find an invitation to read a book or paper attractive in so far as it is linked (implicitly or explicitly) with better-known and 'important' sociological works and authors. For instance, the reader who encounters the following paper, 'Meanwhile Backstage: Public Bathrooms and the Interaction Order' may well do so in the expectation that it will draw on the well-known generic distinction between 'frontstage' and 'backstage'. Such an expectation will likely be sustained by the abstract (in that journal, printed before the title):

This article, based on observational research, provides a microsociological analysis of the behavior that routinely occurs in public bathrooms. Our findings indicate that occupants of public bathrooms routinely perform a number of interpersonal rituals and engage in a variety of backstage behaviors. Analysis of these routine bathroom behaviors reveals the degree to which members of this society are oriented to certain shared values and behavioral standards. These shared values and behavioral standards are identified, and some suggestions regarding their broader sociological significance are advanced.

(Cahill 1985, p.33)

We can note in passing that this – like many abstracts – is itself primarily a claim or announcement of 'significance' rather than a description or précis of the paper's contents. Here the reader is promised that the paper is going to 'indicate', 'analyse', 'reveal', 'identify', 'suggest' and 'advance'; the general categories which will be the predicates of these performatives are: 'interpersonal rituals', 'backstage behaviors', 'shared values', 'behavioral standards'. The reader is not spared reading the paper, however, as the nature of these values, behaviours and so on is not revealed.

One assumes that the reader will thus embark on a reading of the paper with the expectation of finding 'microsociological' significance, and the work of Goffman informing the analysis of interpersonal ritual. Such an expectation would be met by the introductory passages of the paper itself:

Thirty years ago the anthropologist Horace Miner...suggested, with tongue planted firmly in cheek, that many of the rituals that behaviorally express and sustain the central values of our culture occur in bathrooms. Whether Miner realized it or not, and one suspects that he did, there was more to his thesis than his humorous interpretation of bathroom rituals suggest. As Erving Goffman ... once observed, the vital secrets of our public shows are often visible in those settings that serve as backstage regions relative to our public performances:

it is here that illusions and impressions are openly constructed....Here the performer can relax; he can drop his front, forgo speaking his lines, and step out of character.

77

Clearly, bathrooms, or, as they are often revealingly called *rest* rooms, are such backstage regions. By implication, therefore, systematic study of bathroom behavior may yield valuable insights into the character and requirements of our routine public performances.

(Cahill 1985, pp.33–4)

Between them, therefore, the title, the abstract and the opening paragraph – with its embedded quote – achieve a good deal of persuasive work with the reader before any evidence is presented of the actual behaviour referred to. The paper establishes intertextual links which will help to 'place' it in relation to a corpus of other concerns and analyses. Such implicit claims may help the reader to construct the paper as a serious undertaking and redeem it from a charge of triviality or flippancy. (After all, public lavatories are the stuff more commonly of jokes than serious scholarly commentary. Studies such as Laud Humphreys' account of homosexual encounters, in the notorious *Tearoom Trade* (1970) are likely to be remembered for their somewhat scandalous circumstances – with a snigger – rather than as major contributions to sociological work.) In this respect it is noteworthy that the paper under consideration begins with reference to a 'jokey' approach to the subject. The text seems to recognize or predict an objection of 'triviality' and to pre-empt such criticism through such recognition. It contrasts the playful remark by Miner with the undoubtedly serious work of Goffman. The reader may thus be brought to a position where he or she is willing to acknowledge that there is something *serious* to be said about public lavatories, and that such commentary can be illuminating of more than just that sort of setting.

It is at this point that the paper proceeds through a tried and trusted textual device. Having persuasively argued for the obvious relevance and importance of the general topic, an apparent absence of relevant treatment in the literature may be projected as a surprising or at least noticeable absence. The paper in question continues, with the beginning of the next paragraph:

Unfortunately, however, students of everyday social life have shown little interest in this topic of inquiry. Although public bathrooms have occasionally served as research settings, the resulting studies have only been tangentially concerned with the behavior that routinely occurs within such settings.

(Cahill 1985, p.34)

Now it would, admittedly, be rash to try to project all of this and more just from the title of the paper; the sociologically informed reader can be expected to fill in a good deal of interpretative work of this sort from a very first encounter with the paper. In fact, that is how I approached writing this brief commentary myself: I wrote what I expected from the title from the contents page, before reading the abstract, and wrote about that before I read the beginning of the paper. At each point the reader (*this* reader) finds expectations confirmed and further expectations projected as the text unfolds. Certainly, the expectation derived from the title is more than sufficiently fulfilled: as the paper proceeds it is sustained almost entirely by a framework of references to the work of Goffman. Indeed, one might hypothesize that in the case of this particular paper, its intertextuality is so clearly projected that a sociologically competent reader will find it all too predictable; that no 'news' will be found in formulating public lavatories as backstage regions.

Such observations should not be read as implying that these are the only ways of reading the paper. One may equally well find in such textual organizations grounds for something like the following: 'Here we go again – sociologists displaying their penchant for making pretentious generalizations about the most trivial of things; dressing up their trite observations in unnecessary jargon and bolstering their flimsy arguments with references to other sociologists.' The identification of persuasive devices does not imply that readers are compelled to endorse the most favourable construction the text will support.

So far I have identified and exemplified one device in the construction and reading of titles, based on the juxtaposition of topical and generic categories. Such an organization is by no means the only one: other types are equally characteristic of the genre. The first device reflects and projects one important feature of ethnographic work. Other title types emphasize other, complementary aspects of the work.

Although it is by no means a universal phenomenon, many ethnographic texts make a virtue of providing an entrée into strange and exotic settings, each of which is characterized by its own cultural categories. It is, therefore, a common device for ethnographic titles to incorporate – even to consist of – terms which conjure up and allude to the esoteric. Take the following:

Woods Working Women: Sexual Integration in the US Forest Service

The Joint: Language and Culture in a Maximum Security Prison

'Making Rank: Becoming an American Police Sergeant'

Ripping and Running

'Slinging Weed: The Social Organization of Streetcorner Marijuana Sales'

'"Trauma Junkies" and Street Work: Occupational Behaviour of Paramedics and Emergency Medical Technicians'

It is noticeable that many of these titles are composed of binary structures, like the previous type. Here we have the two parts Esoteric: Descriptive. The contrast structure here reflects one of the basic organizing features of ethnographic texts: the passage from the mysterious world or another culture to the public knowledge of a shared descriptive language. The coding of such titles can also be thought of in terms of the related binary oppositions:

Implicit:Explicit / Concrete:Abstract

Metaphor:Metonymy / Local:General.

As we have seen, some of the first parts in such pairings are derived from the 'native' categories of the culture in question. This is not the only provenance of such pairs. Often they are made up of metaphorical or allusive terms which are used by the author to encapsulate a theme or a perspective. As with the members' terms referred to above, these normally generate short, punchy and idiomatic titles. For instance:

To Dwell Among Friends: Personal Networks in Town and City

Off Balance: The Real World of Ballet

Distant Water: The Fate of the North Atlantic Fishermen

Mountain Experience: The Psychology and Sociology of Adventure

Titles such as these may convey the sense that the author/text has taken the subject-matter referred to and compressed and shaped it into a coherent, condensed message.

These and titles like them are highly characteristic of the ethnographic genre. There is a strong reliance on the use of compressed, allusive titles. The 'main' title captures allusive connotations, while the sub-title, if any, furnishes the more explicit denotations.

The use of titles, of course, provides a *sign* which enters the text into relations with others. In some instances, authors and readers can draw on the naming practices to place texts in systematic relations of similarity and contrast with other texts. Titles may be generated by means of various strategies of transformation and contrast with other titles and texts. The following examples demonstrate some of these strategies.

Take the well-known ethnography of medical education at Kansas University medical school – *Boys in White* (Becker *et al.* 1961). The first point to note is that this short, memorable title itself accomplishes a good deal of work in indexing the sociological character of the text. It stands in contrast with the text *The Student Physician* (Merton *et al.* 1957). Whereas the latter portrayed the medical student as a junior colleague in a partnership of professional training and sponsorship, the former emphasized the subordinate status of students. The titles of the respective monographs thus declare their adopted perspective on the problem. Between them, these two titles can be used to map out a domain of sociological discourse; other titles may be inserted into this domain by processes of echoic allusion and transformation. For instance, the evident 'bias' of Becker *et al.* may be echoed, highlighted and ironically commented on by invoking the title 'Girls in White'. (The authors' original stress on subordination is reworked into a stress on gender.) Or the title 'From "boy" to "colleague"' (Shuval 1975) similarly takes titular elements and translates them into a new patterning; the sub-title 'processes of role transformation in professional socialization' implies that the implied contrast is to be treated as facets of a more dynamic process.

In ways like this, then, titles can partake of systematic relationships of similarity and contrast. When Emerson writes of 'Behavior in Private Places' (1970), then her title is a direct allusion to and play upon Goffman's *Behavior in Public Places* (1963). The reader is alerted to the possibility that Emerson is offering a Goffmanesque, dramaturgical perspective – but perhaps offering a new slant or variant on that theme. In a slightly more obvious way, perhaps, Klockars' *The Professional Fence* (1974) is a direct echo of Sutherland's *The Professional Thief* (1937). Indeed, Klockars explicitly refers to the earlier text, and the 'intertextuality' of the work is emphasized by the fact that he showed a copy of Sutherland's book to his informant in order to illustrate for him the kind of research product he had in mind.

The title of the ethnography may seem to be a matter of little significance. And yet there can be little doubt that successful titles – along with other rhetorical resources – have contributed to the reception of well-known books. If our appreciation of qualitative research is strongly influenced by diffuse aesthetic criteria (cf. Lofland 1974) then no element of the text is *a priori* too small or fleeting to merit attention. Indeed, as I have tried to show in this chapter, the sociology itself may be sustained by various 'literary' devices. Arguments are conveyed and coded implicitly in the descriptive writing that ethnographers employ. The authenticity of the account itself is claimed in and on behalf of texts that vividly construct their social worlds.

Chapter five

Voices in the text: exemplars and the poetics of ethnography

It would be wrong to think of ethnographic texts as simple affairs. Whatever their overall degree of sociological or literary sophistication, they can present the reader with a complex and variegated surface. To some extent the complexity reflects commitments and tensions which derive from the ethnographer's socio-logical and epistemological convictions. They reflect issues of 'evidence' and 'proof' in the organization of an ethnographic account. It is highly characteristic of many (though by no means all) such texts that they are extensively and densely illustrated with extracts from the author's field notes, stretches of talk (verbatim or reported) from informants, documents, and similar sources. These are used to furnish evidence and support for the author's argument. The use of such materials, and their interweaving into the ethnography are sometimes regarded as a methodological 'problem' or shortcoming by critics of qualitative sociology. While such methodological debates are not of prime concern here, the following observations – indeed all of this work – will bear upon the most general issues of inference, evidence and proof.

In essence my argument will be that the inferences to be drawn are as much the work of the reader as the work of the writer. The exemplars which will be the focus of this chapter have the following characteristics and discursive functions. First, they provide the reader with concrete – sometimes vivid – if fragmentary, vicarious experience of the social world in question. Second, they allow for the introduction of multiple perspectives and voices in the text. Third, they allow for a polyphonal and collaborative text, constructed between the sociologist, the reader, and the social actors represented in the setting. I shall refer to this material as 'exemplars', while recognizing that they are far more than mere exemplifi-cation. I shall show how there may be an interplay between the various elements of the text, and that the 'argument' can be read through the relations of identity and difference to be found in the text.

Although the distinction is not a hard and fast one, there is a contrast to be drawn between the explicit sociological argument of the author's texts and the implicit, concrete mode of the observer's texts, and the accounts of the actors or informants. The force of the argument can often rest on the contrasting and complementary functions of the implicit and explicit, the concrete and the abstract, the general and the local. The argument of the ethnographic text proceeds not by the accumulation of evidence as discrete elements in an inexorable progression either of hypothesis-testing or of inductive reasoning. The text is not built up from the marshalling of 'evidence' in an additive manner. Rather, its argument is essentially rhetorical. It is *persuasive*. It is therefore the function of the exemplar to contribute to its persuasive character.

The construction of an ethnographic text is, even in its most elementary forms, a matter of some complexity. There are at least two levels to the writing in the course of the study, and the finished product, *the* ethnography, is woven out of these textual elements. Frequently (though not universally) the physical representation of the argument distinguishes those levels. As Fowler (1977, pp.56 ff.) points out, the 'typographical shape' of the printed page can give the reader all sorts of clues as to how it may be read. The typographical convention whereby the fieldwork excerpt or interview quote is cited as 'data' and set off from the main body of commentary – by means of indentation, italicization or similar marks of difference – is important in the production of the ethnographic account.

This chapter will explore the 'dialogue' that derives from such difference. The text embodies and renders in graphic form an internal dynamic at the heart of the enterprise. This 'dialogue' reflects a shifting temporal order, from the 'events' that occurred and were reported 'then', to the reflection and reportage that occurs 'now'. The former is a temporal frame inhabited by the actors and the ethnographer. The latter is a temporal frame shared by the text and its readers. The 'ethnographic present' thus always implies and embeds the ethnographic past. In the first the ethnographer constructs his or her understanding in the company of the actors there described. In the second the ethnographer, as author of the text, and the reader of that text jointly construct meanings and interpretations. Through the latter the 'real meaning' of the embedded field reality is reconstructed.

While adopting a rather different overall perspective from mine, Edmondson (1984) provides an admirable characterization of this aspect of things, under the rubric of 'rhetorical induction'. She suggests that rhetorical induction 'does not argue from a few cases to the next one....It argues from a selection of cases to what we are to expect in the foreseeable future' (p. 59). Through the deployment of exemplars, therefore, the ethnography itself has features of negotiated meaning between text and reader. The text persuades in so far as the reader concurs or acquiesces in the dialogue between the exemplar and the commentary, and draws on the exemplar so as to find the commentary adequately plausible.

The exemplar gives us, as readers, fragments of recorded talk, reported talk and action, which we can take to 'stand for' the social world under scrutiny. The reader can thus encounter persons, events and the like which are profferred as representative of the given culture. It will be apparent that the use of 'representative' here is not equivalent to the notion of 'representation' as used in 'standard' versions of sociological methods. The exemplar is 'representative' in the sense that it signifies or 'stands for' cultural themes or social types. The 'significance' of the ethnographic exemplar is therefore essentially a semiotic one. Indeed, this notion of 'significance' is perhaps more apposite than its more commonplace usage in conventional methodological discourse. If we take seriously such a perspective, then we can view the 'exemplar' as a *sign*.

Icon, index and symbol

It may be helpful to draw on elements of Peirce's account of semiotics here (1931-58). Peirce proposed a triad of signs: *icon*, *index* and *symbol*. These are distinguished in terms of different relationships between the sign and what it signifies: they contrast in *how* they signify. The *icon* depends upon a relationship of similarity between the sign and its signified. An iconic representation is thus based upon common qualities between the two. The *index*, on the other hand, is a sign which points to something else, in terms of a concrete and causal sequence. A *symbol* depends upon an arbitrary, conventional relationship between the sign and its signified. In practice, many cultural, conventional forms of representation depend upon combinations of iconic, indexical and symbolic modes of relationship.

When the ethnographer deploys an exemplar, then, what sort of 'significance' is he or she reporting or claiming? The relationship may depend upon iconic representation. The microcosm of a localized social domain may be proposed as an iconic representation of some more general social phenomenon. Similarly, the 'representativeness' or particular 'cases' – of events or settings or persons – may rest on such a relationship. The 'case' may be held to incorporate essential features of some more general state of affairs. The case may thus come to stand for a range of equivalent phenomena by virtue of a 'community in some quality', as Peirce describes the iconic relationship.

By the same token, the significance of a particular event may rest on a more indexical form of relationship: actions or statements are read as 'pointing to' or as symptomatic of a state of affairs. In the context of the present discussion, this is not normally the physical relation of a signpost or label. The 'labelling' is of a more conventionalized nature, based upon relations of cause-and-effect, or 'appearance-and-reality'. These are, however, not arbitrary, though they may rest on stocks of cultural knowledge. Further, the stock of cultural resources and assumptions on which the exemplar rests will embody the arbitrary – *symbolic* – relation of cultural meanings and connotations.

Here, then, I am not referring to that fundamental level of the linguistic sign, but to higher levels of representation which are realized through such systems of signification. The point is to try to understand the *work* of illumination and explanation which is achieved through such systems; the primary interest is in the iconic and indexical levels.

Consider the following example. It is taken from near the opening of Liebow's monograph, *Tally's Corner* (1967):

A pickup truck drives slowly down the street. The truck stops as it comes abreast of a man sitting on a cast-iron porch and the white driver calls out, asking if the man wants a day's work. The man shakes his head and the truck moves on up the block, stopping again whenever idling men come within calling distance of the driver. At the Carry-out corner, five men debate the question briefly and shake their heads no to the truck. The truck turns the corner and repeats the same performance up the next street. In the distance, one can see one man, then another, climb into the back of the truck and sit down. In starts and stops, the truck finally disappears.

(Liebow 1967, p.29)

Earlier, in the introductory chapter, Liebow has told the reader enough for us to know that the book's topic is the life of poor black inhabitants in Washington, DC. We also know that the main scene of the action is a street corner in downtown Washington, where the New Deal Carry-out shop is located. Liebow announces that 'The main body of the data comprises a record of the day-by-day routines of these men as they frequented the alleys, hallways, poolrooms, beer joints and private houses in the immediate neighbourhood' (p.11).

Now the brief episode of the cruising truck can be read on the basis of a substantial number of significations. In a general sense we have no difficulty in recognizing that this reported scene bears an iconic relationship to other actual or possible events of a similar nature. Precise details of the events may be treated as incidental. What is 'significant' is that a white truck-driver encounters a substantial number of black men 'idling' on the street, attempts to recruit them for casual labour, and is turned down by the majority of them. At least, I take it that this – or something like it – is how many readers would make sense of the passage. If so, then it may be found to have a general significance beyond just one such occurrence. Actually Liebow does not say if this scene is enacted only once, or is a recurrent sight at and around Tally's Corner. While I find no explicit evidence for the reading, I assume that this is a commonly witnessed event. The episode presents itself as an exemplar of repeated and common events. It is worth reporting because it is a faithful representation of essential features of that state of affairs.

Within the episode there are further 'symbolic' features. The contrast between the one white driver and the (apparently) numerous black men may be interpreted as indexing more general, underlying, social characteristics. It points to the separation between the two: Tally's Corner is in a predominantly black neighbourhood – and it is noticeable here that Liebow only bothers to tell us that the driver is white, so that the identification of the other persons as black is an implied contrast. One suspects that the reader may readily flesh out the brief remarks on 'a man sitting on a cast-iron porch', 'idling men' and the clutch of five men at the Carry-out corner. Whether or not the reader has encountered such a scene at first hand, it is eminently 'recognizable'. The reader may use such brief traces to indicate a more general social reality: high rates of unemployment among urban black males, the uncertainties of casual labour, the work-shyness of the poor black, or whatever their own stock of assumptions brings forth.

Indeed, it soon becomes apparent that Liebow himself wishes to trade off such indexical features, for the text continues:

> What is it we have witnessed here? A labor scavenger rebuffed by his would-be prey? Lazy, irresponsible men turning down an honest day's pay for an honest day's work? Or a more complex phenomenon marking the intersection of economic forces, social values and individual states of mind and body?
>
> (Liebow 1967, pp.29-30)

Here we can see a particularly telling use of the exemplar, and a device which is much used in ethnographic accounts. The exemplar is proffered as an iconic representation, as a microcosm of the social world, elements of which can be apprehended by the reader as indexes of social phenomena. It proceeds at one level by virtue of its familiarity as a social scene, and it is inhabited by familiar social types; in this case by anonymous unemployed or underemployed black men. But the text then turns back on such familiarity and confronts it. The reader of the first paragraph is left to draw what inferences he or she may wish from the description of events. It is a description couched in realist terms: there is no overt claim to knowledge or understanding different from that available to any observer who might happen to be present. The second paragraph is of a totally different order. Here the reader's possible inferences are explicitly addressed; or at least, some possible 'commonsense' inferences are canvassed. The text proposes a more explicit interpretation of the events, if only in an interrogative mode. It then goes on to propose that such inferences might be superseded by a more complex version: the use of the word 'intersection' itself has connotations of complexity, reinforcing the overt message of this last phrase. It is worth going on to the next paragraphs of the Liebow extract to see how these initial themes are continued.

> Let us look again at the driver of the truck. He has been able to recruit only two or three men from each twenty or fifty he contacts. To him, it is clear that the others simply do not choose to work. Singly or in groups, belly-empty or belly-full, sullen or gregarious, drunk or sober, they confirm what he has read, heard and knows from his own experience: these men wouldn't take a job if it were handed to them on a platter.
>
> (Liebow 1967, p.30)

At this point a footnote points out that some social scientists have arrived at similar conclusions, attributing 'underprivilege' to faults in the men themselves. But it continues:

> Quite apart from the question of whether or not this is true of some of the men he sees on the street, it is clearly not true of all of them. If it were, he would

not have come here in the first place; or having come, he would have left with an empty truck. It is not even true of most them, for most of the men he sees on the street this weekday morning do, in fact, have jobs. But since, at the moment, they are neither working nor sleeping, and since they hate the depressing room or apartment they live in, or because there is nothing to do there, or because they want to get away from their wives or anyone else living there, they are out on the street, indistinguishable from those who do not have jobs or do not want them.

(Liebow 1967, pp.30-1)

Here the exemplar is transformed. The observed 'facts' remain the same, in the sense that the actions of the truck-driver and the men on the street are still taken as given. But the relationship between appearance and reality, between assumption and understanding is questioned. The initial exemplar was readily recognizable as one thing; now we are told to recognize it in a quite different way. The indexical relations of the exemplar are transformed. We no longer see idle men, but working men in their free time. The exemplar may still be read as an iconic microcosm, but is now understood as the representation of a quite different generality. This is not an instance of irrational laziness, but of rational behaviour by workers. Note how the text emphasizes the motivated, reasonable quality of their behaviour by listing reasons and with a repetitious use of language: 'But since...and since...or because...or because'. To begin with 'anyone' might 'see' a street full of men refusing to work; by this later stage, a couple of pages on in the text, anyone can equally see a quite different picture.

At this point, the reversal of perspective in *Tally's Corner* is emphasized by a reversion to the concrete exemplar. The focus now shifts from these general statements about 'the men' , or 'most of the men' or 'some of the men', to named individuals:

Some, like Boley, a member of a trash-collection crew in a suburban housing development, work Saturdays and are off on this weekday. Some, like Sweets, work nights cleaning up middle-class trash, dirt, dishes and garbage, and mopping the floors of the office buildings, hotels, restaurants, toilets and other public places dirtied during the day. Some men work for retail businesses such as liquor stores which do not begin the day until ten o'clock. Some laborers, like Tally, have already come back from the job because the ground was too wet for pick and shovel or because the weather was too cold for pouring concrete. Other employed men stayed off the job today for personal reasons: Clarence to go to a funeral at eleven this morning and Sea Cat to answer a subpoena as a witness in a criminal proceeding.

(Liebow 1967, pp.31-2)

Here then the text shifts focus, from generalities to the specific, named individuals. These men are themselves treated as exemplars, each made to stand for a category of lower-class worker. It is as if each were a totemic sign for the mapping of the division of labour. Each is revealed as having a perfectly good reason for being on the street which has nothing to do with being work-shy.

The introduction of individuals continues in the succeeding pages. Stoopy has a polio-withered leg, and Raymond, despite looking 'as if he could tear out a fire hydrant', coughs up blood; they represent the halt and the lame. Bumdoodle is a numbers man, and represents all those who are working hard at illegal occupations, 'buying and selling sex, liquor, narcotics, stolen goods, or anything else that turns up' (p.33). Tonk stays on the corner to keep an eye on his wife, whom he suspects of infidelity, while Stanton has stayed off work for the past four days since Bernice disappeared.

This Runyonesque collection of names leaves only a minority, a handful who would correspond to the truck-driver's stereotype of the work-shy and the idle. By this time, the text has woven a complex series of shifts of perspectives. We have been drawn from an apparently easily understood social scene, to a revelation of complex, yet rational motives. At the same time, the persons involved have resolved themselves, from seen but unknown, anonymous figures to named individuals. We have moved from the erroneous attribution of motives by observers such as the white truck-driver and the social scientist and – by implication – the reader, to the revelation of rational action.

In the course of this there is a constant movement between the implicit message of the exemplar and the expository voice of the sociologist. Sometimes they are in agreement, at other moments the exposition challenges the implicit meaning. The two modes of exposition combine, however, to lead and persuade the reader of the rationality of the characters' actions. By implication, of course, we are invited to concur with a view that the author is equipped with greater insight and more plausible understanding than the casual observer, the truck-driver, or the other social scientists referred to.

It is in this sense, then, that one can speak of the ethnographic account proceeding by means of persuasion, and the exemplar is an important textual device. It does not rest solely on such implicit forms of argument, of course. The text will normally include more explicit statements of sociological propositions and generalizations. Each mode of analysis seems to feed off the other, and the text includes different styles of presentation.

Exemplar and exposition

The tension in the ethnographic text which contrasts exemplar and exposition results in a highly characteristic shifting of voices within the text itself. This is often portrayed typographically, as the language shifts from the author-sociologist to the actors in the social setting. The following is an example from an early classic (Cressey 1971):

The most distinguishing aspect of the taxi-dance hall is the position of prominence and prestige occupied by the successful taxidancer. Far from feeling herself exploited commercially, the taxidancer responds to the stimulation of the situation and the admiration of the patrons and for a time finds satisfaction in them.

> Of course it's an easy life, no work, sleep late in the morning, more money than I could earn by day work – and all that. But that's not all that makes me like it. There's something about the hall that makes me feel good. I may be as blue as indigo when I go down there but before long I feel all peppy again. I don't think it's the music. I like to be with people and up at the hall the fellows – especially the Filipinos – treat me real nice.

Especially where the patrons are seeking to win a girl's favour, with the hope of securing late night engagements, they are polite and courteous. Since the girl's society outside the dance hall – so much sought after by many of the patrons – can be secured only through the dubious process of courtship rather than through the more dependable method of bargaining, the popular taxidancer has a favourable status in the taxi-dance hall which seems to arrive in part from the very noncertainty of her favours.

(Cressey 1971, pp.197-8)

In this extract – as in many others – the text shifts from the voice of the sociologist, to the voice of an actor in the social scene, and back again. Usually the extracts are inserted as 'examples' which relate to the more general sociological propositions which the author is putting forward. The use of informants' words, as in the Cressey extract, may be substituted by the sociologist's words as an eyewitness reporter. That is, extracts from field notes may be interpolated into the discourse. The following is illustrative of this second strategy: it is also taken from Cressey's account and uses the 'impressions of an investigator on his first visit to a taxi-dance hall':

> For those who attend the taxi-dance hall, even irregularly, it is a distinct social world, with its own ways of acting, talking, and thinking. It has its own vocabulary, its own activities and interests, its own conception of what is significant in life, and – to a certain extent – its own scheme of life. This cultural world pervades many avenues of the habitué's life, and some of its aspects are readily apparent to even a casual visitor at the halls.

> I had expected almost anything at this dance hall but even then I was surprised. It was the most speckled crew I'd ever seen: Filipinos, Chinese, Mexicans, Polish immigrants, brawny laborers, and high-school boys. More disturbing was the cynical look which the men directed at the girls and the matter-of-fact way they appropriated the girls at the beginning of each dance. The girls themselves were young, highly painted creatures, who talked little – and when they did speak used strange expressions to accentuate their talk. They spoke of 'Black and Tans', 'Joe's Place', 'Pinoys', 'nigger lovers', and used other terms with which I was not

familiar. My attempts to get acquainted with several of the girls met with indifference on their part, while at the same time they each seemed very much alive to a few men and several girls in the place. To everyone else they seemed polite, coquettish, but really quite indifferent. I left the place feeling that I had been permitted to witness but not to participate in the real life revolving around the hall.

So well is the vital world of the dance hall veiled by conventionalized conduct that a person may attend regularly without perceiving it. Unless he is initiated into the meaning of certain activities, of certain words and phrases, of certain interests and standards of conduct, he may as well not try to understand the human significance of the taxi-dance hall. For many factors aid in making the world of the taxi-dance hall a moral milieu rather completely removed from the other more conventional forms of city life.

(Cressey 1971, pp.193-4)

It would be easy to think of such textual devices as mere 'examples', used either as 'evidence' or as 'illustrations'. It would further be easy to regard such evidence as inadequate, when judged against some conventional criteria of inference and proof in scientific reasoning. To do so would be, at best, only part of the story, however. For such an approach would be highly insensitive to the discursive organization of the ethnographic text itself.

Indeed, it is not always clear that the textual fragments constitute 'evidence' in any strict sense. They are often hard to read as furnishing 'data' which can be used to provide empirical support for a given generalization: by the same token, that text's generalizations are not definitively projected by these 'examples'. Consider the first of the Cressey examples. The taxidancer's remarks certainly echo the author's introductory remarks on sources of 'satisfaction' in the taxi-dance hall. But the author also proposes much more than that – for instance, concerning the 'power' and 'prestige' of the successful taxidancer. Further, he goes on after the extract from 'Case 12' to offer more descriptive generalizations about the setting and the taxidancer's 'favourable status', for which no 'examples' or 'illustrations' are offered at that point in the text.

Yet we have no special difficulty in reading passages such as these. Indeed, we do not really expect the author of an ethnography actually to provide 'data' or 'illustrations' in support of each and every proposition and generalization. Were an author to do so, then we should probably find it a very tedious account, and the text would be found to break the normal canons of ethnographic writing. The solution is that these devices have discursive functions which are of a rather more complex character. (Though, on reflection we should almost certainly discover that the presentation of 'evidence' of more conventional scientific types is less straightforward and more discursively context-dependent than is generally thought.)

Edmondson has gone some way towards an adequate understanding of the function of such exemplars in the presentation of qualitative sociology.

Edmondson suggests, as I would, that we disregard the notion that they are intended to be 'evidence' in the sense of being 'typical' in the statistical sense. She goes on:

If instead we regard such citations as rhetorical devices for enabling and encouraging readers to perceive the force of general remarks, we can expect examples to exhibit particularly concentrated cases of what happens generally but, perhaps, less remarkably.

(Edmondson 1984, p.50)

In the first instance, then, such 'forceful' examples are provided as rhetorical devices which may help the readers to enter into the author's argument. These examples, she then goes on to argue, 'function rhetorically as signs: signs as symptoms of states of affairs, signs as encapsulating states of affairs in some way which enables the reader to interpret future situations, and only very rarely necessary signs of states of affairs' (p.52). Edmondson refers to these signs as 'actual types'. Drawn from reality (as opposed to 'ideal types') such signs are selected so as to relate to more general states of affairs. As Edmondson also says: 'actual types do not communicate in an *exhaustively* conventional way; they frequently rely on the reader to take active steps to combine associations in a creative manner'. In other words (though Edmondson does not use this terminology), the ethnographic text here relies upon the *documentary method*. The reader is required to 'make sense', actively, of the text by interpreting particular fragments of text as 'indexes' of some underlying pattern or state of affairs. The 'authenticity' of the text is thus provided not by the 'scientific' canons of evidence, but by the active involvement of the reader in the construction of the text. The sociologist furnishes fragments of 'another' text: these fragments are – as it were – glimpses, seen through the gaps in his or her sociological account. The reader draws on these fragments in order to reconstitute that 'other' text of everyday life in the setting in question.

In this way, the ethnographic text parallels the forms of life it reports. For the 'documentary' method is a mode of reasoning characteristic of everyday, mundane experience. It is through such active constructions that 'everyman' and 'everywoman' actively make sense of and socially construct their own social worlds. Moreover, the ethnographic text is a direct reflection of its essentially pragmatist epistemology. The ethnographer's understanding is warranted not by the accumulation of 'facts', but through his or her active involvement in and interpretation of the social world. Likewise, therefore, the reader's understanding of the social world is to be furnished by his or her active involvement with the text and deployment of interpretive strategies of everyday life.

The instances and exemplars are, therefore, discursive rather than extra-textual features of the argument. They are deployed in persuasive ways. They are, however, more than simply exemplification inserted into the text. They form part of a complex layering of the text. The 'voices' in the text enter into relationships of echo and anaphora, dialogue and development. Sometimes the voices are those of the sociologist – as author of the text and as observer/describer of the social scene. Sometimes the voices are those of the sociologist and the actors.

Multiple voices

Consider again the second extract from Cressey's taxi-dance account. There are two major voices at work here (and never mind whether the 'investigator' is Cressey himself or another sociologist). First we have the 'main' text of the voice of sociology. It enunciates a set of propositions about 'the taxi-dance hall', and certainly not just any old taxi-dance hall. *The* taxi-dance hall is introduced as a generic category. As such it has general features which the 'sociologist' can state boldly. They are known and understood. He is in a position to tell us authoritatively. He provides us with a short list of sociologically relevant attributes which make it a distinct 'social world'. The sociologist speaks confidently, and assures the reader that at least some of these aspects are 'readily apparent' to even a 'casual visitor'.

It is at this point that the 'exemplification' introduces a quite different voice, and a different tone. The knowing sociologist is replaced by an 'observer', whose account is one of puzzlement and unconfirmed expectations. The sociologist tells us that things are apparent to 'even a casual observer' – but what is most apparent in the account is that there are things which are *not* apparent to the observer: there is language which is not understood and attempts to get acquainted are rebuffed with displays of indifference. The positive sociological remarks which open the account imply knowledge: knowledge, that is, of the folkways of the social world of the dance hall. In a paradoxical fashion, such understanding is 'illustrated' by a lack of understanding. Indeed, it is the counterpoint between the knowing voice of the 'sociological' text and the puzzled, even frustrated, voice of the observer which moves the overall argument forward. Assured that things are readily observable, the reader is then thrust into the alternative voice in which things are hidden and escape understanding or engagement. The sociological voice then picks this latter theme up – employing the metaphor of the 'veil' to convey the arcane nature of this social world. In fact, it now appears that all that is apparent to the casual observer is how impenetrable that domain is. The voice of the sociologist now tells us that the social world will be penetrated only by one suitably initiated into its language and activities. By implication, the casual observer will be quite unable to pierce the veil of ignorance (or, at best, superficial acquaintance).

Of course, the only 'conclusion' which we have been offered by Cressey up to this point in the composite text is the observation that the taxi-dance hall is an enclosed social world. On the way, however, the mode of presentation has provided us with valuable glimpses of the text of the reported action. Through the uncomprehending observer's account, the reader may overhear the talk and glimpse the appearance of the social scene. We are given a concrete list of social identifications: 'Filipinos, Chinese, Mexicans, Polish immigrants, brawny laborers, and high-school boys'. We are allowed to witness – but not participate in – the glances and transactions between the girls and their clients.

This account – of a 'witness' but not 'participant' of the real social scene – thus provides a form of warrant or authenticity which would be denied the authorial voice of the totally disengaged sociologist. The 'evidence' which it provides seems all the more sure in so far as it is grounded in an account which might be produced by 'anyone'. It is demonstrably naïve, and almost makes a virtue of it: 'They spoke of "Black and Tans", "Joe's Place", "Pinoys", "nigger lovers", and used other terms with which I was not familiar.' Evidence here is not warranted by the sociologist-as-expert but by the observer-as-everyman.

In so far as it operates as an example of the 'actual type', the 'evidence' of the observer's account is not to be read as actually representative or typical in every respect. The sociologist does not expect us to infer that the clientele consists only of the ethnic groups mentioned – that there are never Lithuanians or Latvians, Italians or Irish – but rather that we should appreciate the diversity of the clientele. What is important, at this point of the argument at any rate, is the fact that it is a 'speckled crew', not its precise composition. But the concrete detail of the list – however short or incomplete – coupled with the vivid use of 'speckled' provides the reader with an image more forceful than just a bald statement of fact (for example, 'The clientele of the taxi-dance hall is ethnically mixed'). Likewise, the contrast between the 'brawny laborers' and the 'high-school boys' provides a concrete way of indexing the mixed nature of the clientele. (I have already drawn attention to the way in which Chicago authors delighted in the use of lists to convey both sequence and diversity in the urban setting. They are one rhetorical analogue of the recurrent theme of the variety of the 'teeming' city streets and buildings.)

The first extract from Cressey illustrates a comparable relationship between the 'voices'. Here it is the relationship between the voice of the sociologist and the voice of the social actor. (In Cressey's work, of course, this is the voice of the taxidancer.) Here again we find that this is more than, or other than, mere exemplification of the sociologist's claim. Likewise, the sociologist's account is not simply a restatement or even an expansion of that of the informant.

Rather, the two voices combine to produce a collaborative, almost antiphonal, account. The two voices are not equivalent, but contribute to the ethnographic text's complexity. It is easy to see that the quotation from 'Case No.12' does not provide anything like conclusive evidence for the sociologist's assertions. Her remarks bear witness to some sources of satisfaction – especially the way the male clients treat her 'nice' and make her feel good. Taken in conjunction with the informant's remarks on the material rewards and 'easy life', these extracts from her speech support the sociologist's observation that 'Far from feeling herself exploited commercially, the taxidancer responds to the stimulation of the situation and the admiration of the patrons and for a time finds satisfaction in them', whether or not this is also evidence for the sociological observations concerning the 'prominence and prestige' of the successful taxidancer. The dancer's reported satisfaction and the attentions of the men do not unequivocally support the contention that the patrons are seeking to win the dancer's favour in the hope of securing special or extra favours. Indeed, no evidence of the patron's intentions is indicated by the young woman's testimony.

Again, we should not really expect there to be a direct correspondence between the two levels of text: their functions are complementary rather than identical. The full force of the passage is derived from the switching of perspective between the two voices. Although it would be a gross exaggeration to imply that the dancer represents a 'naïve' perspective, there does seem to be a difference between the knowledge-claim of the sociologist and the experience of the dancer. For the dancer's account speaks fairly simply of the hedonistic satisfaction of the life-style and the 'peppy' effect of being treated 'real nice'. The voice of the sociologist surrounds this with accounts which should give a contrasting note of caution. While the dancer says nothing to the effect, the sociologist introduces her voice with a major qualification. The satisfaction of the dancers is said to exist 'for a time'. Although it is not amplified at this point in the text, the remark seems to invite the reader to fill in the implied contrast: that after a time the satisfaction palls. A darker note is struck even as the dancer's brightly cheerful self-revelations are introduced. This embryonic tension is repeated and amplified when the sociologist's voice takes up the account once more. He now introduces a further theme: that the patrons' attentions had an ulterior motive. They are deployed in the interests of securing the young woman's company outside the dance hall, and the sociologist implies that the courtship which gives the women satisfaction is a calculated matter; perhaps even that it is a second choice to the more simple calculation of the commercial transaction.

The juxtaposition of the voices here creates the possibility of a complex interpretative scheme. The themes of 'satisfaction' and 'exploitation' are intertwined. The sociologist's voice announces that the dancer does not feel herself exploited, but on the contrary derives satisfaction. The satisfaction theme is taken up by the voice of the dancer – though without the sociologist's caveat on its temporary state. When the sociologist's voice resumes the theme it is implied that the 'niceness' of the male patrons is calculating and, to that extent, exploitative (perhaps more insidiously exploitative than the overtly commercial transaction). Simultaneously, the sociologist hints at the reverse: the successful dancer exploits her position and her scarcity value. The two voices combine and conjoin to produce a more complex picture than a univocal account might convey.

This foreshadowed theme is indeed developed more explicitly later in Cressey's presentation. It is argued that there is a certain symmetry between the interests of the taxidancer and those of her patrons. Cressey encapsulates it thus:

Thus, from the special interests of the patrons and the commercial aims of the taxidancer a competitive struggle develops between man and woman for an advantage over each other. In many instances the struggle is a conscious one in which any means, fair or foul, are used in exploiting the other.

(Cressey 1971, p.200)

The ethnography, then, can be a complex text with various levels and voices. The viewpoint can thus shift as the author engages in dialogue with him or herself, and can combine or counterpose the voice of the sociologist with that of social actors. The deployment of exemplars from field notes, interview transcripts, documents and the like, can be used to give the reader the 'actual type' – a way of confronting the reader with the unfamiliar, or the recognizable, the striking, the exotic, the mundane, or whatever suits the purposes of the argument.

Edmondson has already drawn attention to one such function of the exemplar as actual type: that is, the establishment of connotations which depend upon familiarity with cultural scenes and conventions. The text of the social world as described is made up in part of familiar stocks of knowledge and types. The exemplar can thus help to guarantee for the reader that the text reports a recognizable, shared world of mundane experience. Its use is one way in which the author and the implied reader can repeatedly renew the narrative contract. It is by no means universal, but the repeated use of exemplars allows the text to project a world of observable reality, against which the 'news' of the sociologist's commentary can be constructed. In this respect, therefore, the deployment of actual types has the function of generating a 'natural attitude of the text'. But they do so *implicitly* – as we have seen, drawing on the documentary method – and depend upon the reader's use of conventionalized cultural knowledge.

Actual-type exemplars gain their force precisely because they are not spelled out explicitly, in so many words, by the sociologist. The reader draws inferences from them (or may do so) as to what sort of actions, actors or settings are under discussion. The voice of the sociologist can thus engage in commentary not just with the exemplar itself, but with the connotations and associations, images and expectations which the reader may entertain. The relationships between the exemplar and the commentary is therefore a potentially multivalent and challenging one.

The exemplar may furnish the reader with a conventionally familiar scene, only to find the commentary and further exemplars challenging that familiarity, or turning it in an unexpected direction. Alternatively, the exemplar can be used to introduce the unfamiliar, only for the commentary to naturalize and account for the apparently strange. The textual arrangement of exemplar and commentary is analogous to the more general epistemological stance of the ethnographer. The constant dialectics of familiarity and strangeness, of membership and marginality, of participation and observation, of action and reflection – these are encoded in the textual arrangements.

Let me try to illustrate some of these features through a further consideration of Cressey's text. The observations of Cressey's which I have already referred to are summary, introductory statements which are subsequently expanded upon.

The first expansion relates to a general sociological proposition – that is, the 'four wishes' thesis of W. I. Thomas. Thomas had, in *The Unadjusted Girl* (1923), proposed four fundamental personal desires: for new experience, for security, for response and for recognition. Cressey uses these as an armature to reinforce the initial proposition that the taxi-dance hall is a self-contained social world, and that it may also be a self-sufficient world for its participants.

Perhaps the most important aspect of this dance-hall world making possible its moral isolation is the completeness of the interests and satisfactions afforded in it. Especially for young girls removed from home influences and living with other taxidancers, the dance-hall life proves sufficient to meet satisfactorily most of their dominant interests and wishes.

> After I had gotten started at the dance hall I enjoyed the life too much to want to give it up. It was easy work, gave me more money than I could earn in any other way, and I had a chance to meet all kinds of people. I had no dull moments. I met bootleggers, rum-runners, hijackers, stick-up men, globe trotters, and hobos. They were all different kind of men, different from the kind I'd be meeting if I'd stayed at home with my folks in Rogers Park.... After a girl starts into the dance hall and makes good it's easy to live for months without ever getting outside the influence of the dance hall. Take myself for instance: I lived with other dance-hall girls, met my fellows at the dance hall, got my living from the dance hall. In fact, there was nothing I wanted that I couldn't get through it. It was an easy life, and I just drifted along with the rest. I suppose if something hadn't come along to jerk me out, I'd still be a drifter out on the West Side.

Not only economic gain, but opportunities for excitement, masculine conquests, intimacies, and masculine affection are all provided in the taxi-dance hall. The dancers may even identify themselves with the dance-hall life so completely that when they return after an absence they experience a feeling of joy and satisfaction in 'getting back home again'.

(Cressey 1971, pp.194–5)

Here we can speculate on the force of the exemplar in terms of the theme of familiarity and strangeness. The dancer's account refers to elements which the reader might be expected to recognize as culturally significant. The reference to bootleggers, rum-runners and the like can be read as indexing that the taxi-dance hall is a social setting associated with varieties of 'low life'. Likewise the reader can interpret the informant's own reference to the kind of life she would have been leading had she stayed at home with her folks in Rogers Park. The reader does not have to be acquainted with a real place called Rogers Park in order to read into it an association with respectable domesticity. The quoted text then sets up an opposition – recognizable to the reader in the terms just outlined – between 'home' and the dance hall, between the respectable and the disreputable. While the taxi-dance itself is not likely to be familiar to the reader on the basis of first-hand experience, Cressey's deployment of such exemplars allows the reader to construct a vicarious acquaintance with it, based on familiar themes and contrasts. What is striking about this particular exemplar, however, is how it then seems to challenge the reader's familiarity. On the basis of the commonplace associations and oppositions, the reader is perhaps unlikely to assume that it is the dance hall which provides the satisfying environment. Cressey invokes Thomas's four wishes not in order to demonstrate the shallow or insubstantial nature of the dance hall, but in order to claim that it goes a long way towards their satisfaction for the dancer. Indeed, he concludes the section by stating that only the desire for security is unfulfilled. Hence the force of Cressey's reporting that girls report a return to the dance hall after a period of absence as 'getting back home again'.

One can see how familiar and conventional signs can be used to construct a plausible and recognizable social setting, only for those very conventional meanings to be confronted, and challenged as a further, plausible – but sociological – account is proffered by the author. In other words, the organization of such ethnographic texts provides for an intricate play of similarity and *difference*. The nature of 'evidence' and 'argument' resides in the deployment of the different 'voices' which are thus dispersed in the text.

Histoire and *discours*

To some extent, the separation of the exemplar and the commentary or exposition is a solution to a major tension to be found in many realist or factual accounts. This is captured in Benveniste's distinction between *histoire* ('the story') and *discours* ('narration' or 'presentation') (Benveniste 1970). The distinction is a useful heuristic device for literary analysts, though in practice the two are closely related and cannot be treated as mutually exclusive aspects of the text. The initial distinction is fairly straightforward. In the case of 'story' the text deals with the presentation of facts or events, without the intervention of a narrator. The *histoire* is presented independently of authorial commentary or interpretation. *Discours*, on the other hand, presupposes a narrator who interpolates an interpretive perspective. Todorov (1972) notes of these two aspects of text that they are complex and closely interrelated, but of fundamental significance:

The interpenetration of these two categories is manifestly great and already poses, in itself, multiple problems which have not yet been broached. The situation is further complicated if we realize that this is not the only possible form under which these categories appear in literature. The possibility of considering all utterance (*parole*) as pre-eminently an account of reality or as a subjective *enunciation* leads us to another important consideration. These are not only characteristics of two types of utterance, they are also two complementary aspects of all utterance, whether literary or not. In every *énoncé* these two aspects can be provisionally isolated: on the one hand an act of the narrator, that is, a linguistic arrangement; on the other hand the evocation of reality, and in the case of literature this has absolutely no other existence than that conferred on it by the *énoncé* itself.

(Todorov 1972, p.131)

Although *discours* and *histoire* are not finally separable, then, they may represent different modes of textual representation. The distinction draws attention to contrasting approaches to narration, or point of view. There are thus two polar types of language used: 'sentences which contain references to the situation of enunciation and the subjectivity of the speaker and those that do not' (Culler 1975, p.198). The contrast is not identical to the separation of the voices in the ethnographic text, but is very closely related.

On the one hand, the typical exemplar permits a separation between the 'objective' presentation of speech and action *(histoire)* and the commentary on it, where the author-as-sociologist explicates and generalizes, organizing the instance into more general categories, patterns and concepts. There may appear the 'I' of the participant observer within the narrative of *histoire*, but textually speaking, this should not be confused with the 'I' of the sociological discourse. These may represent 'the same person' in the world, but in the text they are the subjects of different voices and of different viewpoints.

Although by no means universal, these shifting perspectives are marked by specific changes in language. To begin with, there is the common use of 'the ethnographic present'. Whereas the *histoire* is presented in time and place, the past tense, the *discours* of commentary is lifted into a generalizing present tense. The following paragraphs from *Tally's Corner* exemplify this very well:

In the springtime, on a Sunday afternoon, Richard's four-year-old son lay seriously ill in Ward E of Children's Hospital. He and the other twelve children in the ward, almost all from low-income Negro families, were being visited by some twenty-five relatives and friends. Not a single man was among the visitors.

The men had their reasons. Some had separated from their wives and children and did not know their children were hospitalized. Others knew but couldn't or wouldn't make it. Richard had intended going but something came up, he would probably go tomorrow, and anyway, he never did like being in a hospital, not even to visit someone else.

But whether the fathers were living with their children or not, the result was the same: there were no men visiting the children in Ward E. This absence of the father is one of the chief characteristics of the father–child relationship.

The father–child relationship, however, is not the same for all streetcorner fathers, nor does a given relationship necessarily remain constant over time. Some fathers are not always 'absent' and some are less 'absent' than others. Moreover, the same father may have relationships of different intensity with his different children at the same time. The spectrum of father–child relationship is a broad one, ranging from complete ignorance of the child's existence to continuous, day-by-day contact between father and child.

(Liebow 1967, pp.72-3)

There is no explicitly marked shift in the discourse: the exemplar is not set off from the commentary or shaped as a 'quote' or diary entry. There is, however, a readily perceived shift in language and perspective from paragraph to paragraph. It begins at a highly specific point, localized very precisely in time and place. There is an implied observer/narrator who can observe and report the number of visitors and the perceptible absence of male visitors. The reported speech of Richard's excuse continues to imply the presence of the narrator, but apart from announcing that the men 'had their reasons' there is little overt commentary. The 'story' is presented as just that. It is presented in a simple narrative format in the past tense. There is a marked shift at the end of the third paragraph, however. The present tense marks the introduction of a different voice, and the enunciation of a general principle. The present tense is continued in the subsequent discussion, where the exemplar is now commented on. It is qualified – in a way we have already encountered: first impressions of 'absent' fathers are modified, and used to develop a sociological generalization. That is: the spectrum of father–child relationships is broad, but includes the absence of the father as a major characteristic.

This is analogous to the linguistic correlates proposed by Benveniste. His analysis rests on the contrast in French between the perfect tense and the aorist, or simple past. His argument is that the perfect tense – like the present – belongs to the realm of discourse, whereas the aorist refers to the 'event'. The ethnographic present contrasts with the past in English in a formally equivalent manner.

It is not just the tenses: the issue is not one of linguistic determinism. The following example is drawn from a text where the move between *histoire* and *discours* is analogous to the shift between language uses. It will also show how even the 'neutral' description can also be implicative of sociological themes, but at an implicit level. The fragment is taken from Zorbaugh's early classic of Chicago urban sociology *The Gold Coast and the Slum*:

In the slum, but not of it, is 'Towertown', or 'the village'. South of Chicago Avenue, along East Erie, Ohio, Huron, and Superior streets, is a considerable colony of artists and would-be artists. The artists have located here because old buildings can be cheaply converted into studios. The would-be artists have followed the artists. And the hangers-on of bohemia have come for atmosphere, and because the old residences in the district have stables. 'The village' is full of picturesque people and resorts – tearooms with such names as the Wind Blew Inn, and Blue Mouse, and the Green Mask. And many interesting arts stores, antique shops, and stalls with rare books are tucked away among the old buildings. All in all, the picturesque and unconventional life of 'the village' is again in striking contrast to the formal and conventional life of the Gold Coast, a few short blocks to the North.

One has but to walk the streets of the Near North Side to sense the cultural isolation beneath these contrasts. Indeed, the color and picturesqueness of the city exists in the intimations of what lies behind the superficial contrasts of its life. How various are the thoughts of the individuals who throng up Michigan Avenue from the Loop at the close of day – artists, shop girls, immigrants, inventors, men of affairs, women of fashion, waitresses, clerks, entertainers. How many are their vocational interests; how different are their ambitions. How vastly multiplied are the chances of life in a great city, as compared with those of the American towns and European peasant villages from which most of these individuals have come. What plans, plots, conspiracies and dreams for taking advantage of these chances different individuals must harbor under their hats. Yet they have little in common beyond the fact that they jostle one another on the same street. Experience has taught them different languages. How far they are from understanding one another, or from being able to communicate save upon the most obvious material matters!

(Zorbaugh 1929, pp.12-13)

In these two paragraphs we find contrasting narrative modes. To begin with, we have what might well pass for the expository mode of the guide-book. It is not quite the voice of the observer alone, since historical knowledge is implied. It is, however, in marked contrast with what immediately follows. The first paragraph adopts a simple expository mode, and deploys verbs in an appropriate way. This 'guide-book' introduction to the social scene is a common device in realist literature and in many ethnographies, as we have seen. Here the author, as a 'stranger', leads an equally strange reader into an unfamiliar setting. The stranger is shown round, as it were. There is little overt interpretation. The major routes and landmarks are quickly established, the major and most 'interesting' populations (artists or would-be artists) are introduced; some prominent sights are pointed out (the quaintly named tearooms and shops). Hitherto we are in the realm of 'neutral' observation, with little evidence of the narrator's presence or interpretative presence.

This stands in contrast with what follows. The style of language changes quite markedly. Now the interpretative mode of sociological *discours* becomes more apparent. The narrative presentation of historical progressions and city sights is replaced by a series of rhetorical flourishes: 'How various are the thoughts'; 'How many are their...interests'; 'how different are their ambitions'; 'How vastly multiplied are the chances of life' and so on. The voice of the author is apparent here and the shift in perspective is marked by the shift in language.

Note too what else has been achieved in the movement from description to commentary. The first paragraph presents us with a portrait of the city which anybody might be able to produce, and recognize quite unproblematically. In the second paragraph the emphasis is thrown rather upon the problematic nature of interpreting motives, ambitions and life chances. It is notable that the second paragraph ends with observations on difficulties of communication. There is thus a contrast between the 'obvious material matters' of the descriptive passage, and the final stress on 'different languages' and distance. Each paragraph is constructed out of a list or sequence. The parallelism in the constructions highlights their contrasting modes of signification. The certainty and simplicity of the first section is turned to a problematic diversity. The problems of sociological interpretation are located in the concrete specifics of a recognizable urban setting.

At this stage we must introduce a further nicety. For *histoire* is a way of signifying: it is not a mode of narrative which is somehow empty or devoid of significance. Although it rests on the relative absence from the text of the voice of the narrator, this in no way implies an absence of meaning other than the bare recitation of objects and events. Zorbaugh's descriptive account of a locality in Chicago itself implies a particular sociological theory. We have already seen that the repetitive ordering of Zorbaugh's description suggests a sense of order and understanding: 'The artists have located...'; 'The would-be artists have followed...'; 'And the hangers-on of bohemia have come...'; and so on. This implicitly reflects one of the major sociological themes of the Chicago School's approach to urban ecology; that is, the notion of successive populations of immigrants inhabiting specific urban zones. Indeed, this introductory section of Zorbaugh's ethnography is a sustained account of 'The Gold Coast' and 'The Slum' which is replete with lists of local districts and lists of social types or ethnic groups who have populated them. It is a dense description of urban and social variety. The deceptively simple introduction to 'Towertown' reflects and encodes an implicit social theory of urban life.

Some authors have made an extreme distinction between *histoire* and *discours*. In most texts, the perspectives are closely intertwined in a complex fabric of exemplar and generalization. In a few cases, however, a different textual arrangement is preferred. There is a sharp caesura between the ethnographic description and the analytic account. The 'exemplar' is thus a single, extended narrative. There are two well-known examples of this sort: Carlos Castaneda's *The Teachings of Don Juan* (1968) and Paul Willis's *Learning to Labour* (1977). Both of these books have been subject to extensive commentary – and this particular feature of their organization has been remarked. A detailed treatment is unnecessary here, therefore.

Castaneda divided his text into two parts. The first recounts his puzzling, sometimes frustrating, conversations with Don Juan. There he appears as a commentator and reflector on the content of these interactions, but the 'I' of these episodes is that of a participant – often uncomprehending – whereas the 'I' of the second part is the author of *discours*. There is a clear separation therefore between Castaneda's reported experiences and his 'structural analysis'. The tone changes in the latter to represent the conventional discourse of academic social science. Whereas the first part of the text represents a puzzling world of unfamiliar experience, in the second, the emphasis is on logic and order. In this analytic section the author is not explicitly inscribed in the text, so that the appearance of an 'objective' analysis is rendered plausible. The general argument is presented thus by Castaneda:

> (1) Don Juan presented his teachings as a system of logical thought; (2) the system made sense only if examined in the light of its structural units; and (3) the system was designed to guide an apprentice to a level of conceptualization which explained the order of the phenomena he had experienced.
>
> (Castaneda 1968, p.25)

Each of the two sections is mutually supporting in terms of the overall reading of the text. The extended exemplar of conversations with Don Juan leads the student into a world of strange, puzzling and disturbing events. The 'analysis', on the other hand, naturalizes the text by placing these events, and the confusion they engendered, within a conventional framework of explanation. On the other hand, the initial *histoire* provides the reader with the 'strangeness' to be explained.

Similar remarks apply to Willis. The first half of his book comprises 'the ethnography' and the second part is labelled 'the analysis'. Edmondson (1984) has commented on precisely this:

> The most striking feature of the order of Paul Willis's book is that it enables the reader to evolve a certain personal response to its subjects *before* the author advances a detailed sociological account of their situation. The response which the first part of the book is clearly intended to evoke is one of sympathy: sympathy not just in the sense of particular feelings towards Willis's subjects, but also in the sense of a preparedness to consider their points of view and to refrain from the dismissive evaluations of their conduct which are usually (the book makes clear) from people outside their own class and group.
>
> (Edmonson 1984, p.42)

Again, therefore, the entire first half of the monograph is presented in terms of *histoire*; the *discours* of explicit analysis is presented as a separate entity.

The textual functions of these extended exemplars is identical to those of the smaller fragments and episodes referred to earlier. They are essentially persuasive in character. They provide the reader with scenes and actions which may evoke interpretative frameworks of familiarity and strangeness. Each of these two latter texts – *The Teachings of Don Juan* and *Learning to Labour* – presents a vividly direct portrayal of the narrator and the protagonists. The extreme separation of two textual elements marks a strong boundary between the explicit expression of sociological discourse and the implicit, concrete coding of narrative. The persuasive character of the latter is, perhaps, all the more potent, since this implicit mode of presentation seems innocent of the overt interpretative work which is presented elsewhere. Yet this appearance of an unmediated presentation of reality belies the persuasive and analytic work which it conveys. Of Castaneda, Silverman (1975) remarks:

> What...are we to make of his reference to the analysis in Part Two as a 'logical sequence'? The intelligibility of this reference arises for me in a way of speaking which assumes that the logic of a text always remains to be explicated *outside* the text or that the meaning of data *awaits* explication....
>
> But what if analysis is always present in the text itself, always present in the recognition of 'data'? What if the text, as an act of production of sense, always displays the grounds of its intelligibility – its 'logic'?
>
> (Silverman 1975, p.61)

Silverman goes on to suggest that the 'structural analysis' is redundant, that there is no need to go 'outside the text' in the search for intelligibility: 'For the text itself sustains a system of intelligibility' (ibid.). I am less concerned than Silverman to evaluate different textual strategies and modes. My view is rather that the ethnography often depends upon the relationships established *between histoire* and *discours*, between the implicit and the explicit, the concrete and the abstract. Both levels of textual format contribute to the rhetorical force of the ethnographic text.

The persuasive force of the ethnographic argument, then, is sustained by the repeated interplay of concrete exemplification and discursive commentary. The text moves from level to level and from voice to voice. The reader is to be persuaded of the veracity and authenticity of the portrayal by the use of these actual types.

Chapter six

Narrative and the representation of social action

Hitherto little has been said about the representation of social action in ethnographic texts. *Narrative* elements in the text and episodes are embedded and dispersed among non-narrative components. It is rare – though by no means unknown – for ethnographies to be constructed entirely in narrative form. The term 'narrative' is itself very broad: in some contexts the study of narrative is taken to encompass many diverse elements or functions in the text. Here narrative will refer to the representation of events (as opposed to the description of settings, for instance). In its employment of narrative forms the ethnography again displays its shared features with the everyday modes of reality-construction, and with more 'literary' discourse.

There are many 'stories' and story-like elements within the ethnographic corpus. On the one hand, the sociologist will often have collected participants' stories about their life-world, and these will be extracted and embedded in the text as exemplars and illustrations. The various voices of the participants which are accorded a place in the text are the tellers of stories (or story fragments). The ethnographic interview and the more casual fieldwork conversation are more or less deliberately contrived occasions when story-telling is facilitated.

As a matter of fact, ethnographers have not paid a great deal of attention to the narrative qualities of the 'data' they collect and report. That is not the main point of this chapter, but it is symptomatic of a more general limitation among socio-logical ethnographers. Informants' accounts are inspected for the information they contain, and for the perspectives or interests that may be inferred. Much more rarely, however, do ethnographers pay close attention to the *forms* of their informants' story-telling, or how such narrative activities are embedded in other types of situated action. For the moment, however, such matters are not the main concern of this chapter. That limitation just referred to is part and parcel of the lack of reflexive attention to textual and discursive forms.

I am more concerned with some of the ways in which the authors of ethnographic texts weave their own and others' observations and accounts into more extended accounts of social action. Whether it be the recounting of a telling incident, the elaboration and resolution of a puzzling series of events, or the tracing through of a complex web of relationships, the ethnography frequently delineates patterns of interpretation and understanding through narrative constructions. It is surely all but redundant in a book such as this to point out that the narrative order is an accomplishment of tellers, hearers, writers and readers. Order and evaluative connotations are not *found* in the world, they are not intrinsic to it. They are made through conventions of telling, writing and reading.

To a considerable extent, therefore, the ethnographic text portrays the world as a series of patterned and comprehensible events (occasions, actions) by virtue of its narrative ordering. Time, causality and agency may all be conveyed at an implicit level in narrative form. As with so many of the other closely related elements of the text, the sociological interpretation is conveyed through the interplay of narrative and more formal, overt statements of sociological theory and proposition. The narration of people's doings not only arranges them in sequence, but also conveys consequence. The narrative has an internal coherence ('beginning, middle, end', and so on.), whereas the relations *between* narratives furnishes a broader framework of relevances and coherence.

A few ethnographies are confined to a fairly straightforward narrative which chronicles the reported events, such as Krieger's *Hip Capitalism* (1979a) (to be explored in detail below). The majority employ a duality of narrative function. They exploit the interplay between two levels: the one reporting observed and recounted events in the field ('on the ground'), the other telling of the ethnographer's own process of discovery and enlightenment. It must be emphasized that these are not hard-and-fast separations in the monograph itself. Episodes and events may be used simultaneously to reveal aspects of the culture and its members on the one hand, and to map the ethnographer's burgeoning awareness (or confusion, anxiety, disorientation, or whatever), on the other.

At this point it is as well to note that analyses of narrative involve a number of abstractions and ideal-types. It has been widely argued in studies of fiction, film, folk-tale and myth that we can identify a more or less autonomous layer. It is independent from the mode of representation (film, ballet, opera, novel, short story). This is the aspect which in English may be referred to as the 'story'. Story is an abstraction. It is part of an analytic classification of the aspects of the narrative. Shlomith Rimmon-Kenan (1983, p.3) draws on distinctions outlined by Genette (1980) to separate out 'story', 'text' and 'narration': '"Story" designates the narrated events, abstracted from their dispositions in the text and reconstructed in their chronological order, together with the participants in those events.' Whereas 'story' is a succession of events, 'text' is a spoken or written discourse which undertakes their telling. Put more simply, the text is what we read. In it, the events do not necessarily appear in chronological order, the characteristics of the participants are dispersed throughout, and all the items of the narrative content are filtered through some prism or perspective ('focalizer').

Of course, these terms – and other analytic categories in the same vein – are employed primarily for the discussion of texts like novels, films or the products of oral traditions. It is not appropriate to apply them all too directly or literally to a non-fictional account like the ethnographic monograph. None the less, the sort of analytic stance they imply can be employed with considerable advantage.

The ethnographer's tale

If we focus on the 'story of the ethnographer', then we can see that intuitively it makes sense to separate that out as one implied 'story' that can be reconstructed through a reading of the ethnography. We can then go on to ask ourselves what – if any – formal properties can be identified in such stories, in particular by drawing on analytic perspectives derived from literary and mythological studies.

Thought of initially as a type of story, the ethnographer's journey of discovery and self-discovery/revelation constitutes an account of personal development. It has features of a *quest* – a sort of voyage of search, adventure and exploration. The narrative of the ethnographer's story portrays him or her through key events and social encounters. He or she embarks on an exploration in which he or she moves from being 'outsider' to 'insider', from 'stranger' to 'member', from 'incompetent' to 'habitué'. There is a recurrent pattern whereby such narratives are accomplished.

The elements are, indeed, well enough established as to constitute almost a folklore or mythological corpus in its own right. Moreover, it has considerable heuristic value to analyse some of these stories in ways which draw explicitly on the analysis of folk-tales, which are themselves often constructed in terms of quests and their vicissitudes. Within the confines of this book there is not space to analyse a full range of ethnographers' accounts of their own quests and discoveries. A full analysis of that corpus awaits separate treatment at length. Here a few examples must suffice to indicate some of the issues involved.

The narrative elements of 'the ethnographer's story' are familiar enough to any student or practitioner of the craft. While elements of the narrative are normally distributed throughout the text, the ethnographer frequently recapitulates them and elaborates on them in a separate narrative – often in the form of a 'confessional' (cf. Van Maanen 1988). The autobiographical account, sometimes appearing as a 'methodological appendix' and sometimes as a separate paper, portrays the vicissitudes and encounters in the field. The ethnographer presents him or herself as anti-hero, blundering and coping in strange and adverse circumstances. There is an implicit contrast with the image of a self-assured 'expert'. The story so often is one of gaffes and near-misses. The entire corpus of these first-hand confessionals is now extensive, in sociology and anthropology alike, and demands serious attention as a genre in its own right. It really needs separate treatment to do it justice: to identify the full repertoire of thematic elements, its characteristic narrative structures. and its evolution as a form within the academic community.

Characteristically the ethnographer is presented as a naïve intruder. The classic anthropological monograph often tells of hardships and dangers, but the anthropologist's first experience as a 'castaway' or 'explorer' could always portray the author in a heroically resourceful light. The ship leaves and the author is left on the island among strangers. He or she may prove culturally incompetent, but there are clear connotations of adventure and travellers' tales to colour the reader's appreciation.

The sociological fieldworker, exploring aspects of his or her own society (however 'alien' or 'strange') has always inclined towards the ironic and anti-heroic. The naïve intruder acts as a social incompetent. Initial efforts to establish contact are often recounted to show the author's cultural incompetence. Whyte's autobiographical appendix to *Street Corner Society* is so famous, and such a well-established model, that some reference to it is inevitable here. Recounting his 'first efforts', he writes of his initial bafflement in trying to find his way into the 'Cornerville' district. As he says, he did not have to 'find' it physically: it was right on his doorstep and he could walk down its street perfectly freely. But he had no idea of how to establish social contact. He acts on the advice of a young economist at Harvard – described as self-assured and knowledgeable about the city – who tells him to drop into a drinking place and 'strike up an acquaintance' with a girl by buying her a drink. Whyte resolves to try this approach and picks on the Regal Hotel:

> With some trepidation I climbed the stairs to the bar and entertainment area and looked around. There I encountered a situation for which my adviser had not prepared me. There were women present all right, but none of them was alone. Some were there in couples, and there were two or three pairs of women together. I pondered this situation briefly. I had little confidence in my skill at picking up one female, and it seemed inadvisable to tackle two at the same time. Still, I was determined not to admit defeat without a struggle. I looked around me again and noticed a threesome: one man and two women. It occurred to me that here was a maldistribution of females which I might be able to rectify. I approached the group and opened with something like this: 'Pardon me. Would you mind if I joined you?' There was a moment of silence while the man stared at me. He then offered to throw me downstairs. I assured him that this would not be necessary and demonstrated as much by walking right out of there without any assistance.

> (Whyte 1981, p.28)

Passages such as this in Whyte and similar authors are instructive from several points of view. They present the author in a pretty sorry light. (How could such an incompetent ever hope to understand Cornerville, or anywhere else, for that matter?) But they do not necessarily destroy the credibility of the text and its author. For they are often used *contrastively*. The incompetence and the *faux pas* are written as things in the past, and stand for a period of naïve misunderstanding before the enlightenment born of the fieldwork itself. Whyte immediately follows the passage quoted above with: 'I subsequently learned that hardly anyone from Cornerville went into the Regal Hotel.'

The theme of then-and-now is sustained immediately afterwards. Whyte's next try at access was via local settlement houses: 'You could walk right into them, and – though I would not have phrased it this way at that time – they were manned by middle-class people like myself. I realized even then that to study Cornerville I would have to go well beyond the settlement house.' The force of 'even then' is redoubled in the next paragraph: 'As I look back on it now, the settlement house also seems a very unpromising place from which to begin such a study.'

In accounts such as these, then, we do not just have the wisdom of hindsight, but the hindsight born of hard-won wisdom. The voice of experience contrasts with that of the callow novice. The fieldworker is more experienced now, and more thoroughly *au fait* with the social world. Early mistakes and gaffes can be juxtaposed with the *savoir-faire* of the seasoned campaigner. The reader is invited to understand that the fieldworker of the text has learned to survive in the field, and is hardened by the experience. The anti-hero is shown as an embarrassment and a liability to those studies: putting his or her foot in it. Keiser (1970) provides a characteristic account of the 'outsider' as a cultural dope. He is, literally, lacking in street wisdom. Keiser's work was with the Vice Lords, black male gang members on the streets of Chicago. At times his autobiography reveals his lack of local knowledge.

On the streets of the ghetto I was functionally an infant, and like all infants, had to be taken care of. I did not know what was, and what was not, potentially dangerous; and I did not understand the significance of most actions and many words. For example, one afternoon while I was standing on 15th Street with a group of Vice Lords, a young man in his early twenties walked up and started yelling that he was a Roman Saint and was going to 'whip' every Vice Lord he found. It was obvious by the way he talked and acted that he was mentally deranged. One of the Vice Lords said, 'The dude's crazy, man! He ain't no Saint. Leave him alone.' Suddenly a dead-pan look came over the young man's face. Abruptly he turned from us, and walked down an alley opposite from where we were standing. Very calmly, and with no show of speed, every Vice Lord in the group walked away, out of line of possible fire. Suddenly I found myself standing alone, looking down the alley at this fellow. Tex came up and pulled me to the side. He said, 'Man the dude get to the end of the alley, he liable to get his jive together and burn you down (pull out his gun and shoot you)!' Besides feeling stupid, I did not know whether to be afraid or not. The fellow reached the end of the alley, turned the corner and was gone. The extent of my helplessness had been made quite clear.

(Keiser 1970, p.234)

Of course, the very existence of Keiser's published ethnography is testimony to his own survival.

Some authors write a catalogue of ineptitude and difficulty. Karp's autobiographical account of his attempts to observe in and around Times Square is another case in point (Karp 1980). His confession of sustained ineptitude is risible. He recounts successive problems and impasses in attempting simply to gain access to informants in that 'public' setting. The reader can hardly fail to assemble the portrait of an earnestly clumsy intellectual, totally out of his depth in the dirty bookshops and among the whores on the street. He writes about his failure in the bookshops, where requests for permission to observe are turned down with barely suppressed laughter. His colleagues offer him a suggestion as to why he is having difficulty:

They suggested that the mistake was in introducing myself as a professor at Queens College. The store managers had probably not heard of Queens College, which is part of the New York City University system. Rather, they understood the word 'queen' in its slang form, meaning 'effeminate homosexual'. My colleagues suggested that I was introducing myself as a kind of 'super queen' or 'super freak', and the combination of 'queen' with 'professor' – 'a professor of queens' – was more humorous still. Quite unwittingly, therefore, an attempt to legitimate myself had exactly the opposite effect.

(Karp 1980, pp.89-90)

Like Whyte, Karp goes on immediately after to indicate what better strategies he developed 'later' (though the unsympathetic reader will wonder whether anything can quite expunge the image of Karp's clumsiness).

The narrative of the ethnographer's quest departs from these stumbling efforts to cope, and unfolds growing competence and acquaintance with the setting and its members. The 'frankness' with which the author recounts embarrassing episodes at least suggests that they were mere passing phases or occasional episodes. The 'pilgrim's progress' of the ethnographer tells the reader stories about personal encounters and social relationships. Often – though by no means universally – the quest is progressed by helpers and sponsors. In some accounts these helpers become major figures. Whyte's 'Doc', Liebow's 'Tally' and their counterparts become heroes in their own right.

The narrative introduces these key characters, who act as guarantors for the ethnographer. They ensure the 'access' that is sought, and – more fundamentally – as characters in the narrative they underwrite the authenticity of the experience. When the author reproduces the spoken research contract between the observer and the sponsor, there is simultaneously an unspoken narrative contract between the text and the reader. Doc's contract with Whyte is well known and widely cited: he guarantees to the sociologist the protection of his friendship and undertakes to ensure that he sees all he wishes to. The social relationships so described are important elements in the narrative itself. The reader can see the author progressing with increasing certainty towards intimacy with the other characters. The story thus moves from faltering first steps, through introductions and sponsorships, to a range of social relations. The connotations are those of a progressive penetration of an 'inner circle', and the initiation of the author into a domain of esoteric knowledge.

The 'confessional' mode, and the personal narrative of the ethnographer, thus establish that the author claims no exceptional powers. He or she makes mistakes as any other person might. After all, what reader of sociology (real or implied) would expect to manage smoothly and competently in everyday dealings with slum dwellers or young gang members? The confessions of fumbling insecurity may be read to imply that 'anyone' would have reacted in a similar way, and invite a sympathetic identification on the part of the reader. The cultural incompetence of the author helps to establish the 'otherness' of the actors he or she encounters. The failure of the ethnographer's taken-for-granted routines highlights the degree to which he or she is 'stranger' or 'outsider', and constructs the newly encountered social world as alien and exotic. In some accounts (such as Kreiser's) the whiff of danger adds even more to the sense of the exotic. The fact that the problems were overcome suggests more than 'everyday' experience, however. The clumsy anti-hero is progressively revealed as a successful survivor.

The personal narrative of ethnographic exploration does not, therefore, detract from the credibility and plausibility of the ethnographic account. On the contrary, its very confessional quality can help to reinforce the narrative contract between the text and the implied reader. The retrospective account of failures resolved and troubles survived thus vouches for the authenticity of the author's experience. He or she claims uniquely to have gone through that baptism of fire in order to achieve the close acquaintance that is the foundation of ethnographic knowledge. The 'discovery' of social relationships and cultural forms is thus paralleled by the *personal* narrative of exploration and survival.

Several authors have drawn attention to the fact that it remains conventional to separate the personal narrative from the narrative of 'the ethnography' proper. Often the confessional is relegated to a separate appendix in the monograph, a totally separate paper, or even a separate book, paralleling 'the real' research monograph. This separation, it has been suggested, maintains the authorial purity of the ethnography proper. It is true that such a separation keeps the account simpler and more straightforward. I disagree with the implication, however, that the autobiographical account is a threat to the purity of that other text. On the contrary, as I have indicated, it serves precisely to strengthen its claims for authenticity. The hard-won facts and insights are warranted in this narrative mode. The narrative form is one elementary way in which social order and social understanding are represented. The ethnography incorporates the twin narrative texts, each of which may be fragmented and mingled with the other. They are the narrative of observed social events, and the narrative of dawning understanding on the part of the author.

The rest of this chapter will be devoted to a consideration of uses of narrative to convey social events: to portray their consequentiality, and to transmit an implicit analytic stance towards those events. Detailed attention will be paid to two studies in which the use of narrative elements and formats is very pronounced. It should not be thought that all ethnographies are so single-minded in their narrative style. As has already been indicated, the majority of texts fragment their narratives and embed them in more explicit commentary.

When narrative succeeds

One of the most striking and successful narrative ethnographies (though its theoretical orientation is rather different from most works in the genre) is *When Prophecy Fails* (Festinger *et al.* 1964). The book has attracted blame and acrimony, as well as praise, primarily on methodological and ethical grounds. Those issues will not be uppermost here, although it will become apparent that even the *ethical* considerations in the conduct of the research have implications for its textual representation. In essence, the story of *When Prophecy Fails* is simply told. It tells of a small group of 'believers' whose tenets of faith include communication with extraterrestrial beings and the prediction of a cataclysmic flood on earth. The members of the cult group believe that they will be taken up and saved from the flood, the date of which is predicted with considerable precision. The story follows the group from the early days of its formation, through a period of anticipation, to the failure of the prophecy and the protagonists' reactions to that failure.

The monograph is prefaced by an opening chapter on the general topic of 'unfulfilled prophecies and disappointed messiahs', in which a general theoretical orientation is introduced: that is, the theory of 'consonance' and 'dissonance'. It is proposed that the disconfirmation of a deeply held belief will not lead to its abandonment. Rather, the adherent will attempt to eliminate dissonance by means of the vigorous reaffirmation of the original belief and the attempt to convert others to the idea. The subsequent chapters provide the substantive empirical content of the monograph, in which is charted the career of the movement and its ideas. The book ends with a brief conclusion, an epilogue and a methodological appendix. For the most part, however, the data and analysis (such as it is) are presented in narrative form. The substantive chapters follow a chronological account of the early inspiration for the group, its formation, the period of waiting for the prophecy's fulfilment, and the aftermath of its non-manifestation.

Two things are striking about the unfolding narration. It is all but devoid of explicit theorizing and commentary. This is not an ethnography in which fragments of reported speech or action are embedded in theoretical exegesis and textual glosses (such as comparative references). Second, much of the narrative is presented with remarkably little implied distance between the narrator and the subject-matter. The two features of this particular text are closely related. The matter-of-fact style of reportage is remarkable, given the substance of the events. The narrative concerns itself with manifestations that are normally thought of as fantastic and impossible. Most readers, one would assume, do not themselves subscribe to beliefs in flying saucers and communication between earth-bound humans and inter-planetary travellers. The text, however, makes no overt acknowledgement of such an implied reader's response. From the outset the text announces events with no special commentary as to their credibility.

That is clearly apparent in the opening passages, in which we are introduced to the source of the belief system and the prophecies.

> The first contact between a prophet and the source of his revelation is likely to be marked by confusion and astonishment, not to say shock. So it was with Mrs Marian Keech, who awoke near dawn one morning in the early winter about a year before the events with which we are concerned. 'I felt a kind of tingling or numbness in my arm, and my whole arm felt warm right up to the shoulders,' she once remarked later, in describing the incident. 'I had the feeling that someone was trying to get my attention. Without knowing why, I picked up a pencil and a pad that were lying on the table near my bed. My hand began to write in another handwriting. I looked at the handwriting and it was strangely familiar, but I knew it was not my own. I realized that somebody else was using my hand, and I said: 'Will you identify yourself?' And they did. I was much surprised to find that it was my father, who had passed away.'
>
> (Festinger *et al.* 1964, p.33)

The text goes on to introduce Mrs Keech, who had had psychic experiences in the past. It continues without any evaluative connotations or interjections. There are no distancing 'she claimed', 'we were told' or 'she believed'. We are soon informed that

> At about the same time that she began to receive messages from nonterrestrial sources, Mrs Keech had become actively interested in one of the major popular mysteries of our time – flying saucers.
>
> (Festinger *et al.* 1964, p.34)

Again, there is nothing here to deny or cast doubt on the factual occurrence of the extraterrestrial message. There is no hint here of controversy or heterodoxy. Indeed, the beliefs are treated as unproblematic, and evaluative description is reserved for the conventional reception on the part of non-believers:

> She soon learned that the world was populated with scoffers and unbelievers. At her father's command she had transmitted his first message to her mother, who answered by reprimanding her and ordering her to stop such nonsense or, at least, to stop inflicting it upon her living parent.
>
> (Festinger *et al.* 1964, p.35)

It is the dead father, note, whose action is treated unproblematically and the living mother who is characterized as a 'scoffer'.

We are told that Mrs Keech experienced frustration waiting for messages and trying to decipher the messages she did receive:

> As she struggled, she gradually became aware that other beings or intelligences were trying to 'get through to' her. 'It occurred to me,' she sub-

sequently said, 'that if my father could use my hand, Higher Forces could use my hand. I have always been interested in my fellow men and I have always wanted to be of service to mankind. I don't mind telling you I prayed very diligently that I would not fall into the wrong hands.' During this early phase of message writing, Mrs Keech apparently came to fear that she would 'fall into the hands' of beings located in 'the astral'. She explained that the astral is overflowing with spirits who are desperate for communication with those left behind, and whose insistent clamor can confuse or obliterate the intelligence available from higher beings, who dwell at higher (that is, less dense) spiritual vibration frequencies.

Mrs Keech's prayers were answered. Within a short time she began to receive messages from a being who identified himself as 'the Elder Brother' and informed her that her father was in considerable need of spiritual instruction in order that he might advance to higher levels.

(Festinger *et al.* 1964, p.36)

The 'answering' of Mrs Keech's prayers and her reception of the messages from the Elder Brother are treated quite unproblematically. It is difficult to think of many other social-scientific accounts which would state quite so literally that somebody's prayers had been answered. It is especially arresting when applied to such an unusual or unorthodox experience of the supernatural.

There is, in other words, a very potent narrative contract available between the text and the reader. Consider the opening: a proverbially phrased observation on the relationships between a prophet and his/her inspiration. Its tone of knowing certainty is reminiscent of the opening of *Pride and Prejudice*. The 'theoretical' orientation is introduced as a commonplace – a *topos* – embedded in a domain of unproblematic everyday knowledge. From the start, therefore, the text establishes a strong narrative contract, inviting the reader to a pact of complicity. It appears to reproduce 'what everybody knows' about religious leaders and their problems.

The cumulative effect of these introductory sections is powerful. The communication between Mrs Keech and the extraterrestrials is established as a natural matter of fact. There is no textual marking of the events as bizarre, incredible or out of the way. The narrator is only minimally present: a few phrases and terms are placed in quotation marks, and there is sparing use of evaluative comment.

The early sections of the narrative are, we learn later, reconstructed, in the sense that the events took place before the ethnographic study itself was undertaken. It is, perhaps, all the more striking that the text contains so few disclaimers or qualifications as to the authenticity of the events reported. The narrative contains simple unvarnished accounts of a series of psychic manifestations. For example:

Toward mid-April she began to receive communications from Sananda, who was destined to become her most important source of information and instruction, as well as her principal link with orthodox Christian revelation, for

Sananda subsequently identified himself as the contemporary identity of the historical Jesus – his new name having been adopted with the beginning of the 'new cycle' or age of light.

(Festinger *et al*. 1964, p.36)

It is not until these manifestations have been chronicled that the text interjects an analytic perspective on the reasonableness or rationality of the growing conviction of Mrs Keech, and the acolytes.

The early reportage of Mrs Keech's messages from alien beings contrasts quite clearly with a particular passage in which another of the group's members is contacted and transmits prophecies to the rest. The episode occurs during the 'long wait for orders'. During a period of meditation, Bertha Blatsky (hitherto a minor character) goes into a trance:

After perhaps twenty minutes more of complete, tense silence, Bertha Blatsky, who was seated on the couch with her head thrown back and her eyes closed, began to breathe very deeply in short, sighing breaths. She continued, almost panting, and interspersing an occasional low moan for perhaps two minutes, and then began to gasp 'I got the words, I got the words' over and over again. Her heavy breathing continued at a more rapid rate, and she began to sob.

(Festinger *et al*. 1964, p.92)

Bertha Blatsky gives a message from Sananda, the source of extraterrestrial contacts. This, the text has already implied, is providential in the sense that a message was urgently expected and needed at that time; the main actors did not know what form such a message might take, nor even who the medium might be. We are told, immediately prior to this episode, that 'Accordingly, they were prepared to consider almost anyone in the group a potential messenger from outer space and almost any declaration in order. They began by focusing their attention on the author present, the last person to arrive' (p.91). The research worker escapes by suggesting meditation, at which point Bertha's message arrives.

The initial manifestation is reported in the same straightforward way as the earlier messages and 'lessons' are delivered to Mrs Keech. What is noticeable is the lack of authorial commentary or imputation of motive. There is no hint that the recipients are anything other than passive mouthpieces for Sananda's teaching. Later Bertha 'returned to the couch, announcing that she would "try it again and see what happened"'. The result is disappointing, as the authors' phraseology implies: 'No one knew it then but the high point of the evening had passed, and the remainder was a tedious, painful monotony as Bertha struggled to live up to the thunderbolt she had hurled....About 10:30 p.m. she resumed her position on the couch, but only empty phrases, tediously repeated, came from her mouth' (p.94). Bertha, discouraged, is persuaded to continue, but no further manifestation is forthcoming. The narrative moves forward to the following night:

The Wednesday night meeting began at 11 p.m. with the same audience, except for the absence of Frank Novick and the addition of a male observer who had called in the morning to arrange his invitation for that night. Although the audience was the same, the performer was not. The group saw a new and forceful Bertha. Gone were the incoherence and repetition, the appeals to Mrs Keech for help. With an air of confidence, even of command, she took her place on the couch, flung one arm over her eyes, and began to speak. No sobbing or panting preceded her performance. She slid into her role with professional ease and began to lecture, confidently, authoritatively, to the meeting.

Her assumption of authority was corroborated when it became clear that the voice speaking through her this night was not that of Sananda, but the Creator Himself. Having thus trumped Mrs Keech's ace, Bertha proceeded to discuss such matters as 'the good', 'the will', 'the I', and the 'Am'. As she progressed in these instructions she became more forceful and more domineering.

(Festinger *et al*. 1964, pp.97-8)

The authors go on to report the Creator's messages. Before commenting on those, I think it is worth pausing to contrast the accounts of Mrs Keech with those of Bertha Blatsky. The cumulative effect of the text's reports of the latter increasingly suggests that she is motivated: 'performing' a 'role' and increasingly pushing herself centre stage. The text is almost entirely non-judgemental about Mrs Keech, but its tone with Bertha is more ambivalent. It is not overtly and crudely dismissive about the latter, however. The text proceeds with a somewhat ironic treatment of the episode.

The introduction of the Creator's voice is accomplished in the normal way. That is, it 'becomes clear', it is not 'claimed', although that sense is undermined by the immediately following reference to 'trumping' Mrs Keech's ace. For the most part, however, the initial pronouncements of the Creator are presented 'straight'. The Creator, indeed, announces that Bertha has been chosen as the greatest of all prophets. Nevertheless the text is not altogether reverent about the Creator's role. Through Bertha the Creator calls for a further, third meeting the following night. A member of the group objects – pointing out that he has already been away from his family and his work for too long: he proposes that the out-of-town members of the group be allowed to meditate at their homes while the instructional message be recorded and copies sent out. But, the text goes on: 'The Creator promptly and flatly vetoed the plan' (p.98). The group member proposes an alternative course of action: that is, three meetings in succession the following weekend. 'After asking if there were any objections to this plan, the Creator announced His willingness to co-operate' (p.99).

The effect of the Creator bargaining with His apostles in this fashion and the language chosen to convey it is bathetic. Again, the authenticity of Bertha's communication is implicitly undermined. The contrast with Mrs Keech's prophetic episodes serves to highlight the text's non-judgmental neutrality *vis-à-vis* the latter. Indeed, the text *When Prophecy Fails* maintains a remarkably detached attitude towards the prophecies which form the basis of the narrative.

The entire structure of *When Prophecy Fails* rests on the unfolding narrative of unfulfilled expectations. The ordering of the monograph traces the chronology of events in the group's story. The presentation of the prophetic *raison d'être* allows the reader's perspective to be aligned with the faith of the 'true believers' in the group. The group's belief in Mrs Keech's pronouncements is rendered plausible. The good faith of Mrs Keech is not called into question, and the text deals sympathetically with her (in contrast to the treatment of Bertha). The effect of the non-fulfilment of the prophecy is produced in a suspenseful way. It is all the more successful for the absence of any overt disbelief on the part of the narrators.

When Prophecy Fails is remarkable for the overall lack of explicit narration reflected through the fieldworkers. It is reticent when it comes to reference to the team of ethnographers who conducted the investigation. They are at best shadowy and anonymous characters. They play very little part in the reported action. They are not identified separately. Each is merely 'an observer'. Despite the fact that (presumably) the ethnographers were at some time or another not merely witnesses but also active participants to emotionally charged events, there is precious little indication in the text of such involvement. The anonymity of the observer is paralleled by a characteristic disengagement from the action, as evidenced in the Bertha Blatsky episode. Anxious for a messenger, it will be recalled, the protagonists turned to 'the author present' and asked him to lead them that night.

> The author-observer, attempting to maintain his neutrality, protested that he could not officiate, that he was not 'ready'. Mrs Keech countered firmly that he *was* 'ready', and she would not be put off by further protests: 'We all have to face our great responsibilities and take them,' she maintained. Finally, the observer agreed to her demand. He was led into the living room and Mrs Keech told the group that he would lead them that night. With nine expectant gazes transfixing him, the observer fought for time: 'Let us meditate,' he ad-libbed, and bowed his head in silence. After a few minutes of silence, he asked Mrs Keech to say a few words. She stated simply that the group had been called together for a special purpose, namely, the receipt of orders. She asked the observer if he had anything to add to that, but he had nothing, so the meeting returned to silent meditation as the tension mounted.
>
> (Festinger *et al.* 1964, p.92)

This is the point at which Bertha Blatsky enters into her trance-like state. There is a striking contrast between the refusal of the author-observer to initiate action and Bertha's act, which places her at the centre of the group's attention and activities.

The textual reticence of the narrator(s) of course parallels the reticence of the field research team. They were – as the extracts above illustrate – unknown observers. The research, indeed, has been criticised from within the profession precisely for the dubious ethical status of such a piece of covert research. Not only did one observer infiltrate the group secretly; but several fieldworkers also participated as part of a plan of systematic deception. It is intriguing to see such reticence reproduced in the textual presentation of the narrative itself. On the other hand, whatever the rights and wrongs of the field research itself, there is no doubt that the narrative voice that is adopted is very effective. By presenting the group and their beliefs in the way it does, the text is able to sustain the reader's engagement with their faith. That is not to say that the implied reader is expected to be converted to those beliefs, but at least to be able to suspend disbelief to the extent of empathizing with the expectations and disappointments of the cult members as their prophecies are unveiled and progressively unfulfilled. Some such alignment of perspectives, some such sympathy, is necessary if the narrative mode of presentation is to sustain the implicit social psychology. For the explicit theory of cognitive dissonance is lightly sketched in, and is not explicitly referred to during the telling of the story. If the reader is to believe in the theory, then he or she needs to believe in the story.

A singular narrative

A singular use of narrative is provided by Susan Krieger's *Hip Capitalism* (1979a). The burden of the account is adequately conveyed by the cover blurb: 'The incredible story of a San Francisco rock music station and its transformation from underground, hippie origins to commercial success. Flower children and corporations clash in this account of chaos in the sixties.' Apart from the mild irony of a factual research report being introduced as 'incredible', the character-ization of it as a 'story' is unusually apposite. Krieger's monograph is constructed almost entirely as a narrative, a chronicle of events – great and small. The under-lying plot is relatively straightforward and can be summarized fairly simply.

It is set in the San Francisco of the 1960s. Under the influence of a man named Donahue, the FM radio station KMPX, owned by Crosby, becomes extremely successful, playing West Coast rock music. Crosby acquires a further station, KPPC. There are troubles at the radio stations, and the KMPX staff go on strike. They move to another radio station, KSAN, which is owned by the Metromedia corporation, and which changes its format to accommodate rock music. The staff become disillusioned, while the station attempts to broaden its markets. A more sympathetic general manager, Duff, is appointed. Ponek is appointed as programme director. There is pressure to introduce a more varied and more commercial style of programming. There are repeated episodes of conflict and various staff members are fired. The radio station is increasingly directed to attempts at improving quality, broadening its audience, and avoiding trouble. There is a final period of 'renewal' when the staff consciously strive to keep in touch with the audience and with their own identity.

Krieger's story does not have a natural 'ending', as the radio station KSAN continued to exist beyond the period of her study. There is, however, a clear narrative shape and purpose to the monograph. It is, as James March's foreword explicates, a story of the process of mutual adaptation of organizations, a story that bears on the trajectory of social movements more generally. It is, above all, a morality tale:

> At a personal, organizational, and social level, this history is a morality play performed as a farce. It is a morality play because the participants saw it and acted in that way. It is a farce because the most obvious social rules were treated as arguable within a general context of social orderliness. The people who performed on the station did outrageous things. They were familiar things, though rarely said and done on the air; and they were things that were important to the rock music culture. But they were unambiguously outrageous. They disturbed public sensibilities, and would have been otherwise almost pointless. Broadcasters were obscene in language and behavior, but their greatest obscenity was not in their actions but in the moral posture they adopted with respect to those actions. Socially acceptable sinners ask for forgiveness for their outrages, claiming human weakness. These sinners asked for praise proclaiming their outrages as a basis for pride. They challenged a rational society at a vulnerable point, its arbitrary beliefs in traditional decency, by attempting to convert articles of faith into subjects for rational discourse and by attempting to force moral and behavioral consistency on individuals and society. By asking what makes an obscenity obscene, they threatened the moral order.
>
> (March 1979, pp.13-14)

The moral clashes and ambiguities are exposed through a myriad of detailed events that are deliberately reconstructed to a degree which threatens to overwhelm and defy sociological analysis. Each chapter is prefaced by a few sentences of summary, and those are collected together to form a 'Conclusion' which is actually a recapitulation of the main events. The narrative is also prefaced by a summary listing of the main episodes. The arrangement of the chapters is strictly in terms of chronological periods and described events. The reader is relentlessly subjected to the chronological, narrative format, displayed in all its detail.

Krieger's text approximates to one type of limiting case, where *histoire* predominates almost to the total exclusion of explicit *discours*. This textual strategy is clearly not accidental. Indeed, it is a deliberate ploy on Krieger's part, which has been replicated in another of her research monographs (Krieger 1983). To that extent there is nothing hidden or implicit in Krieger's writing. On the contrary, she has celebrated her chosen textual strategy in published papers (Krieger 1979b, 1984) and March's commentary in the foreword to *Hip Capitalism* shows that Krieger has resisted any – more orthodox – approaches.

Krieger has a conscious rationale for her work. She represents social life directly in terms of its minutiae. In her study of the KMPX and KSAN radio stations, it is, indeed, almost a day-to-day, blow-by-blow recapitulation of the events in question. The result is not at all 'readerly'. The fact that Krieger models her texts apparently on literary forms does not guarantee a lively read. Approached as a piece of 'literature' (in a commonsense way), it is likely to be found flawed. The welter of detail, the lack of authorial commentary, the noticeable absence of the narrator as an actor in the social setting, all combine to render the monograph somewhat unreadable. Obviously this is defensible on sociological grounds: the text mirrors the intricate and finely grained texture of everyday life. Everyday life is constituted through the concatenation of many *small* events, and occasional more dramatic episodes. It is not readily available to totalizing, summary statement.

Krieger's text therefore has a somewhat 'transparent' quality. We do not need to dig deeply or struggle for the harvest of sociological theory. There is no distinction here between 'theory' and 'data'. The chronicle and its representation stand for both. That is not to say, however, that there is nothing instructive to be learned from a closer scrutiny of Krieger's writing. From this preliminary characterization of the work one can already discern that any interpretation of the events at KMPX and KSAN reflects the organization of the text and the readings it invites. In so far as the extended chronicle has a 'point', a sense of direction and closure, it is largely dependent on the reader's retrieval of classic narrative elements of plot and character.

For, through all the details, there is a strong story-line, and a range of character types. The construction of the narrative is far from artless. It is certainly not just the raw spillage of 'data'. Krieger's account is highly contrived – designed to represent social actors, actions and accounts in a particular way. The narrative style itself is remarkable. Krieger herself describes it as a 'multiple-person stream of consciousness narrative' (p.23). She explains that the choice of style was made deliberately in order to produce a mode of explanation which was faithful to the 'intimate scale' of the process of co-optation (p.24). This narrative mode is justified at greater length in her paper on the textual construction of the research (Krieger 1979b).

There Krieger explicitly reflects on the processes and decisions that went into the writing of her monograph, outlining a series of 'rules of a text'. They are outlined as follows. First Krieger writes about 'creating and peopling a world', in which were addressed a number of issues: 'sensibility, character and naming'. Under 'sensibility' Krieger mentions the desire to create a particular representation of that social world:

My desire was to make it a place which could fairly easily become familiar and perhaps friendly, and so I sought to include details about ordinary things: telephone calls, rooms in buildings, affections people had for one another. A second problem has to do with location. I wanted to indicate that the station was to be found in different kinds of places: in the building at 50 Green Street, at 106.9 on the FM band, in relations a disc jockey had with a promotion man or a salesman with an advertiser, in the original owner's paranoia, in the regard a benefactor had for Donahue. A third and possibly more essential problem had to do with specialness. I wanted the world of the station to seem peculiar, not altogether unlike other worlds, but one in which one was struck by certain things and saw them perhaps more clearly.

(Krieger 1979b, p.176)

Here, then, Krieger articulates, possibly more self-consciously than most sociological authors, the textual construction of a social world and the narrative contract between the text and the reader. The ethnographic text is to produce a social domain which is recognizable or knowable for the reader, yet constituted through its unique particularity. It is to be given an adequately dense ambience of descriptive detail; the reader is invited to seek familiarity, even identification, with this milieu. The issue is a generic one for ethnographic writing, and Krieger tackles it in a particularly direct and explicit fashion.

The introductory description of the KMPX station is adequately representative of how Krieger attempts to weave together concrete descriptive detail in order to construct her triptych of sensibility, character and naming:

KMPX was broadcasting in stereo with a power of 80,000 watts, non-directional, in March 1967. Its transmitter was located on top of Mt Beacon in Marin County at a height of 1,250 feet. Listeners could tune it in at 106.9 on the FM band. The station was operated out of a modernized warehouse building at 50 Green Street in a section of San Francisco just off the Embarcadero, in view of the piers, and close to the base of Telegraph Hill. These were good quarters. For a period before, Crosby had operated the station out of a hotel room with not much more than a turntable and a microphone as equipment. The hotel quarters were such that listeners could occasionally hear when the toilet flushed and when money was deposited in a pay telephone nearby, or so it was said. For reasons having something to do with his hardship in running the station, and something to do with a tenacity one might not expect from a man of his appearance, Leon Crosby had a profound personal attachment to KMPX. The strength of that attachment was tested a year later, in the spring of 1968, when Donahue and a majority of the KMPX staff walked off their jobs and threatened to take Crosby's radio station away from him. What follows is a story of how that happened and of what became of the station in the next four years.

(Krieger 1979a, p.30)

In passages like this, then, Krieger tries to reconstruct her chosen social world, to invite the sympathetic engagement of the reader, and to foreshadow the major topic of her book. The concrete detail of description is used to establish the 'sensibility' of narrator, reader and participants. The homely origins of the KMPX station may be contrasted with the introduction of (and to) KSAN, the radio station to which the striking staff were recruited:

Prescott arrived at 211 Sutter Street shortly before 6 a.m. on Tuesday, May 21, in time to do the morning shift. When he opened the door to the radio station on the fourth floor, one of the first things he saw was the wallpaper, Metromedia wallpaper, a muted multicolored print, undistinguished, yet somehow awful. When the rest of the staff arrived later, they found themselves faced with the same paper and moving in on the station's former classical [music] staff.

(Krieger 1979a, p.106)

For the participants and the narrator the wallpaper is treated as indexing the new corporate identity of KSAN, under the Metromedia empire. The new physical location is introduced with extreme precision, and just that one characteristic is singled out for special significance.

Krieger is quite explicit about her concern with 'characters'. She acknowledges how important was the narrative function of various personae: 'My guiding questions had to do with the text and the problem of developing characters who would be capable of carrying its narrative' (1979a, p.177). Since Krieger's account of 'character' is not intended to be a study of individual psychology or biography, the elements of individual actors are sketched in and hinted at in a highly selective fashion. As Krieger herself puts it, 'I found myself accepting a sketchiness in the description of characters, and the problem then was how to do each sketch.' The characters in *Hip Capitalism* are introduced in terms of very brief pen-portraits. Of some of the key characters, for instance, we learn:

Tom Donahue was looking for work. Donahue, at 38, was a large and imposing man. His hair was dark and full, combed back. He had a close cropped beard. There was an air of command about him, a seriousness, a presence which suggested the world should be his and would have been if someone else had not already dealt the chances.

(Krieger 1979a, p.29)

Leon Crosby was 43, a small man, balding, with an attitude of wariness about him, an uneasiness, as if he were surrounded by troubles which might at any moment get critically worse.

(p.29)

Leath kept his position as KSAN general manager to the end of June. In the start of July, it was announced that he was taking a three-months leave of absence. He was replaced by the general manager of KNEW, Varner Paulsen, who called KSAN 'the FM'. Paulsen was medium sized and bald. He had been with Metromedia long enough to feel committed to the company and with KNEW as general manager for just over two years.

(p.108)

Duff was 32 when he moved from Boston to San Francisco to become the third general manager of KSAN. He had a wife and two sons. He had been born in Texas, gone through the Air Force Academy, attended three universities in

> Texas, and written a 60-page handbook on talk radio. He had hung around radio stations as a kid....Duff wore glasses, had a moustache and a trim beard and short brown hair when he came to KSAN.
>
> (p.130)

The 'characters' are sketched in terms of a few 'signs': most notably here coded in terms of their hair. Whether or not this was deliberate on Krieger's part, it is congruent with the style of San Francisco culture of the period that hair length and style, presence or absence of beard, should be used as a marker of personal character. It is noticeably deployed as a marker of 'straightness', and of the tension between 'hip' and 'straight'. The use of a few character and personal traits to establish characterological reference is an obvious use of the figure of synecdoche: allowing the part to stand for the whole. It is also translated into a more symbolic, metaphorical function, standing not just for personal front and self-presentation, but for more general cultural traits.

It is characteristic of the entire narrative style here that metonymy and synecdoche should predominate over metaphor. The narrative is sustained through sequences of social action – related through contiguity rather than thematic (metaphorical) relationships of similarity or analogy. When the broader social context of social change in America is introduced, for instance, it is done through synecdochal allusion, rather than explored in detail, or invoked in terms of generalizing images. The combination of minutiae from the radio station and the laconic references to national events has an almost bathetic effect:

> The station got a new chief engineer in October, replacing the one who had stayed on from the classical format who, Donahue felt, hated the guts of the rock music staff. Richard Nixon was elected President of the United States in November. The campus of San Francisco State College was closed down indefinitely. There were executive changes in Metromedia.
>
> (Krieger 1979a, p.117)

The style serves to point up the emphasis elsewhere on the tiny – almost pettifogging – detail of the main narrative. The elements (such as they are) of national context are reduced to further elements in the narrative voice. The sympathetic reader may become embroiled in the frustrated wranglings between the participants; or may become frustrated in turn at becoming so enmeshed.

As Krieger's narrative unfolds, the moral contest is that between the *authenticity* and spontaneity of the original inspiration, and the corporate values of the stations' newer owners and managers. Here is played out (without explicit invocation) the struggle between *Gemeinschaft* and *Gesellschaft*. The spontaneous seeks escape from the pervasive tendencies of rationalization and economic calculation. The tale of 'co-optation' is one in which major 'characters' have important narrative functions. And there are few unequivocal heroes.

Finally, there is one stylistic feature that gives Krieger's text an unusual character and flavour. The particular mimetic function that is pursued most vigorously is not the descriptive representation of persons and places, but the representation of their accounts and reflections. There is a multiplicity of voices in the text. Krieger herself reports the approach in this way:

> I dealt with the problem of converting reports to narrative in the text, in part, by techniques of paraphrase. The rule was to use what people said they remembered and thought and felt about events in a stream of consciousness fashion, in passages attributed to them but presented without quotation marks....The nature of the interview notes I had taken seemed to lead to paraphrase as a common form, since what people said was often not complete enough in itself in the notes or not suitable for direct quotation. In the interviews, each had discussed the history of the station in their own ways. To make a narrative that would draw on them all and space them out over time, I had to chop them up and take selections from them, and given the amount of discretion and interpretation involved, use of quotation marks, even if only for strictly textual purposes, seemed misleading.
>
> (Krieger 1979b, p.181)

The result of this strategy is to represent a great deal of the narrative through elements of 'indirect discourse'. Indirect discourse, of various types, approximates to the more mimetic forms of speech representation in narrative text, short of the reproduction of 'direct discourse', under the appearance of verbatim quotation of utterances. A range of representational methods from the 'purely diegetic' to the 'purely mimetic' is outlined by McHale (1978). (See also Rimmon-Kenan 1983, pp.109ff.)

McHale's range of types runs from the 'diegetic summary', which is the bare summary report of speech, with no attempt or claim to represent the content and style of the speech itself. McHale's example is: 'When Charley got a little gin inside him he started telling war yarns for the first time in his life.' Further along the scale is the 'summary', which refers to the content of the reported speech, but makes no attempt to preserve it in style or detail: 'He stayed till late in the evening telling them about miraculous conversions of unbelievers, extreme unction on the firing line, a vision of the young Christ he'd seen walking among the wounded in a dressing station during a gas attack.' Then there is 'indirect content paraphrase', where the content is reproduced independently of style or form: 'The waiter told him that Carranza's troops had lost Torreon and that Villa and Zapata were closing in on the Federal District.' Yet more mimetic is the variety of indirect discourse that preserves some elements of the original speech act, and not just its reference; 'When they came out Charley said by heck he thought he wanted to go up to Canada and enlist and go over and see the Great War.' 'Free indirect discourse' preserves yet more of the stylistic form and vocabulary of the supposed original: 'Why the hell shouldn't they know, weren't they off'n her and out to see the goddam town and he'd better come along.' Finally, there is direct discourse, conventionally represented in quotation of dialogue, and a variant of it, 'free direct discourse', used to represent first-person speech, often as private inner monologue. (All the examples, from the original discussion by McHale, are taken from various works by Dos Passos.)

Krieger makes a good deal of use of indirect discourse in representing the action from multiple perspectives. This device allows her to weave the various accounts into a multi-layered, multi-voiced narrative. The following passage from the KMPX strike episode illustrates the technique:

> Donahue ignored Crosby's offer that he take one station. He felt arbitrarily relieved of his duties. Whether he had brought it on or not, he did not care. Crosby had just taken back what was not his to reclaim. The world for a moment collapsed. Donahue walked out of the office and left 50 Green Street. A while later he talked with Melvin. They decided to go on strike. They did not think of going to another station. They did not want to kill this one. They wanted to keep it from being destroyed. You do not kill what you love, Donahue said.
>
> (Krieger 1979a, p.71)

The style of reportage mixes the authorial statement of events, times and places; the indirect summary of speech; free indirect discourse, more directly mimetic of the reported talk.

The use of free indirect discourse is something that has attracted a good deal of attention. It is especially remarkable as a device for the combination of narrator's and character's voices. It has a number of possible functions in fictional texts. In particular it has been noted that free indirect discourse allows for the development of polyvocal text. It allows the textual representation of multiple perspectives of the situation (McHale 1978), which are also re-capitulated more explicitly in Krieger's combination with more overtly marked allocation of speakers:

> When Crosby came back from his court hearing and sat down with Hunt on Monday, Hunt thought Crosby was just plain mad. He was not realizing the future. He simply wanted to fire them. Hunt said he told Crosby he thought they should talk to the strikers, for the sake of the station's image. Crosby agreed. He said they would try to negotiate the reasonable demands. Some of the money ones would have to be met, but not the others.
>
> (Krieger 1979a, p.75)

The literary-critical treatment of indirect discourse illuminates how it is used in an ethnographic context like Krieger's. As various authors have pointed out, it is useful in representing the idiom or idiolect of individual speakers. It can, therefore, be used to preserve the style of speech of individual actors, or the register of a given group or sub-culture. Reported speech may also be represented in this indirect mode so as to create the equivalent of 'interior monologue', so that personal feelings or responses can be constructed. The following is again representative of Krieger's usage:

Bear, like Pigg, felt he could tell when a show he did was good and drugs helped. If you were high and feeling fine you could put out good music and make people on the outside feel good. Street felt, drugs or not, when she walked into the studio, nobody was going to bring her down, nobody. She was going to do her show and she was not going to be brought down by any program director complaining about the miserable shape of the equipment or any listener phoning in objecting to her music. Pigg said he hated it when people called in to tell him he sounded in a down mood on the air. It was his show and he did not like them personalizing it like that. One reason he used a radio name was to make the show something apart from himself, and he knew, they all knew, there was this implicit rule you should not bring people down on the air. You should not make a show an ego trip for yourself at their expense. Your ego was involved, but you did not want to become too much that. A lot depended on your musical taste, but that was just personal.

(Krieger 1979a, pp.179-80)

This passage again illustrates Krieger's characteristic pattern of usage. Often she explicitly introduces a character's speech or perspective with a reporting verb ('said', 'felt', 'thought', and so on). That verb is then followed by an indirect content paraphrase. The character's attributed speech or personal reflection is then expanded and continued with indirect discourse, occasionally blending into free indirect discourse. There is therefore the potential for quite complex patterns of reportage and discourse. Two or more characters' voices may be represented simultaneously as one reports that of the other – the whole framed by the narrator's voice, yet all the voices combined into the indirect style:

Duff said Paulsen told him he had a high opinion of the staff at KSAN but that the corporation might bug him about superficialities. Paulsen said he believed by the time he left and Duff came on that the staff had more discipline than they had when he started as general manager 10 months before, and the discipline had to do with what they considered were their roles. Duff said he noticed immediately that the staff had an us–them attitude toward Metromedia. They seemed to expect autonomy within the corporation. They were fetishist about drugs. Also they were megalomaniac. They thought they were great. They expected to be number one in gross ratings. At first he disagreed.

(Krieger 1979a, p.131)

Ultimately Krieger's narrative style has difficulties. The relentlessly detailed chronology of *Hip Capitalism* lacks a sense of shape and purpose. Paradoxically, perhaps, the focus on sequences of events detracts from other – equally important – temporal features. There is no sense of *durée*, no sense of rhythm. The text divides the narrative into different periods, but with the exception of the KMPX strike, the narrative is not well ordered into episodes. There is little development of actors' projects and strategies over time. Likewise, the use of indirect reported discourse, while successful locally in the representation of voice and idiom, is cumulatively unsatisfactory. In the absence of authorial commentary, or non-chronological thematization, the detail and the shifting voices leave the reader searching for an interpretative framework. The sociological import of the text is hard to keep in focus.

Fragmented narratives

This chapter has concentrated on two particularly extreme examples of narrative presentation: the highly personalized 'confessional' and the extended chronicle of events. For the most part, the published ethnography combines narrative elements in less 'pure' forms. The implied narrative of the fieldwork experience is fragmented and dispersed. The strict chronology of events is disrupted as the text of everyday life is re-ordered in thematic categories. Events and narratives of social action are presented in extended 'exemplars' (cf. Chapter 5). The significance of events is thus found not primarily in their narrative sequence, but in their relations of similarity and difference with other narrative units. In other words, the 'conventional' ethnography places events in paradigmatic relations, rather than the mere recapitulation of their syntagmatic, diachronic relations.

Whereas 'narrative' ethnographies like *Hip Capitalism* achieve their force through a linear arrangement, the majority of ethnographic texts – extended monographs in particular – achieve their effects through the repetitive accumulation of equivalent episodes. The repetitious, cyclical character of such narrative conventions thus lifts the conventional ethnography out of the mundane world of lived experience and invests the reported world with additional – almost mythical – significance. For as Lévi-Strauss pointed out, there is a radical distinction between the directionality of history and the 'suppression of time' in the realm of myth-logic (Lévi-Strauss 1972; cf. Leach 1970). While the analogy is not exact, one can use Lévi-Strauss's metaphor of the orchestral score to represent 'myth-logic': 'an orchestra score, to be meaningful, must be read diachronically along one axis – that is, page after page, and from left to right – and synchronically along the other axis, all the notes written vertically making up one gross constituent, that is one bundle of relations' (Lévi-Strauss 1972, p.212). Lévi-Strauss's original formulation of the model suggests that the 'myth' is encountered as a repetitious linear sequence of elements (episodes). A successful decoding necessitates the re-grouping of elements into synchronic arrangements of similarity and contrast.

This is almost precisely parallel to the intellectual work that goes into the conventional ethnography. The diachronic, syntagmatic relations of everyday events are rearranged in atemporal, paradigmatic relationships. (The diachronic element remains more strongly represented in the 'confessional' account of personal development, however.) It is enshrined in practical advice to ethnographers, who are encouraged to cut up or otherwise fragment and rearrange the chronologically ordered episodes of their field notes and journals.

John Lofland (1971) provided a classic example of such procedural advice, recommending that in addition to preserving a complete, chronologically ordered account, the ethnographer should get 'the material *out of the sheer chronological narrative* of one's field or interview notes and into a flexible storage, ordering and retrieval format' (p.118, my emphasis).

When we read the majority of 'conventional', 'realist' ethnographies, then, the interpretative work of the author is already coded in the arrangement of narrative elements into larger paradigmatic units or 'bundles' (themes, chapters) and their sequential arrangement. Although a complete analysis of even one text would be very lengthy from this point of view, some indication of the issues can be illustrated here.

There are some intriguing parallels and differences between *When Prophecy Fails* and a monograph (more explicitly sociological in inspiration and execution, perhaps) dealing with a similar social phenomenon: *Doomsday Cult* (Lofland 1977). This too is an ethnography of a 'deviant' cult, in this case a rather small group of adherents of what Lofland calls the cult of the 'Divine Precepts' (DP), as revealed to a Korean prophet. (Since Lofland's research the movement has become much more successful and widespread. The pseudonym has become redundant and somewhat ritualistic, but – like Lofland – I shall retain the original nomenclature: cf. Lofland 1977, pp. 279 and 345.)

Like Festinger and his colleagues, Lofland describes a process of conversion, proselytization and the maintenance of faith among a small network of believers. The time-span of his account is longer – and in the long run Lofland's follow-up must acknowledge a period of 'success' for this millenarian movement. (Lofland suggests that in the even longer run, it is still doomed to become one of the 'main "has been" movements that linger in America' – 1977, p.280.)

Many of the reported events that are central to Lofland's account, however, are directly comparable to those in Festinger's text. These include stories of *failure*. Like the believers in *When Prophecy Fails* the adherents of the DP are followed through a succession of abortive or inconclusive events. The substance of these occurrences differs: in the one case we trace successive failures of extraterrestrially inspired prophecy; in the other, a succession of failures to attract potential members through repeated attempts at proselytization. As in the Festinger, there is a repeated ironic contrast between the cult members' aspirations or expectations and the events that transpire (or fail to). The narrative effect is conveyed largely through the form of *repetition*.

The arrangement of some key chapters illustrates the point. It combines the paradigmatic collection of formally similar items *and* their syntagmatic, chronological arrangement. Lofland discusses a range of strategies used by the adherents of the DP to try to attract new recruits to the cult. He distinguishes, *inter alia*, between different types of 'access' that the proselytizers sought to establish. Here are two binary oppositions: 'disembodied' and 'embodied', and 'overt' versus 'covert':

> The embodied–disembodied distinction refers to the problem of whether to approach individuals face to face or to impart information through such means as radio and newspapers. The overt–covert presentation distinction refers to the problem of whether to make it clear to the transmitter that the access was instituted in order to 'sell' a millenarian doctrine (overt) or to withhold the apocalyptic content and stimulate interest in some other presentational basis, such as sex (covert).
>
> (Lofland 1977, p.66)

Each of these strategies thus provides a collection of events, actions and decisions, each with its outcomes and consequences. The collections (chapters) on each theme also embed chronological accounts of the successive attempts to implement each strategy.

There is, therefore, a repetitious accumulation of types and instances. The effect of at least some of them is bathetic. The DP members are repeatedly subject to failure. Advertisements are not answered, meetings not attended, and so on. The cumulative effect is similar to that of *When Prophecy Fails*, though it is achieved through different means.

The figure of repetition is an extremely important component in ethnographic narrative in general (see also Edmondson 1984). In the absence of a quantitative aggregation of discrete data, the rhetorical induction of the ethnography relies upon the narrative accumulation of types and instances. Its rhetorical forms — themes and examples, cycles and sequences – gather together the fragments of evidence under various thematic rubrics. The arrangement of the text itself provides the auspices for finding relations within and between its constituent parts. Repetition transforms the disparate components into 'evidence', imparts weight and significance, and provides the reader with interpretative keys. The collection and repetition of events within thematic assemblages constructs a cyclical, predictable and ordered social world. The ethnographer claims to discover order in the day-to-day world of passing moments. The ethnographic text displays and constructs that order in its very narrative.

The structuralist interpreter of mythological narratives and the author of ethnographic accounts are both engaged in similar kinds of hermeneutic work. They find and transcribe the repetitious chronicles of everyday life or mythic recital, and transform them by re-ordering their thematic units. The 'significance' of the analysis is inscribed in those thematic reconstructions, their arrangement and their contrasts. The chronicles outlined at some length in this chapter – *When Prophecy Fails* and *Hip Capitalism* – are unusual in claiming significance for their chronological ordering alone. The majority of ethnographic monographs construct the repetitive myth-form out of the sequence of reported events. In both narrative modes, however, the figure of repetition is central to the rhetorical production of sociological findings and analytic import.

Chapter seven

Character and type: the textual construction of actors

Modern literary theory has not always been especially successful in dealing with issues of character and the textual representation of persons (cf. Culler 1975, p.230). Structuralist and post-structuralist analysts have proved at ease with more straightforwardly narrative elements. Indeed, there has been a marked tendency to assimilate characters to elements or functions of narrative. None the less, it is important to devote some attention to the treatment of persons in the ethnographic genre. The warrant of ethnographic knowledge, after all, rests on the claim of an intimate knowledge of social actors and their everyday lives. It comes as no surprise, therefore, that some ethnographic texts convey much of their substance through the detailed representation of individual persons. This is by no means universal, however. Although all of these texts report and comment on social interaction in some given settings, they vary in their treatment of individual actors.

Some ethnographies contain memorable 'characters'. Indeed they may prove the most enduringly memorable features of the monographs. The 'message' may, in effect, be that, contrary to naïve expectation, actors in the setting lead their lives rationally, morally (or vice versa). The sociological analysis may be conveyed, therefore, through the construction of character: motives, values, emotions and other traits are displayed in detailed accounts of social action. Some ethnographies, on the other hand, contain no major 'characters'. Although social action is portrayed, the actors themselves remain more or less anonymous.

At one extreme, therefore, it makes sense to identify the 'heroes' of some sociological research: at least, there are memorable individuals with whom the reader may identify. In texts of that sort, 'plot' and 'character' are intertwined and 'persons' are treated in some detail. At the other extreme, we have texts in which 'character' is subordinated to action, or to the relatively undifferentiated collectivity of shared beliefs, habits or conventions.

In terms of this distinction, therefore, we can draw on Forster's well-known dichotomy between 'round' and 'flat' characters in novels (Forster 1927, p.75). In that formulation, 'flat' characters are uni-dimensional: they have a single character trait which constrains and dominates their part in the novel.

Such a character is therefore highly stable, and therefore predictable. Forster makes the point that characters of this sort are often 'typed' – that is, drawn in accordance with cultural expectation, or stereotypes. 'Round' characters, on the other hand, are multi-dimensional. They are assembled by the writer and the reader out of an accumulation of varied manifestations of the person. Characters of this complexity may be shown to change, to be inconsistent and so to surprise the reader. While rounded, multiplex characters do not escape our conventional assumptions, they may be less susceptible to 'typing'. The reader is unlikely to interpret them merely as realizations of stock types.

To a degree, the distinction drawn here between polar types of ethnographic writing parallels the contrasts drawn by Todorov (1977) between plot-centred, or 'a-psychological' texts on the one hand and character-centred, or 'psychological' narratives on the other. The parallel is not exact, but it represents a comparable attempt to capture the sort of contrast to be dealt with here. These distinctions do not demarcate different types of novel, of course. Within the same literary work we are likely to encounter characters of different degrees of complexity. Likewise, although they are different types of ethnography on this dimension, within the same work we are presented with 'flat' characters even when more rounded ones are portrayed. The protagonists of some ethnographies, indeed, achieve their individuality and 'depth' in contrast with more shadowy one-dimensional characters.

It is a matter of some analytic import just how the representation of persons is managed in the text. The contrast between complex, individualized characters and a penumbra of much less differentiated ones is significant for how we read the interests and commitments of the ethnography (and, by implication, of the ethnographer). In other words, the treatment of persons as characters in the text is inseparable from the analytic theme of 'point of view'. The distinctions just outlined inevitably direct the reader towards different categories of social actor. They may demarcate social boundaries and distinctions which invite or resist the sympathetic recognition of a reader. The differences between character-types and their implied points of view may also contribute to the ironic interplay of 'expectation' and 'experience', 'appearance' and 'reality'.

Character and action

Likewise, 'character' is frequently represented through the narrative representation or reportage of social action. While the ethnography may baldly state actors' personal traits, or the more general cultural attributes, these must normally be manifested in concrete sequences of social settings, and interaction. The relationship between characters and narratives is central to one traditional treatment of the topic in literary theory. This is grounded in the formalist and structuralist tradition. Its origins lie in Propp's analysis of the folk-tale. There are identified a small, finite number of narrative 'functions' which characters may realize. (There is not necessarily a simple one-to-one relationship between individual characters and unique functions.) Propp's own categories necessarily reflect the folk materials from which they were derived. They are: the villain, the helper, the donor, the sought-for-person, the father, the dispatcher, the hero, the false hero. They are evidently somewhat specific to the restricted code of folk narratives. That has not prevented other theorists from postulating a restricted number of general (if not universal) functions of that sort (for example, Tomashevski 1965). Greimas (1966) also proposes a small number of primitive functions, arranged in basic relationships of contrast. Among many possible problems with any such system is that the application of them to a broad range of texts and genres often implies such diffuse and metaphorical interpretations of the categories that their analytic value is substantially, even fatally, weakened. It remains, however, an intriguing possibility, not pursued here, to examine the sociological corpus for a restricted repertoire of functions and types, in terms of a formal analysis of the ethnography as a 'folk-tale'. It is not my purpose to be diverted into a general discussion of the utility of formalist analyses of 'actants' in narrative texts. The issue is raised here to introduce the notion that at least within a genre there may exist a limited number of character-types or functions. The possibility is open that among ethnographic texts we can discern a number of recurrent functions of characters or 'actants' – without assuming that they will be exhaustive, or generalizable beyond the genre.

To begin with, the discussion will focus upon ethnographic texts in which there are multi-dimensional, individualized characters. These are texts in which the sociological argument is furthered through the representation of a limited number of individual social actors: the social world is treated as *their* social world and there is a close correspondence between the perspective of the ethnographer and that of the central character(s). Moreover, the sociological 'discovery' may reside in the detailed discovery and revelation of individuals' 'character' – possibly to the surprise of the narrator (and, by implication, the reader too).

At one extreme, of course, there is a genre of sociological text intimately related to the ethnography, which consists wholly or largely in the reportage of 'life-histories' (for a general review, see Plummer 1983). These individuals are among the most fully documented persons in the entire corpus of sociological literature. While not, perhaps, as famous as some of the individual 'subjects' of other descriptions (the Elephant Man, Freud's Anna O., Luria's Mnemonist), sociology boasts its classic case-studies of individuals. Undoubtedly the most famous of these individuals is 'The Jack Roller' (Shaw 1930). Shaw's account of Stanley – or rather his presentation of Stanley's autobiography – became widely read, especially after the publication of a paperback edition in 1966: 'The text thus became a classic in the field of juvenile delinquency and has been re-quired reading for generations of sociologists training in the field' (Snodgrass 1982, p.3).

The sociological commentary which packages Stanley's life-story is dis-appointing to many readers; it is underdeveloped and often banal. The success of the appeal lies elsewhere. As Geis (1982) remarks:

To my mind the appeal of *The Jack-Roller* must be credited not to its sociological insights and contributions but to the extraordinary nature of Stanley himself. The protagonist is truly Dostoyevskian in his complexity and in his appalling ability to act in ways that seem stunningly self-destructive and self-defeating by almost anyone's standards. Stanley tells us that he cannot tolerate the smallest degree of monotony, that he cannot abide the 'stares of snobbish people,' and that he will not take reasonable orders especially if they are issued by a woman. In addition, Stanley describes how he is hooked and drawn, lemming-like, to the sordid and gaudy Loop area of the city. We read, hardly believing his reports of blowing up emotionally, walking off jobs, and starting fights over trivial matters. Stanley seems to know precisely what he is doing, as he unselfconsciously recites his experience and is simultaneously presumably unaware of the likely consequences of his actions. There is something extremely perplexing in so forthcoming, guilt free and self-righteous a tale, with the teller able to state the connections between choice and consequence but obviously incapable of doing much about it.

(Geis 1982, p.123)

Burgess's commentary on the jack-roller's life-story explicitly emphasizes the significance of Stanley's character (Burgess 1930). The life-story, so focused on the individual, provides a perfect exemplification of the interplay between temperament and circumstance.

There is every likelihood that the satisfaction apparently experienced by many readers of *The Jack-Roller* derives from the aesthetic-cum-ethical resolution of the story. Geis summarizes the responses of the original reviewers:

Kimball Young, as did virtually all the reviewers, revelled a bit in the seeming happy resolution of Stanley's early troubles, pointing in his review to the jack-roller's 'final reorientation to normal social participation.' The reviewer for the *New York Times* marked as well the 'treatment which apparently has ended in the boy's complete redemption,' while T.V.S. (probably T.V. Smith, a well known social philosopher of the time) in the *International Journal Of Ethics* noted that Stanley had become a 'socially oriented person on the road to conventional success.' Read Bain thought it 'almost unbelievable' that the combination of Shaw and a loving landlady, the anonymous Mrs Smith, 'could snatch the brand from the burning.' Indeed, the *Christian Century* was so taken with Stanley's redemption that it headnoted its review 'A Modern Prodigal's Return,' and observed in its text that 'for the past five years [Stanley] has been going pretty straight... [and] is an adjusted member of society and no longer an enemy of it or an irresponsible drifter on its surface.' It appears singular that Stanley's alleged reformation, only one element in the book, preoccupied the reviewers. Perhaps Shaw sensed that the final reckoning hardly was in, so he downplayed this item *vis-à-vis* the reviewers, who liked the up-beat denouement of the title, however uncertain they must have known it to be.

(Geis 1982, p.127)

There is little doubt that the 'literary' quality of this early classic far outweighed the sociological originality or acuity of its accompanying commentary in producing the effects it did. The autobiographical life-history in sociology – as in other non-fictional genres, and in comparable fictional genres too – provides the reader with the sense of detailed understanding of another individual.

The 'heroes' of life-histories and ethnographic monographs provide the reader with two parallel sets of potentially satisfying experiences. On the one hand they furnish the sense of intimate acquaintance with characters that most readers themselves would not encounter at first hand in their everyday lives. On the other hand, these characters illuminate a range of settings in which, again, the respectable reader may have no direct involvement. The individual character may thus embody opportunities for social exploration and discovery, such as Rock alludes to: 'Matza's deviant, Paul Cressey's taxi-dancer, Donald Cressey's embezzler, Sutherland's professional thief, Marvin Scott's jockey and Becker's marihuana user are assembled and then set free to bring back intelligence about the nature of social life' (Rock 1979, pp.79-80). The detailed portrayal of individuals – usually through a mixture of their own words and the observations of the ethnographer – thus helps to establish the warrant for credibility and authority in the text.

The life-story, which covers the entire biography, or some partial 'moral career', provides a particularly potent version. It is possible to portray, or at least project, an outcome – a resolution – to the biography, and a fulfilment of the character. This is much less likely in the conventional ethnography. Just as its narratives are likely to be brief and episodic, so the reader glimpses the characters over a restricted span of time and circumstance. There is thus little opportunity for such a sense of resolution through the psychology of individual development.

In the conventional ethnography – as in much realist literature – characters and plot are displayed simultaneously. Individual actors are encountered through episodic engagements and glimpses. Some characters are foregrounded and occupy much of the narrator's and reader's attention; others are much less substantial characters, more distantly perceived; yet others exist only through the reports and perceptions of more central characters. The construction and representation of social actors is one of the many ways in which implicit sociological arguments are conveyed. It parallels and overlaps with the use of descriptive writing outlined in Chapter Four, and is embedded in narrative writing, as discussed in Chapter Six. It also develops the argument of Chapter Five, as the narrative representation of social actors is frequently progressed through the use of episodic exemplars. The discussion therefore continues with an examination of character in realist ethnographic writing.

Anonymous ethnography

At the other extreme from the ethnography peopled with heroes is that peopled almost entirely by anonymous individuals. Here the authenticity of the account is warranted not by the intimate knowledge of individuals, but by the aggregated accumulations of an 'outside' observer. There is little or nothing here of the 'rounded' character and the 'psychological' text.

Such a textual type reproduces the anonymous, fleeting encounter of behaviour in public places. A case in point is Edgerton's ethnography of an urban beach in southern California, *Alone Together* (1979). (The title is itself evocative of the pervasive atmosphere which is conjured up throughout the monograph; the co-presence of strangers in a public setting.) The analysis is concerned with social order on the beach, the nature and management of threats and disruptions to that order.

The persons who populate the beach, its piers and promenade, are described in terms of general social categories, such as gender, age, ethnic membership and so on. More specific categories include the life guards, the police officers who patrol the beach and its surroundings, drug users, surfers, criminals, transients and tourists. The descriptions of even the most singular of individuals serve only to emphasize the passing scene of anonymity:

> Three young men walked along the waterline. All wore costumes that were bizarre enough to startle the most flamboyant rock star. One carried a guitar in a case that was painted to resemble an American flag. One played a flute and the third sang rather loudly while doing dance steps in the sand.
>
> They gave a brief impromptu concert for a minute or two, then seriously, even rather glumly, walked back through the sand away from the beach. Only a handful of beachgoers appeared to notice, and these only glanced up briefly and then turned away. Their apparent disinterest *(sic)* was difficult to fathom, since the strangely costumed men and their music were conspicuous, even bizarre, and few musicians of any sort stroll along this beach.
>
> (Edgerton 1979, p.108)

This is one of several similar passages describing troublesome persons at the beach. In so far as it is remarkable, it is so for its lack of engagement with the scene and the persons referred to. The overt function of the passage is to introduce the reader to outlandish and colourful characters, whose presence may potentially be disturbing to ordinary beach-users. The textual realization is almost perfectly the reverse. Rather than a text of colourful presence, we have a text of absences. The 'flamboyant' costumes are not described and the sparse description of their behaviour is not such as to excite a great deal of response in the reader. The description of the event and the audience of beach-users is marked by absence and negation. So 'only a handful' notice, who 'only glanced up briefly'. The lack of interest is hardly remarkable. Even from the point of view of an 'outside' observer, then, the narrative withholds rather than supplies information. It emphasizes anonymity and a *lack* of detailed understanding: the actions of the bizarre young men and the lack of response from other beach-goers are rendered as motiveless, inconsequential.

Even when more individualized characters make an appearance on the beach it serves to sustain the same effects:

A 50-year-old man, wearing an Aloha shirt, bermuda shorts, white socks and street shoes, was observed meandering across the sand with an enormous pair of binoculars fixed to his eyes. His odyssey was made stranger still by the fact that he was stooped forward at almost a 45-degree angle. So extreme was his forward tilt that when he peered into his binoculars it was difficult to under-stand how he could see anything but the sand at his feet, yet he marched onward and looked through his binoculars. On closer inspection it became obvious that his odd posture served a purpose, since he did indeed locate the targets of his inquiry very close to his feet. For example, he almost literally stood over a voluptuous young woman and stared at her through his glasses. After a few moments, he moved on to the next attractive woman and repeated his inspection. He was observed doing this for 40 minutes, yet at no time did any beachgoers display marked concern about his activities. A few men noticed him and smiled, but then went back to whatever they were doing. Various women obviously saw what he was up to, but they all avoided giving any clear sign that they knew he existed. One of the lifeguards commented that the man, who was known as Mr Peepers, was a harmless and regular visitor to this part of the beach.

(Edgerton 1979, p.109)

The beach scene is portrayed through a series of such vignettes, all of which serve to establish the *lack* of personal intimacy in the setting. Even a 'character' identified by name appears only under the guise of a nickname bestowed by others.

Throughout *Alone Together* the individuals on the beach are portrayed entirely as anonymous characters, observed from the outside – from a distance. These characters have no 'inner life', and their actions are devoid of understandable motives. Even the categories of person who are regularly part of the beach scene, the life guards and the police, are depicted in the most anonymous terms. The ethnographer's claim to intimate first-hand knowledge of the urban beach is not based on close relationships between observer and observed. Its implicit claim derives, rather, from the detailed chronicle of observed persons and events. While anybody can observe the comings and goings of the urban beach scene, only the dedicated and purposeful observer would do so in the sort of protracted detail that is reported in *Alone Together*. The warrant for authority lies in the detailed transcription of time and place: the logging of times and the mapping of beach locations. These details, indeed, contrast with the relatively vague impression of the persons depicted.

Implicit sociology: 'corner boys'

One of the classic examples of implicit, persuasive sociology rendered through descriptive-cum-narrative writing is to be found in Whyte's *Street Corner Society* – itself a classic of the genre. As with many ethnographies of this type, it begins with a general introduction which explicates some of the background and import of the study. In 'Cornerville and its People' Whyte devotes a bare six pages to an introduction to the 'little Italy' slum setting of his study in 'Eastern City'. The readers learn something of the context, and a major theme is introduced: the division among younger men in Cornerville – between 'corner boys' and 'college boys':

> Corner boys are groups of men who center their social activities upon particular street corners, with their adjoining barbershops, lunchrooms, poolrooms, or clubrooms. They constitute the bottom level of society within their age group, and at the same time they make up the great majority of the young men of Cornerville.... The college boys are a small group of young men who have risen above the corner-boy level through higher education. As they try to make places for themselves as professional men, they are still moving socially upward.
>
> (Whyte 1981, p.xviii)

Following this brief introduction, the ethnography proper is launched with a vivid account of a group of corner-boys, 'Doc and his boys', the gang known as the Nortons. They – Doc in particular – must be among the best-known hosts or informants in the sociological literature. Doc is certainly the best-remembered and most often cited sponsor of an ethnographer in the field.

The reader who believes him or herself to be familiar with Whyte's work might well think, in retrospect, that the book begins with a detailed account of the boys' everyday lives and characters. In fact, Whyte gives a remarkably selective portrayal. A brief characterization of the Nortons and social relations within the gang is followed by two detailed accounts: 'Bowling and social ranking' (pp.14-25) and 'The Nortons and the Aphrodite Club' (pp.25-35).

Whyte does not say so at the outset, but the reader is presumably entitled to assume that such selected topics are in some sense – yet to be determined – significant. The reasonable assumption on reading these accounts is that these aspects of everyday life in Cornerville are microcosmic of the generality of the younger generation of Italian-American men in the 1930s. The account of *bowling* is especially remarkable. Whyte begins as if in a story:

> One evening in October, 1937, Doc scheduled a bowling match against the Italian Community Club, which was composed largely of college men who held their meetings every two weeks in the Norton Street Settlement House.
>
> (Whyte 1981, p.14)

Whyte recounts that particular bowling match in brief terms:

> Doc was captain of the Nortons. He selected Long John, Frank, Joe and Tommy for his team. Danny and Mike were not bowling in this period. Chick and Tony led the Community Club team.
>
> Feeling ran high. The Nortons shouted at the club bowlers and made all sort

of noises to upset their concentration. The club members were in high spirits when they gained an early lead but had little to say as the Nortons pulled ahead to win by a wide margin.

After the match I asked Frank and Joe if there was any team that they would have been more eager to beat. They said that if they could pick out their favorite victims, they would choose Chick Morelli, Tony Cardio, Joe Cardio (Tony's brother), Mario Testa, and Hector Marto. The last three had all belonged to the Sunset Dramatic Club.

Frank and Joe said that they had nothing against the other three men on the Community Club team but that the boys had been anxious to beat that team in order to put Chick and Tony 'in their places.' Significantly, Frank and Joe did not select their favorite victims on the basis of bowling ability. The five were good bowlers, but that was not the deciding factor in their choice. It was their social position and ambitions that were the objects of attack, and it was that which made victory over the Community Club so satisfying.

Lon Damaro and Fred Mackey had cheered for the club. Although they were club members, the boys felt that this did not excuse them. Danny said: 'You're a couple of traitors – Benedict Arnolds....You're with the boys – and then you go against them....Go on, I don't want your support.'

(Whyte 1981, pp.14-15)

As Whyte recounts it, this was the only such confrontation between the corner boys and the college boys. There were, however, bowling encounters with individual members. He goes on to enumerate some of them, and also tells us that after the Community Club match the Nortons took up bowling more enthusiastically: 'In the winter and spring of 1937–38 bowling was the most significant social activity for the Nortons' (p.17). At this point Whyte does not immediately provide further exemplification of the Nortons' actual bowling performances, but provides a brief characterization of the culture of bowling:

A high score at candlepins requires several spares or strikes. Since a strike rarely occurs except when the first ball hits the kingpin properly within a fraction of an inch, and none of the boys had such precise aim, strikes were considered matters of luck, although a good bowler was expected to score them more often than a poor one. A bowler was judged according to his ability to get spares, to 'pick' the pins that remained on the alley after his first ball.

There are many mental hazards connected with bowling. In any sport there are critical moments when a player needs the steadiest nerves if he is to 'come through'; but, in those that involve team play and fairly continuous action, the player can sometimes lose himself in the heat of the contest and get by the critical points before he has a chance to 'tighten up'. If he is competing on a five-man team, the bowler must wait a long time for his turn at the alleys, and he has plenty of time to brood over his mistakes. When a man is facing ten pins, he can throw the ball quite casually. But when only one pin remains standing, and his opponents are shouting 'He can't pick it,' the pressure is on, and there is a tendency to 'tighten up' and lose control.

When a bowler is confident that he can make a difficult shot, the chances are that he will make it or come exceedingly close. When he is not confident, he will miss. A bowler is confident because he has made similar shots in the past and is accustomed to making good scores. But that is not all. He is also confident because his fellows, whether for him or against him, believe that he can make the shot. If they do not believe in him, the bowler has their adverse opinion as well as his own uncertainty to fight against. When that is said, it becomes necessary to consider a man's relation to his fellows in examining his bowling record.

(Whyte 1981, p.17)

In what is probably the most memorable aspect of Whyte's analysis, he goes on to show the correspondence between bowling success and social standing within the corner boys' clique. Bowling is portrayed as a means of social differentiation and a marker of it. Whyte makes relatively little explicit cross-reference between more general sociological themes, the 'culture of bowling' reproduced above, and the narratives of bowling occasions he includes in the text. Implicitly, their inclusion and the various juxtapositions convey a vivid introduction to the entire ethnography.

To begin with, these vignettes of Cornerville life establish a powerful narrative contract between the reader and the text. A series of 'characters' are introduced and some of their key 'characteristics' are exemplified. From the very beginning of the book Whyte has mentioned an antagonistic, competitive relationship between the corner boys and the college boys. He does not construct his text in terms of detailed expositions of these contrasting social types. He does not occupy the reader with descriptions of the (presumably) relevant demographic data: we do not start out with a discussion of, say, the college boys' educational opportunities and successes (where do they go to college? what do they study? how are their studies financed? do they differ in background from the less educated corner boys?). Indeed, from a strictly sociological perspective the unsympathetic reader might complain that Whyte sidesteps a great many sociologically important questions. On the other hand, most readers have proved sympathetic. Any such critical perspective seems not to arise, or to be suspended or superseded. For Whyte's book is not sustained by a detailed propositional form of argument. Rather, he invites the reader's sympathetic engagement with the text through a close marriage of description and narration.

The selection of bowling is far from fortuitous. It provides a concrete narrative of conflict between the main social categories. Narrative thus stands for the sociological argument of contrasting life-styles and value systems in Cornerville. It achieves more too. The culture of bowling seems to establish a cultural framework for reading the rest of the text. The social context of bowling, as it appears in the narration, and as glossed by Whyte (without specific reference to the corner boys' subculture) provides a concrete manifestation of competitiveness, and the need to remain cool under pressure. As Whyte explicates it, these are the main features of success at bowling. Bowling is not just a clue to the internal structure of the corner boys' group, but is also a metaphor of a more general cultural *Gestalt*. The assemblage of character and ethos through the apparently 'trivial' narration of bowling is strongly reminiscent of an equally classic cultural description: Geertz's account of Balinese cock-fighting. Here too the author offers a detailed narrative account of a particular sporting contest which is used to convince the reader of more general cultural traits or themes.

Similar cultural themes and codes are laid down in the second section of narrative where Whyte presents 'The Nortons and the Aphrodite Club' (pp. 25-35). It establishes themes of social differentiation, relations between the sexes, and male pride: 'The girls moved in a different social orbit, and the Nortons considered them "high-toned" and conceited. Still, they could not help finding them attractive' (p.26). Nevertheless, members of the Nortons become socially involved with girls from the Aphrodite Club. Consider the brief episode of Doc and Alec, Helen and Mildred:

> Alec was always boasting about his powers with women. Doc paid little attention to him, but the other boys felt that something should be done to put him in his place. One night in April they were kidding Alec, when, as Doc says, Alec challenged him:
> 'If you're such a great lover, I challenge you to show your stuff!'
> I said, 'Alec, I might not be as handsome as you are, and I don't have all the hair that you have, but I can outbull you any day.'
> Alec says, 'No! No!'
> 'Well,' I said, 'I'm older now and I don't want to take a girl away from a man just to show I can do it.'
> But then Danny says, 'Doc, I think you're slipping.'
> *Maron!* When Danny says that, I must do something. He only said it to steam me up, but I said, 'All right, Danny, I pick Helen. Saturday night. You watch'....Alec wasn't there to see it Saturday night. That was too bad. We were bowling one floor below the girls. I went up to see Helen, and I asked her to come down, I had something to tell her. In a few minutes she came down – by herself. She sat next to me all the evening, the only girl among all those fellows. Danny was impressed. Later he told me, 'Doc, you're still the great lover.'
>
> (Whyte 1981, p.32)

The themes of bowling and relations between the sexes interpenetrate: both speak of competition among the male members of the Nortons. As Whyte himself sums things up:

> Association with the girls was, like bowling, a means of gaining, maintaining, or losing prestige in the group. As in bowling, Alec had to be kept in his place.

It was essential to the smooth functioning of the group that the prestige gradations be informally recognized and maintained.

(Whyte 1981, p.35)

In a third section of the chapter Whyte provides a third narrative: 'Doc's Political Campaign' (pp.35-42). Involvement in politics heightens Doc's sensitivities; for example,

> The political campaign only increased Doc's problems. Now, more than ever, he felt he must get a job. He was sensitive about his lack of formal education and unemployment was an added burden. He needed money for the campaign, and he did not want people to say that he was running for office just to get himself a job.
>
> (Whyte 1981, p.36)

Finally, Doc's lack of money and security undermine his own political ambitions. He withdraws from the campaign, explaining himself to Whyte:

> Bill...as a politician, I'm supposed to go to dances and meetings, and I can't go because I haven't got the money. Fellows come up to me and ask for cards with my name on them and stickers and signs. I can't give them any....You can't be that way in politics. They hold it against you. If you don't buy their ticket, they call you a cheap bastard.
>
> (Whyte 1981, p.40)

Again, the theme of *pride* emerges from the background of unemployment in Cornerville. The reader will probably have little difficulty in reading the various fragments as evidence of character *traits*. Moreover, those traits can be put together to compose a plausible character – a person. Furthermore, as we shall see, the persons and their traits are read against a background of cultural characteristics. Just as the narrative fragments stand for traits which are collated into a character, so those traits and the characters may be inspected for evidence of shared values and sentiments (related to ethnicity, class, gender, region, occupation and so on).

What, then, might the reader have learned of Whyte's street-corner 'boys' from their initial appearances in the book? To begin with, the reader encounters them as a collection of individuals *and* as representatives of social categories or types. The understanding of the text rests on the duality of characterization to be found there. Indeed, each aspect is mutually reinforcing. The 'type' provides the cultural code against which the individual is assessed, while the person realizes and validates the typification. There is little doubt that 'Doc' and his boys are presented in such a way as to invite a sympathetic identification with them. At the outset, the ethnographer/narrator's point of view is aligned with theirs. The world of Cornerville is initially seen from the corner boys' perspective: they are portrayed as individual men, while the rest of the social world is much more sketchily rendered. Moreover, the corner boys' moral evaluations of others are implicitly conveyed in the text.

For the reader, potential expectations concerning members in a slum quarter are likely to be challenged by Whyte's portrayal of the men (although it must be acknowledged that, given the general impact of Whyte's work and that of subsequent sociologists, actual readers are likely to be sensitized to potential ambiguities, ironies and challenges to common-sense presuppositions).

Doc is allowed to introduce himself. Whyte reproduces Doc's own account of his early years. By his own initial account, he was not liked as a young boy, and had to win 'respect' through powers of fighting. Doc, right from the beginning, embodies an agonistic ethos. He is more than just a fighting, competitive young man, however. Whyte comments on, and exemplifies, further complexities in Doc's 'character'. Doc has had to work to overcome physical disability – a withered arm. He is intelligent and 'found school work easy'. He left school to take a job with a stained-glass firm. He lost that work in the Depression. Reference is made several times to work and teaching in stained-glass work. He is the leader of the Nortons. Like other leading figures in the gang, Doc was respected for his intelligence and his skill in argument: 'On the infrequent occasions when he did become involved, he was usually able to outmaneuver his opponent without humiliating him', Whyte tells us (p.12). His position is upheld in the bowling rankings and in his success with women.

In a competitive male world, then, Doc is portrayed as a leader. His character is available to the reader through a series of observations and narratives provided by the ethnographer. He is only one of several corner boys whom we glimpse in this way, but he is the most prominent, and most rounded. All those who have read the monograph to the end – and many who have not – know that Doc was Whyte's 'sponsor' in the fieldwork. A social worker in Cornerville arranged a meeting between Whyte and Doc, and Doc provided the entrée that Whyte needed:

> 'Well, any nights you want to see anything I'll take you around. I can take you to the joints – gambling joints – I can take you around to the street corners. Just remember that you're my friend. That's all they need to know. I know these places, and, if I tell them that you're my friend, nobody will bother you. You just tell me what you want to see, and we'll arrange it.'

> (Whyte 1981, p.291)

The relationship between Doc and Whyte is one of the most famous of such ethnographer–sponsor pairings in all the methodological appendices, research papers and monographs.

Although Whyte's text is not exclusively concerned with Doc, the Nortons and their corner, there is every indication that in so far as their world is presented, the reader encounters it largely through their perspectives. To a considerable degree, Whyte treats the characters of his text relatively unproblematically. He seems to have no qualms about the construction of his personae. To a considerable extent Doc – like his fellows – is allowed to 'speak for himself'. Whyte treats the evidence for character as transparent. Doc emerges from the fragments of reported action and speech.

Doc is not likely to be found a figure of perfection, yet he appears as a sympathetic character – at least to a reader employing an uncritical 'natural attitude'. His potential is manifested against a background of social and economic limitations. The reader finds Doc exercising leadership and authority on the corner. By conventional standards he is a 'failure', and his political 'failure' underlines that. Yet, in that context, his decision to quit reflects personal pride. Doc and his friends in the Nortons show the reader that unemployed men in the slum have pride and individualism; that there are fine gradations of social standing and moral quality even among these lowly social orders; that social 'failures' have admirable qualities – qualities that would be more amply rewarded in other, more advantageous, social strata.

These are not the only themes of Whyte's monograph. Much of his later analysis centres on 'racketing' in Cornerville. The themes I have just referred to are, however, important. The narrator's identification with the point of view of the Nortons invites an equivalent sympathy on the part of the reader. The first chapter on the Nortons is paralleled by an equivalent account of 'Chick and His Club' (pp.52-93). Chick Morelli, the central character here, has already appeared in the chapter devoted to the Nortons. He is a college boy, a member of the Haliau Community Club. He is socially upwardly mobile, attending 'Ivy University' Law School. Whyte tells the reader that the time has come 'to step inside the club, observe their actions, and listen to the accounts they give of themselves' (p.52). It is not altogether obvious, however, that the narrator has completely abandoned the perspective of the Nortons in favour of Chick and his fellows. The reader is likely to feel that throughout the work, the point of view of the corner boys is more sympathetically constructed than any other. If that is true, what textual clues or evidence might contribute to such a reception?

In reporting the perspectives of Chick Morelli, the narration seems more consistently to establish distance between the author and Chick. Note, for instance, how features of Morelli's life-history are introduced.

Chick Morelli told his story in this way:..(p.52).

I asked him if he had found it hard to adjust when he came from Italy (p.53).

I asked him if there had been a gang of fellows with whom he associated. He said there had been. Was he the leader of it...(p.53)?

Concerning his personal contacts, Chick told me that he valued especially his friendships with...(p.55).

Chick said that...(p.56).

I asked Chick how he happened to go to Ivy University Law School...(p.56).

Each of these is used to introduce or continue Chick Morelli's own account: he is certainly allowed to speak in his own words. But the quasi-interview format of the text at this point establishes a clear separation between the voice of the informant and the voice of the narrator. If that introduction is contrasted with the introduction of Doc, then a subtle difference is discernible. The contrast is not total; to some extent similar devices are employed:

Doc spoke of his early years in this way...(p.3).

As he told me...(p.4).

According to his story...(p.6).

On the other hand, there are more passages where the narrator presents elements of Doc's life-history *not* as the voice of another but as the *narrator's* knowledge, in the *narrator's voice*. For instance:

Doc was born on Norton Street in 1908. His mother and father, who came from the province of Abruzzi, were the first non-Genoese Italians to settle on the street...(p.3).

Doc was always sensitive about his arm, and he would not permit anyone to make allowances for his disability...(p.4).

Doc found school work easy. He read widely both at school and in the branch library...(p.8).

Doc lived with his sister and brother-in-law, so that he had food and shelter, but he hated to impose upon them...(p.9).

The narrator less consistently establishes a distance of reportage between the two voices: the authorial voice speaks for Doc's experiences and motivations. Doc seems to be 'known' in a way that Chick Morelli is not.

Sociologically speaking, this does not in itself surprise us. We know well that Doc was Whyte's point of entry into Cornerville. The reader may well assume that Doc and the Nortons were closer than the college boys to the ethnographer. Morelli and his circle are encountered initially through the Nortons and in competition with them. What is remarkable is that these differences are actually inscribed in the text, represented by slight but perceptible differences in the writing. At this point it remains to be seen to what extent this is idiosyncratic to Whyte.

The differences in treatment here should not be exaggerated. To a considerable extent, the representation of Chick and the college boys are parallel. The narrative elements which are used to convey the culture of the social circle are, of course, different in content. Like the Nortons, the Italian Community Club is a scene of interpersonal competition. Moreover, we meet the Nortons again, themselves competing for membership. (Tellingly, we read of Whyte himself being put up for membership with his chances of success resting in the balance.)

The theme of competition and agonistic ethos is again revealed in narrative format.

The persons represented in *Street Corner Society*, Doc and Chick especially, are assembled through a series of fragmentary items of 'evidence' presented through a mixture of descriptions and narratives. Not all are represented equally. As we have seen, Doc is at the centre: although he is not precisely a 'hero', there is a close identification between the voice of the narrator and the voice of Doc. Other individuals have their own voices, though they are presented as interlocutors with the narrator. Others effectively have no presence or voice of their own. As a category, the characters who most noticeably suffer the latter fate are the women ('the girls').

Absent characters and silent voices

The girls of the Aphrodite Club are visible only through their being objects of the Nortons' attention. From the identity of Doc and narrator we move through to the relation of difference between the narrator and the female characters – Helen, Mildred and the others. Sociologically speaking, this is something which Lyn Lofland (1974) has commented on in relation to urban ethnographies in general; women are present but unseen in these social settings, or if 'seen' it is only through the eyes of male characters. Lofland points out that this is a feature of most, if not all, of the sub-genre of urban community studies; (for example, Suttles' *The Social Order of the Slum* (1968); Gans' *The Urban Villagers* (1962); Liebow's *Tally's Corner* (1967)). Women have major roles to play in the social order, but are not represented as social actors. They are *objects*, not subjects of their own actions in their own culture.

Lofland writes of the 'thereness' of women in these texts. It is a general characteristic of the sub-genre of urban 'community' studies that the male characters are represented in a 'rounded' fashion. They appear in the text as *subjects*; the narrator – the ethnographer-in-the-text – is personally and conceptually aligned with them. By contrast, the female characters are the objects of other characters' (males') desires and perceptions.

In this regard it is illuminating to focus upon some of the more subtle textual inscriptions of gender differences. The following section from Gans' *The Urban Villagers* (1962) is illuminative of the ways in which male and female subjects may be assembled differentially. Here the author deals in generalities rather than specific individuals, but subtle differences in the treatment of male and female actors are discernible. Consider, for instance, the depiction of cultural patterning on 'male–female relationships':

In many working-class cultures, the man is away from the home even after work, taking his leisure in the corner taverns that function as men's clubs. But, since the Italian culture is not a drinking one, this is less frequent among West

Enders. Consequently, much of their segregation of leisure takes place within the home: the women sit together in one room, the men in another. Even when everyone gathers around the kitchen table, the men group together at one end, the women at the other, and few words are exchanged between them. Men are distinctly uncomfortable in the company of women, and vice versa, but the men find it harder to interact with the women than the women with the men. At social gatherings I attended, whenever women initiated conversations with men, the men would escape as quickly as possible and return to their own group. They explained that they could not keep up with the women, that the women talked faster and more readily, turning the conversation to their own feminine interests and they tried to dominate the men. The men defended themselves either by becoming hostile or by retreating. Usually, they retreated.

The men's inability to compete conversationally with women is traditional. Second-generation Italians grew up in a patriarchal authority system with a strictly enforced double standard of behavior for boys and girls.

(Gans 1962, pp.47-8)

Now, the point here is *not* the 'patriarchal' character of Boston Italians: there is little to be gained by objecting to (or indeed by endorsing) the culture in question. I do not expect the ethnographer to gloss over aspects of everyday life which do not automatically accord with the values of a liberal intelligentsia. Rather, I wish to draw attention to how the text here implicitly reinforces that overt sociological message, and invites a particular point of view on the part of the reader.

In the first paragraph cited above, Gans apparently outlines an aspect of the culture from a 'non-aligned' perspective – an outsider's view of 'Italian culture'. As the paragraph progresses, however, the reader and the implied observer/ narrator are increasingly implicated in the division between the sexes. As the men and the women separate out into their respective groups, so the participant observer becomes present ('At social gatherings I attended...'), and is implicitly aligned with the male participants. At this juncture the men (though apparently cowed into silence by the women's more fluent talk) find their own voices. *They* explain their own withdrawal and their reticence; *they* defend themselves. The women, by contrast, are spoken about or spoken for. Despite their supposed verbal skills they do not speak in their own right. In the absence of an alternative 'explanation' to that of the men, Gans takes it as given. Indeed, at the beginning of the following paragraph it is translated into a sociological generalization ('The men's inability...is traditional'). In such ways are the subtle inscriptions of gender incorporated into the sociological discourse. These aspects of published texts are but instances of more general features and devices whereby the texts, their implied authors and audience of implied readers are gendered. It is not just that many (though by no means all) are about men, rather than women, nor that many influential authors happen to be male. (Indeed, ethnographic sociology, like social anthropology, is noteworthy for the contributions made by female scholars.) Rather, the point is that so many of the texts construct and presuppose a male perspective on the social world.

The portrayal of the social world thus treats 'male' as the taken-for-granted, or 'unmarked' value; the female experience or perspective has to be singled out as the one which expresses 'difference' or 'otherness'. There is a well-known stylistic usage, until recent years taken for granted among English speakers, of the 'generic male'. The pronoun 'he' is used to stand for the entire population. 'He' is understood to incorporate male and female alike. The usage of the socio-logical text frequently invokes the generic male. It is, for example, pervasive in authors like Erving Goffman, whose ideal-typical actors are continually expressed as the male pronoun. The introductory paragraph to one of his famous essays, 'On Face Work' (1967) is characteristic:

> Every person lives in a world of social encounters, involving him either in face-to-face or mediated contact with other participants. In each of these contacts, he tends to act out what is sometimes called a *line* – that is, a pattern of verbal and nonverbal acts by which he expresses his view of the situation and through this his evaluation of the participants, especially himself. Regard-less of whether a person intends to take a line, he will find that he has done so in effect. The other participants will assume that he has more or less wilfully taken a stand, so that if he is to deal with their response to him he must take into consideration the impression they have possibly formed of him.
>
> (Goffman 1967, p.5)

Once noticed, of course, the concentration of masculine pronouns becomes not merely obtrusive, but is also productive of a vertigo of frustration. When the textual device is apprehended, then one can no longer read the 'Every*man*' to represent all social actors unproblematically. Does Goffman, in this example, intend to speak for us all, or does his usage betray the fact that *his* ana-lysis of 'face work' is one grounded in a man's experience of a male-dominated world?

For the 'generic male' in sociological usage goes far beyond the 'mere' quirk of using the masculine form to categorize the entire population. It gives us a clue to a wider phenomenon. The ethnographer – sociological or anthropological – uses other conventions too. Frequently we construct 'the ————' (whatever) as the object of our discourse: 'the Nuer', 'the drug user', 'the gang member', 'the race goer', 'the Navaho' and so on. These too partake of the generic maleness of human actors in conventional texts. *Unless otherwise and specially marked*, the ideal-typical social actor is generically male. So, 'the' gang-member is taken to be male – unless designated 'the female gang-member'. In the same way 'the' Street Corner Society is the society of men, and female actors are expressed in terms of their difference from that masculine world. The converse of the 'thereness' of women – their invisible presence – is the fact that the 'hereness' of men is so unremarkable for the majority of our ethnographic texts, however sensitive they may be to other problems and multiple-realities.

Some feminists would argue, moreover, that the very style of most conventional ethnographic reporting is 'masculine'. The style of realism and objectivism, implying a single authorial stance, is a rhetoric of objectivity. For all their sensitivity to social actors' own perspectives and accounts, the majority of ethnographers employ a mode of writing that privileges *their* analytic perspective. The quotes, examples and perspectives are given unity by the persistent commentary of the author's voice.

It is noteworthy that some attempts to diverge from that style of writing include work by women about women. It is *not* the case that all male sociologists write in one way and all women in another. Rather, the point is that an explicit concern for feminist discourse *can* include a commitment to alternative varieties of textual organization that disrupt the taken-for-granted authority of the single viewpoint. It implies an ethnographic text that does not rest its claims for authenticity on the superior wisdom or more comprehensive understanding of the impresario sociologist. Such a feminist perspective (not necessarily confined to women) would celebrate a more reticent, but more complex, text. A prime example of the style is Krieger's ethnography of a lesbian community, *The Mirror Dance* (1983). Here Krieger explicitly adopts a multiple, 'stream of consciousness' approach. The voices of the women interweave with one another. Krieger does not impose the 'analysis' we have come to expect from the sociological author. The reader is certainly aware of the work that has gone into production of the text. It is clearly not a random arrangement of observations. It is as contrived as any textual representation of social realities. But Krieger seeks to depart from the conventional role of the observer and reporter.

The following extract is representative of Krieger's style in *The Mirror Dance*: it is taken from a chapter on 'parties and gatherings'.

> She liked to feel she could act natural at parties, said Ellen, or at the bar. She liked to just float. She liked to be in the woodwork and to come out of the woodwork. She didn't like to be pinned down as so-and-so's lover, even when she was. There was something about relationships, that she felt vulnerable about them around other people, that she felt uncertain. She liked to be flexible in the minds of outsiders. She liked to be by herself. She didn't like to have to be responsible for anyone else. It worked out well going places with Marla. They each already knew a lot of people in the community, so when they went to something, they would each go their own way. It was like they came together, but they were alone.
>
> (Krieger 1983, pp.53-4)

The next paragraph catches up the reported feelings of another woman, Sarah, and so the entire text is woven together. The author arranges the women's reported speech, but there is minimal authorial commentary and analysis. The use of indirect reported speech is apparently intended to convey a shifting of perspective and subjectivity from one member of the community to another.

The resulting monograph is awkward. That is partly because the chosen style is somewhat alien to the ethnographic genre. It is also a reflection of Krieger's ultimate failure to break free of some conventions of more 'mainstream' texts. The result is flat and featureless: it lacks verve as an experimental text, and results in too great a reliance on the bland reporting of the women's speech. Nevertheless, *The Mirror Dance* deserves some attention as a rare attempt to fracture the 'writing as usual' of the traditional ethnographer. As a woman, Krieger implicitly challenges the authorial stance of her male colleagues, and the rhetorical forms of her avowedly feminist colleagues whose texts retain that stance.

The full implications of feminist critical theory for academic writing go well beyond the scope of this monograph. The 'gendering' of ethnographic texts is a topic that I have barely touched on here. We shall undoubtedly continue to debate the textual implications of feminist scholarship in sociology, and the ethnographic genre is an obvious and important terrain for such reflection. It is, after all, often argued that there is an affinity between feminist discourse and qualitative methodology (cf. for example, Clegg (1985), Stanley and Wise (1983)). (One need not be persuaded by all the epistemological and political arguments to recognize that tendency.) If feminism is to adopt many of the principles and practices of ethnographic fieldwork, then its proponents will not be indifferent to ethnography's textual devices too. Indeed, the claims of feminist scholarship already direct attention to the reading and writing of sociology.

These brief observations are not intended to convey the idea that no ethnographic texts treat seriously the everyday lives of female social actors. On the contrary, many do. Some of them are written by women, some by men. But it is noticeable that even a monograph explicitly concerned with 'Women's Work in a Man's World' (Spradley and Mann 1975) embodies implicitly masculine perspectives (the authors were male and female respectively). We have already encountered the introductory scene-setting passages of that text, *The Cocktail Waitress*. That introductory sequence, based on a vivid first-hand description of an everyday scene in the bar, is written from the point of view of an 'outsider', not one of the waitresses themselves. The observer/reader/narrator enters the scene from the 'man's world', and the enquiring gaze is constituted by that world. The text tells us that the scene can be observed 'in bars and cocktail lounges throughout the country' (p.2). It does not invite explicit reflection on whether it is equally accessible to male and female observers or whether its features are equally, transparently obvious to male and female observers. It universalizes the setting, Brady's Bar, and in doing so it implicitly universalizes the implied observer. This is all the more remarkable given the fact that Brenda Mann not only co-authored the monograph, but had worked as a waitress in the bar as part of the research project. The stance of objectivity incorporated in the text is explicitly celebrated by the authors (p.13).

In the passage cited, the implied observer feels free to comment on the 'image' conveyed by the waitress's appearance and demeanour: again, the image is one that is read from a male perspective. Hey (1986) has commented, in a similar vein, how the universalized, anonymous recorders of Mass Observation felt free to incorporate gender (and class) specific connotations. Hey suggests that:

> The effect of the observer's 'scientific' detachment frequently reduces the observed to the status of objects and this objectification of women is also secured by the ability of the male observers to both share and collude in the male chauvinism of pub cultures....
>
> (Hey 1986, p.42)

Spradley and Mann escape such crude stereotypes as can be found in Mass Observation. On the contrary, their text is highly sensitive to the sexual division of labour – and the semiotics of sexuality – in the bar. Yet their text never quite escapes the generic perspective of 'a man's world' within which their protagonists comport themselves.

Indeed, the feminist versions of post-structuralist theory radically question the taken-for-granted textual practices that constitute 'authority'. The various contributions of Cixous, Chodorow, and Kristeva all challenge the conventional assumptions concerning language, knowledge and power (cf. Moi 1985; Weedon 1987). The combination of feminism and post-modernism produces a powerful critique of the complacency of texts that claim a privileged insight into a universe of stable meanings. The feminist critique of the social observer is parallel to that levelled against the traditional literary critic and 'the institutional dominance of liberal-humanist criticism, with its insistence on truth and universality through which it claims to speak for humanity as an ungendered whole' (Weedon 1987, p.140). The 'universalization' of human nature, the 'generic male' and the implicit representation of gender in the text together produce powerful textual devices for the marginalization of 'unvoiced' women.

The 'thereness' of women is just one striking example of the contrast between actors who are fully 'present' in the text (albeit through selective synecdochal representations) and those who are perceived only in their *absence*.

A widely read modern ethnography that clearly exemplifies the voiced/unvoiced contrast is *Learning to Labour* (Willis 1977). That monograph has enjoyed considerable success, and has also been subject to various stringent criticisms. Among the critics are those who point out the extreme bias in the 'point of view' implied in the text. Willis's work is based on fieldwork with a small number of working-class boys. It is abundantly clear that Willis himself identifies closely with 'the lads', as they designate themselves. Although they have unattractive qualities (most notably, racist and sexist attitudes) that are duly acknowledged, the lads are characterized in such a way as to invite the sympathy of the reader. Willis indeed invests the voices of the lads with a special weight. Albeit in underdeveloped ways they articulate a critique of class society. They thus speak not just for themselves, but become class heroes who voice an 'indigenous cultural theory' (Marcus 1986, p.181). They are allowed to express themselves vigorously and idiomatically. The reader is likely to feel an immediate acquaintance – if not affinity – with the twelve foregrounded individuals.

By contrast, however, the despised conformist boys who are contrasted with 'the lads' have *no* voice or presence in the text. The ethnographer's perspective is aligned almost entirely with that of his heroes. Sociologically speaking, this is a major methodological flaw. Textually, it facilitates the single-minded and spirited celebration of the lads' oppositional form of working-class culture. It is paralleled by the equal absence of female voices from the entire text. *Learning to Labour* endorses and inscribes a masculine, patriarchal culture. Females are accorded a presence only at one remove: they are the object of the lads' speech and are subject to their sexist values. They do not have a presence in their own right.

The arrangement of textual presence and absence in Willis thus conveys a very strong sociological message. His account is highly circumscribed. It is summarized succinctly by Marcus:

> Centrally he is concerned with a representation of the oppositional culture among his twelve lads, and with some shifting from shop floor and home environments (discussions with parents) to show how the focally represented oppositional culture created from school experience resonates in these other critical locales....So there is a very strategic circumscribing of the system portrayed in the text for the purposes of Willis's argument. He pays some attention to middle class culture, as manifested in staff and other students, and he recognizes distinct perspectives for girls, West Indians, and Asians, but mainly he keeps to a school-situated ethnography of his twelve nonconformist boys.
>
> (Marcus 1986, pp.174-5)

The form of the argument, however, invests the nonconformist boys' experiences with a privileged existence, quite different in quality from those other categories of actor referred to by Marcus.

Character and code

Our reading of 'character' in the ethnography is inextricably mixed with the description of social scenes and the narrative portrayal of social action. Indeed, these elements are always separable only for analytic purposes – although in any one text one aspect may come to predominate over others. We can arrive at some tentative understanding of these features with reference to Barthes' dissection of 'codes' (Barthes 1974). In his 'slow reading' of Balzac's novella 'Sarrasine' Barthes isolates and traces out five codes. Barthes' own procedure involves the fragmentation of the text into minimal constituent parts ('lexies') and relating them to the five systems of signification. This painstaking approach is beyond the scope of this work – and doubtless well beyond the patience of most readers. Rather, I shall sketch how Barthes' analysis can be drawn on in a more general fashion to illuminate processes of signification in the ethnography.

To begin with, then, Barthes' five elementary codes are summarized:

1 The *Proairetic*. This is the code of *actions*. This is the major code of a narrative mode of 'storytelling'. In Barthes' analysis any and every action is attributable to the code. According to this code, acts are named and arranged in sequence.
2 The *Hermeneutic*. This is the code of questions and *enigmas*. Together with the sequence of narrative this code generates suspense, and hence resolution.
3 *Cultural* codes. These are multiple, and are *referential*. Here Barthes draws attention to a text's appeal to shared cultural knowledge – what a more sociologically inclined author might be inclined to refer to as the 'stock of knowledge' held in common by writer and audience by virtue of their shared cultural competence. The 'codes' thus embody and reproduce 'recipe knowledge' and cultural typifications. The specific actions and characters in the text are played out against a backcloth of such cultural codes.
4 The *Semic* code. This is primarily the code through which the reader assembles semantic features relevant to persons and 'characters':

> the character is a product of combinations: the combination is relatively stable (denoted by the recurrence of the seme) and more or less complex (involving more or less congruent, more or less contradictory figures); this complexity determines the character's 'personality', which is just as much a combination as the odor of a dish or the bouquet of a wine.
>
> (Barthes 1974, p.67)

5 The *Symbolic* code. This level of signification permits interpretation of the text to a wider set of *connotations* or themes.

Clearly, any fragment of a given text may, in principle, partake of any or all, of these codes. We should not use Barthes' scheme, or any like it, as a deterministic grid. It is a useful heuristic device which directs our attention towards various aspects of the text and demands that we treat the various aspects of signification with due care and attention. For the reading of sociological texts as sociological – that is, for evidence of cultural themes, social problems, or whatever – then the relationship between specific instances in the text and the various *codes* is of great importance.

While ethnographies do, as we have seen, embed narrative episodes and stories, the narrative function is often subservient to the other four codes Barthes identifies. They intersect and are cross-referred in the assembly of social actors who also undertake plausible social action in comprehensible cultural settings. To a considerable extent, the ethnography must *tell* the reader what codes he or she is to bring to bear in understanding its accounts of persons and their doings. As we have seen, however, it is surely not enough for the text simply to announce its codes. They are realized and warranted through concrete descriptions and narratives. But there can never be an exhaustive relationship between the interpretative codes and the concrete 'evidence'.

These observations can be illustrated and developed through a consideration of 'character' and narrative in the ethnography of a black urban ghetto in Pittsburgh, *On the Street Where I Lived*, by Melvin D. Williams (1981). Williams' entire account of the inhabitants of the ghetto is explicitly structured in terms of three *types* of life-style: 'genuine', 'spurious' and 'mainstream'. The last of these refers to black members whose way of life is virtually indistinguishable from that of their white counterparts anywhere. Williams devotes little attention to them. The 'spurious' blacks 'are often involved in neighborhood projects, political activities, volunteer programs, and large church congregations...in order to remain close to opportunities and possibilities for upward mobility and, therefore, closer to "mainstream" patterns of behavior' (p.9). The 'genuine' black on whom Williams concentrates 'is the one most socialized in distinctive cultural patterns that differ from values and norms in the wider society....His perception of the world and his concomitant behavior are to some extent determined by isolation and long-term restrictions in poor Black ghetto ecological niches' (p.10).

Williams goes on to list the traits of the 'genuine' life-style:

1 A defiance of social distance among themselves.
2 Defilement of mainstream symbols of value.
3 Bodily expressiveness for identity and interactional cues.
4 Public interaction within large groups and with loud oral communication.
5 Reciprocal distribution of scarce goods.
6 Mutual humiliation for group pleasure.
7 A propensity for physical contact (touching, 'the press of flesh').

These criteria are listed in order to explicate an interpretative framework according to which the reader can approach the succeeding descriptions and characterizations.

The 'life-style' of the 'genuine' ghetto inhabitant is conveyed through a small number of pen-portraits of 'household styles' (pp.49-63). 'Golf-stick George' is the first of these. The author tells us that a first impression of George is that he has a lonely life: he has no wife or children living with him and has no visitors to his two rooms. 'Thus, to a newcomer to the neighbourhood, George appears to be a recluse in a third-floor attic, a welfare recipient with no family and no friends' (p.50). The reality, Williams hurries to assert, is quite the reverse:

In reality, however, George is not lonely, for once one discovers, observes, and analyses George's behavior over a long period of time, one is able to discover that George has a very viable social network within Belmar. When he is not at his corner tavern, he walks the streets of Belmar swinging a golf club, a symbol to some extent, of the style that he is extremely successful at demonstrating; he makes a conscious effort to swagger or 'swing' as he walks rapidly up and down the streets of Belmar. This is how he spends most of his time, visiting his network of other taverns in Belmar, or visiting a few of his streetcorner buddies at their homes. George's style is perspicuous (*sic*). As he walks along the street of Belmar, he invariably speaks to everybody, whether the person is standing at a window or in the doorway; sitting on the porch, driving down the street in the car; or walking on the sidewalk. Indeed it is not unusual to see George stop a car in the middle of the street and carry on a conversation with the driver by leaning through the open window. Further-more, it is common for George to borrow cigarettes from the drivers he stops or for George's comrades driving down the street to stop and summon George to ask for a cigarette or just exchange some minor thoughts or opinions in conversation. George interacts with almost everybody in Belmar, and he very clearly lets everyone know that he is well-known. His style of interaction is distinctive. He talks loudly to make sure that not only the person who is listening hears him, but that everyone on the block also hears him and recognizes that he is engaging in conversation with someone in the area. He is always loud and boisterous, but most of the time he is pleasant.

(Williams 1981, p.50)

The description of Golf-stick George continues in this vein for several more pages. We learn that he does not act his age (fifty-seven), but adopts the dress and style of a younger man. His style is described as 'expressive'. His expressive style is directed towards women: 'When he is feeling his best, George makes a point of demonstrating to all those who see him that he is capable of interacting very intensively with the women of the neighbourhood' (p.51).

Here the narrator reverses the connotation of reality and appearance, since it is revealed that these are only casual encounters. Indeed, it transpires that the women speak to George only because he forces his attentions on them, and he can prove obstreperous and embarrassing. In general, Golf-stick George is portrayed as a 'street-corner man'. He is described as intelligent, and as enjoying a wide social network. His life-style is explicitly related to that of other descriptions of street-corner men, such as Liebow's or Whyte's. Specific aspects of this culture are described in terms of: sexual stimulation; the sharing of financial resources; privilege as a source of information in the neighbourhood. We are told that he is 'pleasant':

It is a pleasure to talk to someone who does not tell his troubles, who shouts that life is great, who bobs and weaves forward and backward, from side to side, as he exhibits his 'down' (ghetto sophisticated) behaviour. George is 'with it'. George knows 'where it's at.' George is not 'a jive cat' (unaware). He walks and talks 'his stuff.' He is good at it, and he knows it.

(Williams 1981, p.52)

In general terms, therefore, Williams provides us with what is clearly intended to be a graphic and sympathetic portrayal of this single (and singular) ghetto inhabitant. This section of the ethnography continues with similar descriptions of further individuals: Deacon Griffin (a 'mainstream' resident); Jody (a street-corner man, 'genuine'); Violent Jim (a heavy-drinking street-corner, genuine man); the Cat Lady and her son, Neil (both 'spurious').

These character sketches ('brief lives') are juxtaposed in order to draw morals about life in Belmar.

> Golf-stick George is a 'man of leisure', not a 'bum'. He strides as if he owns the world and he does (at least, his expressive one). He thinks he should talk to kings and walk with presidents, and so he does, with the street kings of Belmar and the presidents of various neighborhood organizations. His style is the only style that gives him access to his perceptions of the American dream.

> The Cat Lady is fearful of the Belmar 'world'. She only leaves her house to purchase necessities. For 4 years, she has trained her son to be fearful and to put his trust in cats and dogs. To them, Belmar is a 'jungle' of people who commit all the evils documented by television and newspaper reporting. They believe the stereotypes of poor blacks in America, and like their white counterparts, they withdraw themselves from a meaningful social context. So 'genuine' and 'spurious' live side by side here, both victims of and responses to the American way.
>
> (Williams 1981, p.63)

On the Street Where I Lived is not an especially distinguished work: it does not offer any very remarkable or sensitive analyses, and its arguments are often couched in rather crude terms. It does, however, provide a useful example at this point in the argument, precisely because it is somewhat 'transparent' in its textual devices and arrangements. It has an especially clear relationship between the codings of character (semic) and referential cultural codings and the other dimensions of Barthes' interpretative schema. It will also permit us to articulate a more dynamic version of Barthes' model than many other exemplifications and derivations from it.

To begin with, we must note – though not bother to recapitulate – the interplay of explicit propositions, illustrative character sketches and narrated episodes. As noted already, the former claim to provide the appropriate framework for understanding frames. The two aspects of the text do not exhaust each other, there is not a perfect one-to-one match between them, and neither constrains how readers interpret the text as a whole.

In the account of Belmar we can read a number of related issues at the level of hermeneutic code. The ethnography can be read as the answer, or resolution, of some problems, puzzles, paradoxes or muddles. They are of the order: How do the inhabitants of the ghetto survive? What dilemmas do they confront? What are the complexities of their lives? To some extent they are posed explicitly in the monograph: they are available to the reader throughout it as a resource for finding thematic coherence. The cultural codes are multiple, and there are numerous referential uses of writing which draw on what every reader knows as a matter of course. There are, however, two 'master codes' in this domain. They are: the cultural code of 'mainstream' American culture, and 'genuine' black culture of the ghetto.

The 'characters', like Golf-stick George and the Cat Lady, can be assembled by the reader, and read against the cultural codes which are explicated and implied. Indeed, the 'significance' of aspects of the characters depends upon the simultaneous presence of *both* master codes. Each, of course, implies the other; for any given reading the presence or relevance of one implies the negation of the other. Given what we know from the description of Golf-stick George, his 'character' can be assembled and interpreted in accordance with the two codes. Read through the 'genuine' code – as Williams explicitly invites – George is independent, with a wide social network, which provides material resources and social relationships. He has a highly individual style, which is a source and expression of personal pride. Read from the 'mainstream' code, however, precisely the same traits and actions add up to a quite different 'character'. George is lonely and inadequate, exploiting and imposing himself on a wide range of individuals, desperate for company, annoying women, essentially dressed in inappropriate clothes. A social parasite who is incapable of supporting himself. Williams summarizes these competing 'readings' by contrasting the designation of George as a street-corner man with that of 'bum'.

Now, viewed from the point of view of these two simultaneous, or alternating, frames or codes, then the 'character' of George stands in a double relationship to the cultural code, while the semic code has the double value just outlined. In relation to the 'mainstream' code, then George's function is that of 'transgression'. In relation to the 'genuine' code his function is that of 'affirmation'. Each code implies alternative functional relations with other codes.

The functions of character in the text concern the revelation of 'authenticity' and its ambiguities. The ethnography may implicitly claim to discover the characters' authenticity by interpreting them according to the most appropriate cultural code. It can thus play an ironic contrast between the implied reader's taken-for-granted assumptions and the 'real' social world of the actors in question. But the display of authenticity is often achieved by the implicit degradation of other actors. The cultural authenticity of Willis's romanticized heroes is achieved in two complementary ways. Not only are the 'lads' celebrated as complex characters, whose voices are extensively introduced, but other categories of social actor are unvoiced. Females and conformist boys (the 'ear'oles') are objects only of the lads' accounts. Willis's own hermeneutic work establishes, through such textual realizations, the authenticity of the lads. Contrary, perhaps, to a supposed 'mainstream' cultural code, the lads emerge as the 'true' bearers of a valid working-class male culture. As the text foregrounds and privileges certain voices, so the reader's sympathetic engagement with some actors rather than others helps to establish the point of view of the ethnography itself.

The theme of cultural authenticity also reflects on the translation of individual characters into emblematic bearers of cultural generalities. Just as the narrative constructs a timeless, mythical realm of the text, so its characters achieve apotheosis into social types and guarantors of sociological generalizations. The function develops that identified by Pratt (1986a and 1986b) and Fabian (1983), who describe the 'normalizing discourse' whereby the embodied 'Other' is translated into a disembodied and generalized 'He'. The temporally specific, locally situated character in the text is simultaneously invested with extra-ordinary consequence. The heroes of the classic monograph do not necessarily *lose* their individuality, but have added to it the halo of sociological significance.

Chapter eight

Difference, distance, and irony

At the heart of the ethnographic enterprise is the following tension. On the one hand there is the contrast between the 'self' of the observer and the 'other' of the observed. Whether or not 'strangeness' is thrust on the observer through an encounter with the exotic, or is achieved through imaginative bracketing of the familiar and the mundane, the confrontation of the self with the other is fundamental. In experiential terms the ethnographer is, in principle, always the 'marginal native'. There is thus a constant tension between the position of 'member' and 'stranger'. Reference has already been made to Brown's observations concerning the 'point of view' of the ethnographer and his or her text. Brown refers back to the long tradition in which the ethnography *of* the marginal in society is paralleled by the self-perception of the ethnographer *as* a 'marginal' actor. As Herzfeld (1983b) expresses this tension:

> The ethnographer's marginality is not simply a passive structural anomaly or a safe perch on the cultural fence; most of the time, the ethnographer is either an insider or an outsider. But – and this is the real crux of the matter – no ethnographer can ever claim to have been one or the other in an *absolute* sense. The very fact of negotiating one's status in the community precludes any such possibility. Anthropologists have to learn to adapt to events in which they themselves are significant actors. This creates a sense of imperfect closure every bit as disconcerting for us as taxonomic anomalies in a symbolic system.
>
> (Herzfeld 1983b, p.151)

Herzfeld here draws attention to the fact that over and above the interpersonal give-and-take of field roles and relations, there is always a *discursive* 'difference'. The encounter, the transactions of social exploration, are predicated on the non-identity of the observer and the observed. Herzfeld concludes his account (derived from fieldwork on the island of Rhodes) with reference to the familiar metaphor of ethnographic description as 'translation'. He points out that such a metaphor carries with it danger: the trap of seeing the possibility of 'literal' or 'faithful' translation. Whereas a common-sense view of translation implies a self-effacing translator, for the ethnographer this is not an adequate representation:

> In ethnographic reporting, despite all the imperfections and inconsistencies, the essence of the text itself depends upon the translator's presence. It must be an aggressively 'open' text...designed to foreground its own lack of closure. Anthropologists are notorious for their yearning to return to the field for that one last question, even though they should know that there is no such thing. Their products are actually more like elaborate tropes than literal translations, in that they depend for their impact upon the maintenance of a strong sense of difference...separating the original experiences from the crafted text that seeks to convey it.
>
> (Herzfeld 1983b, p.163)

As Herzfeld's remarks indicate, the ethnographer inscribes himself or herself in the text. He or she does not simply 'read' an inert and passive 'field'. The ethnographer is an element within the field as well as its 'observer'. The writing of 'difference' between the observer and the Other is paralleled by the reflective contrast of the I, as subject of discourse, and the Me, as the object of reflection. This Meadian contrast between the I and the Me is central to the symbolic interactionist tradition and to the epistemology of ethnography (cf. Rock 1979).

In this chapter I shall deal with one collection of textual effects that stem directly from the writing of difference; that is, the uses of irony and paradox in the construction of sociological 'news'. I do not argue that such features are unique to ethnography as a genre. On the contrary, they are generic to sociology. I do want to suggest, however, that the devices to be described are particularly characteristic of this variety of sociological writing, and reflect tensions of engagement and distance, familiarity and strangeness. We have already seen some of the ways in which 'difference' and 'the other' are constructed and inscribed in the ethnographic text. The dialogue between the commentary and the exemplar, the shifts of tense from past to ethnographic present, and the various devices for the construction of character, all contribute to the rhetorical effect.

Ethnographic irony

Given these methodological and textual features it is hardly surprising that *irony* is one of the master tropes of ethnographic writing. Within sociology, irony is not confined to the ethnographic genre. Indeed, it has been argued that it is especially characteristic of sociology in general. The importance of 'dialectical' or 'dramatic' irony in sociological argument generally has been recognized by Brown (1977):

> The 'logic' of dramatic irony consists of three elements. First there is a juxtaposing of opposites, of thesis and antithesis, the association of which was unexpected. Then the peripety, or reversal from one term to its opposite, must be as inevitable as their initial association was unforeseen. Finally there is dramatic resolution, a synthesis of thesis and antithesis on a higher level. For

example, theory, as dramatic closure and unity, shows us how and why Puritan ascetics become bourgeois men of affairs, how capitalism becomes socialism, how socialites become oligarchs. The unanticipated juxtaposition makes the theory a discovery; the inevitability of the outcome is the dramatic equivalent of its logical cogency or empirical proof.

(Brown 1977, p.174)

Brown goes on to outline some of the contexts in which such arguments have gained a central place in sociological theory and interpretation. He instances Merton, for example, on manifest and latent functions, where he argues that an eye for the unintended consequences of social practices is the distinctive contribution of the sociological imagination. He then provides a wide-ranging discussion of irony in sociology (Brown 1977, pp.180-220), including detailed analyses of irony in the work of Goffman and Sorokin.

Although not unique to it, an ironic tone is, however, pervasive of much ethnographic writing. As Van Maanen (1988) puts it: 'Irony, gentle or brash, is typically the highlight for the general reader of ethnography, who learns, contrary to prejudice, of the "rational savage", the "superstitious scientist", the "emotional bureaucrat", the "moral thief", the "tribal executive", or the "faithless priest"' (p.33).

It is therefore one of its most characteristic and arresting devices that ethnography employs a sort of tragic irony. Actors seek and attain their goals, but in their very success they are frustrated. Far from achieving the hoped-for benefits of their actions, they suffer the very reverse. This is well illustrated in Jerry Jacobs' ethnography of an American 'retirement community' – a self-contained settlement for the over-fifties (Jacobs 1974). (The average age of the residents is sixty-three.) 'Fun City' is a purpose-built environment for the elderly, 'envisaged as an activities-centred planned community, designed to help over-come some of the shock one was likely to experience upon being subject to the abrupt transition from a work to a leisure life style' (p.2).

Some aspects of the community 'work' in this spirit, Jacobs reports, but the overall effect is one of desolation and isolation:

From the street the homes show no signs of life. The inhabitants themselves are rarely, if ever, seen walking the sidewalks, sitting outside their homes, tending the yard, or making repairs. The only sign of habitation is the row after row of large, late-model American cars stationed in the carports. If viewed from a distance, Fun City appears to be a cross between a suburban tract community being readied for habitation and a large, cleverly camouflaged used car lot.

(Jacobs 1974, p.1)

There is, too, a major paradox in the very organization of the community – which has no local government, no fire department, no police department and no major medical provision. As Jacobs remarks:

That an ageing population of white middle class property owners, many of them in poor health, seek 'security' in an isolated social environment which has no police department, fire department, or major health facilities is an enigma.

(Jacobs 1974, p.4)

Even the supposedly 'healthy' climate – one of the major attractions of the Fun City – carries its own ironies. The community certainly does 'enjoy' a warm, dry, smog-free climate. Frequently it is very hot, and herein lies a major difficulty for the inhabitants:

First, because of the heat, all of Fun City's facilities, the Town Hall and shopping center areas, are air conditioned. For many this has a kind of boomerang effect. Residents who have sought Fun City's climate because of its salubrious effects upon their rheumatism or arthritis, cannot avail themselves of the social and recreational facilities because of the untoward effects of the air conditioning upon their physical complaints. As a result they spend most of their time at home, or outside in shaded areas, which restricts their movements and social life considerably. Many people can not participate in formal club activities because of their air conditioning. For those not troubled by it there is the problem of getting from homes to Fun City's two main areas of social life.... Many do not drive and there is no public transportation. If not for the heat, some might have walked, but because of the 'healthy climate' they have become essentially 'shut-ins'.

(Jacobs 1974, p.55)

The irony of the situation is captured in the second paragraph of the monograph. After the briefest of openings, Jacobs writes:

The city itself is organized around wide, well-kept streets that are remarkable in several ways: (1) they are all about the width of a four-lane highway; (2) there are no cars parked in the streets; (3) there are few cars driven on them; (4) they are all immaculately clean – no cigarette butts, gum wrappers, toothpicks, match sticks, bent beer cans, broken bottles, animal excrements, or less seemly items (the usual tell-tale signs of urban or rural life) are to be found in the streets of Fun City; (5) they are all lined on both sides with sidewalks that no one walks on; (6) all of the city's streets and sidewalks can be observed at any time of the day or night in the same state of eerie desolation.

(Jacobs 1974, p.1)

This description manages to move from elements which could be taken to imply spaciousness, to emptiness, from the desirability of cleanliness to the 'eerie desolation' of empty streets. Hence the irony of *Fun City* (and how ironic the very title of the ethnography is!) is encapsulated in the organization of this brief description. There are ironic contrasts and absences within the various descriptions: streets with 'few cars driven on them'; 'sidewalks that no one walks on'. Indeed, the recurrent feature of this passage might be called the 'noticeable absence' of certain 'normal' features of everyday scenes such as might reasonably be expected in contemporary society.

Following David Lodge (1977), one might parallel this description of absences with a passage from E. M. Forster's *A Passage to India*:

> Except for the Marabar Caves – and they are twenty miles off – the city of Chandrapore presents nothing extraordinary. Edged rather than washed by the river Ganges, it trails for a couple of miles along the bank, scarcely distinguishable from the rubbish it deposits so freely. There are no bathing steps on the river-front as the Ganges happens not to be holy here; indeed there is no river front, and bazaars shut out the wide and shifting panorama of the stream. The streets are mean, the temples ineffective, and though a few fine houses exist they are hidden away in gardens or down alleys whose filth deters all but the invited guest. Chandrapore was never large or beautiful, but two hundred years ago it lay on the road between Upper India, then imperial, and the sea, and the fine houses date from that period. The zest for decoration stopped in the eighteenth century, nor was it ever democratic. There is no painting and scarcely any carving in the bazaars.
>
> (Forster 1959, p.1)

As Lodge says, 'the dominant note of the description is negativity and absence' – *nothing extraordinary; scarcely distinguishable; no bathing steps; happens not to be holy; no river front; shut out; temples ineffective; defers; never large or beautiful; stopped; nor was it ever democratic; no painting and scarcely any carving* (Lodge 1977, p.97). Clearly there are many things which such an Indian city would not have (a fish-and-chip shop or a pub, for instance), but there would be no point in recounting all of them – an inexhaustible task anyway. The absences which are remarked on make sense if they are read as features which might reasonably be expected to be present. By telling us what Chandrapore *lacks*, Forster manages also to indicate what an Indian city could predictably have in the way of amenities and attractions (bathing steps, painting and carving, temples and so on). Hence the description achieves a contrast between what one might hope of Chandrapore and its 'disappointing' reality.

The passage reproduced from Jacobs above is not dissimilar. The description of Fun City simultaneously establishes what is predictably characteristic of 'normal' street scenes, and hence to the abnormality of this particular community. The crux of the Jacobs passage is this: '(4) they are all immaculately clean – no cigarette butts, gum wrappers, toothpicks, match sticks, bent beer cans, broken bottles, animal excrements, or less seemly items (the usual tell-tale signs of urban or rural life) are to be found in the streets of Fun City'. At the outset this sentence sounds like the description of a delightful, Utopian scene. A street which is clean, wholesome and safe, where one can walk or live in comfort and security: surely this is a widely shared ideal with which the reader might well

161

identify. Yet it reveals an absence – *the* major absence at the heart of the monograph, that is, of 'normal' social life.

The passage achieves a high degree of ordering and symmetry, arranged round this central crux. The numbered points 1–3 in the first half establish the contrast – of streets like four-lane highways, but with no cars; in the second half point 5 balances this with sidewalks which nobody walks on. There is, then, a reasonably high degree of coherence within this paragraph – of the repetition and balance of matched antithesis – which belies its apparent baldness. There is, too, another implied irony underlying this balance: we learn at the beginning that despite the broad highways, in fact there are no cars, and might reasonably expect to find that everyone gets about on foot. In the second part we find this expectation dashed as well. The logic can be expressed in a series of propositions:

(a) There are broad highways

  Therefore

(b) There are a lot of cars

  But

(c) There are no cars on the streets

  Therefore

(d) Everyone goes on foot

  But

(e) The sidewalks are empty

  Therefore

(f) People do not go on foot either

  Therefore

(g) People do not get about at all.

Throughout this tightly organized little passage, then, we find a good deal of 'interpretative' work being done by an apparently innocuous description of Fun City. It is a characterization of absences and negatives, of paradoxes and disappointed hopes, and of deviation from the 'normal' conditions of social life. (Jacobs notes that the squalor he mentions is characteristic of urban *and* rural life – which seems to leave no place at all for Fun City in the normal typology of social living and thus underlines the negativity of the description.)

A great many ethnographic, 'interpretative' accounts are arranged like Jacobs' description of Fun City. That is, they trade on contrasts between what 'everyone' (including the ethnographer, in many instances) regards as 'normal', and the supposedly unusual features of a given setting. Likewise, they may be organized in terms of a contrast between actual states of affairs, and what is portrayed as 'reasonable' under similar circumstances.

Insider and outsider

The ethnography repeatedly plays on the contrast between the 'insider' and the 'outsider'. The authority of the text rests on the premise that a stranger has become intimate with the culture in question; occasionally it is the habitué who has stepped out of a social world and into sociology. The reader is constructed as 'outsider'. The text and the ethnographer-in-the-text must convey their intelligence across that divide. There is therefore a constantly rehearsed dialectic between 'inside' and 'outside'. The implied reader, as stranger, is thus constituted as in need of enlightenment. He or she may reasonably be expected to embrace naïve prejudices and presuppositions. By contrast, the ethnographer can be taken to have transcended the shallow understandings of the outsider, in favour of more complex and hence more authentic versions of social reality.

The revelatory power of insider/outsider distinctions is captured by an introductory passage to Suttles' *The Social Order of the Slum* (Suttles 1968). Rhetorically, the passage rests upon a balanced antithesis:

> The Addams area is one of the oldest slums in Chicago and researchers have invaded it almost as often as new minority groups. Like most slums, however, it remains something of a mystery hovering between two divergent interpretations. In some ways it is easiest to describe the neighborhood by how its residents deviate from the public standards of the wider community. There are, for example, a high delinquency rate, numerous unwed mothers, and several adolescent 'gangs'. Measured by the usual yardstick of success it is tempting to think that the local residents are simply inadequate and disadvantaged people suffering from cultural deprivation, unemployment, and a number of other 'urban ills'. If the residents insist upon the irrelevance of public standards and the primacy of their own, this can be dismissed as sour grapes or only an attempt to make necessity a virtue.
>
> Seen from the inside, however, the Addams area is intricately organized according to its own standards and the residents are fairly insistent on their demands. These demands require discipline and self-restraint in the same way as do the moral dictates of the wider community.
>
> (Suttles 1968, p.3)

The rhetoric here is very clear. The spatial metaphor of 'inside' and 'outside' is particularly apt for Suttles' own analysis, as his exposition of social order in the 'Addams' area is couched very largely in spatial terms. It emphasizes the segmentations and the boundaries whereby identity and loyalty are constructed by its various residents. In the course of this introductory passage Suttles also draws fleeting attention to the contrast between himself and other researchers. The implication is that they remain on the outside. Like many such introductory passages, the Suttles paragraphs set up the 'mystery' to be resolved in the ensuing monograph.

The general argument pursued in *The Social Order of the Slum* exemplifies an approach – itself ironic – that is highly characteristic of sociological and anthropological writing. Confronted by the surface appearance of disorder and disorganization, the text progressively constructs an *ordered* social universe. Suttles' argument is strongly reminiscent of the work of anthropologists like Evans-Pritchard, in the demonstration of order through nested segments of social structure (cf. Suttles 1968, p.31). The argument itself proceeds by successive contrasts, mirroring the social structure there portrayed. The theme is introduced in the opening sequence and amplified in later pages where Suttles contrasts the 'public view' and the 'local view'. Suttles sets up a sequence of ideal-typical 'knowers', who stand for a continuum of acquaintance with the area, without ever escaping the stereotyping of an outside observer. In the public view the Addams district is portrayed as only vaguely and imprecisely delineated.

> For many Chicagoans the Addams area is only an indistinct part of the 'West Side'. At that distance, it is generally labelled an impoverished Negro slum....
>
> The newspapers and, among those who know of the West Side, a smaller number of individuals make a finer distinction by referring to the 'Near West Side'. Here the emphasis shifts from Negroes to Italians....
>
> Among a more select group of people who live adjacent to the Addams area, it is known simply as 'Taylor Street'. Above all, this name implies a connection with the Outfit and Italians....
>
> Doubtless, all these preconceptions are a sort of myth....
>
> (Suttles 1968, pp. 24-5)

Suttles presents these as essentially vague, diffuse and over-generalized perspectives. It is striking to compare them with the section that follows, on 'the local view'. Here the identifications given above are replaced with a lengthy rehearsal of very specific references to places and social categories. Although it is not necessary to reproduce it here, a map at this point (one of a series) helps to reinforce the aura of precise insider knowledge, in contrast with the previous diffuse caricatures:

> To the northeast is 'Greek Town', where the remnant of a Greek neighborhood survives in a few restaurants, nightclubs, and coffee shops. The residents are mostly Mexican, and Addams area residents usually acknowledge that it is the stronghold of a Mexican 'gang' called the 'Potentates'. Directly to the north, across the Eisenhower Expressway, along Van Buren, there is a small Puerto Rican area, which acts like a Balkan 'buffer state' to fend off the Negroes further north....This is the stronghold of the Van Buren Royals, too insignificant to threaten the Addams area, but sufficient to ward off the Negroes between Van Buren and Madison Street....Madison Street itself is

sufficiently far away that Addams area residents can regard it half humorously and half sympathetically; it is the rialto of derelicts and drunks who are a nuisance but not dangerous.

(Suttles 1968, pp.27-8)

And so it goes on. Suttles provides two more pages of detailed topographical information on Addams and its environs, carefully matching dimensions of social difference to the spatial arrangements of streets and blocks. The gang names are provided: 'the Village Deacons', 'the Falcons', 'the Egyptian Vipers', 'the Honchos', 'the Red Ambers'. The formerly vague picture is brought into sharper focus. The contrast is heightened by the accumulation of local references and identifications. In turn the locality is invested with connotations of greater significance: a Balkan buffer state, a Rialto. These latter metaphors are themselves ironic; 'the rialto of derelicts and drunks' especially so.

The contrast between the insider's precise knowledge and the outsider's erroneous common sense constructs a major warrant for the authoritative claim of the ethnography. Sociologists are familiar with the inversions whereby the effects may be achieved. The rhetoric is part and parcel of the recurrent tension between the familiar and the strange. While the sociologist strives to gain familiarity with the setting or culture to be researched, he or she must strive repeatedly to treat it as 'anthropologically strange'. There is a tension between the desire to become a member, thoroughly conversant with the culture, and the desire to maintain a degree of 'distance' from it. It is the pull between 'surrender' and 'discipline' (Lofland and Lofland 1984).

The textual production of 'social worlds' and their difference tends always to what Boon (1982), writing about anthropology, describes as 'the exaggeration of cultures'. The writing of cultural differences, he suggests, is hyperbolic, though the realist monograph and the other genres of anthropology repeatedly overlook their own rhetorical over-statements. Boon concludes that 'ethnographic writing about other cultures consists, like cultures themselves, in an exaggeration of differences' (p.26). The sociologist who trades in contrasts, ironies and differences, no less than the anthropologist who describes the 'exotic', relies upon the rhetorical construction of 'otherness'. They both 'exaggerate' cultures in various ways.

Urban exotica

The urban ethnographer finds weighty significance in the apparently most trivial of scenes and activities. The observer thus overturns implied common-sense perspectives while celebrating his or her sociological insight. Wiseman (1979), for instance, employs such a device while pursuing a classic theme – the discovery of primary 'communities' in the metropolis. Her chosen arena of observation is that of second-hand clothing stores:

Although urban life has been characterized as discouraging primary-type interaction except in areas where people of similar interests see each other on a long-term basis, this is not entirely accurate. Quasi- or fleeting relationships of a primary nature *do* occur in some city settings, either by design (as in the case of some entertainment sites) or by the accident of their social structure and ecology. Furthermore, despite their limited nature, these latter contacts can be very enjoyable. The ... study of second-hand clothing outlets sets forth in some detail how transitory sociability emerges in a mundane setting where people need each other to attain shopping goals as a result of various store policies. There are obviously many similar such special-purpose enclaves of limited *Gemeinschaft* in the supposedly harsh, alienating atmosphere of big city life.

> (Wiseman 1979, p.44)

The analysis and the vocabulary in which it is couched thus play on the contrast between the 'supposed' reality of city life, and the 'accurate' representation to be offered by Wiseman. The concatenation of abstract sociological terms codes the difference between the mundane and the esoteric. This rhetorical function of sociological terminology is not always recognized, though its aesthetic effects are often the subject of adverse comment. No doubt some of the opprobrium heaped on sociological discourse reflects actual readers' sense of exclusion: they are constructed as naïve or mistaken outsiders by the text's contrastive rhetoric.

A very precise parallel can be provided from Nash (1975), who describes the bus ride in somewhat portentous sociological terms. His theme is equivalent to Wiseman's: the 'community'-like social relations to be found in bus-riding. He explicitly contrasts his analysis with prior assumptions: 'Bus riding seems an unlikely setting for feelings and thoughts ordinarily associated with communities or stable groups' (p.99). So the paper begins. By the end of it Nash has established a weighty view of the matter:

Bus riding can be considered a strategic arena and can reveal a great deal about the taken-for-granted knowledge and membership feelings of participants within a particular social setting. Often the quality of *lebenswelt* is much more *gemeinschaftlich* than previously thought. Depending on the inter-relationships among objective conditions of the scene, there is a degree of conduciveness to the acquisition of community in the phenomenon of bus riding.

> (Nash 1975, p.122)

The overall effect may be illustrated from yet another account of an urban 'scene' – the flea market (Maisel 1974). The social significance of the setting is emphasized: it provides the opportunity for capitalist entrepreneurial activity and a sense of adventure:

People play the entrepreneurial game for all it is worth, share in the excitement of trying to outguess the market and outwit one's neighbor. Though flea market vendors are reluctant to specify their usual profits, it is clear that anticipation of a 'good day' – that is, high profits – is the main source of their ambition and labour.... For the market functions fundamentally in the same manner as the high risk, fateful enterprises described by Goffman – it provides participants with a sense of risk, uncertainty, consequential chance – and thus produces vivid experiences usually absent in ordinary social life.

(Maisel 1974, p.503)

The ironic display of unsuspected complexity and seriousness is yet another variant on the theme. It is well exemplified by Marvin Scott's account of horseracing and its associated gambling (Scott 1968). His analysis rests on the exploration of complexity in a social domain that might otherwise pass for 'mere' entertainment. It is a world of intricate culture and calculation. Typically, Scott announces his theme with a shifting viewpoint and a graphic representation of its subject matter (using the figure of hypotyposis):

Heads apart, three glistening thoroughbreds thunder toward the finish line, their riders crouched low with whip arms flailing. As the action on the track reaches its conclusion, the shouting of the fans rises to an ear-splitting crescendo. Driving toward the wire, the three horses are bunched so closely that it is a tossup which will win. To the fans, this is a magnificent struggle of nature – flesh and blood and pounding hoofs – clearly, nature in the raw.

But what appears a natural reality also can be viewed as the construction of man's activities. That is, natural events are often as they ought to be because they are the products of human constructions: social organization makes nature follow our needs.

(Scott 1968, p.vii)

The contrast is sustained when we encounter some of the key elements in the action. What is a horse? one of the chapters asks. It disrupts any taken-for-granted view that 'horse' is an unproblematic category, emphasizing that what a horse is depends on one's point of view: so that

from the standpoint of the player, a horse is an animal that runs 'hard' – regardless of age and sex. The other animals are 'pigs', 'dogs', 'beetles', or 'goats'. What makes a horse a 'horse' is heart. According to this criterion, to be a horse – as fans put it – 'he's gotta have heart'.

(Scott 1968, p.13)

Scott then goes on to introduce another 'insider' perspective: 'From the viewpoint of the breeder, a horse is a thoroughbred' (p.13). He elaborates this by drawing out the strict definitions of 'thoroughbred' employed by the jockey club, emphasizing even more the presence of specialized usage and knowledge. Implicitly, therefore, Scott lays claim to this esoteric knowledge of close acquaintance, contrasting this with the implied outsider's everyday assumptions.

These variations are similar to what Anderson and Sharrock (1983) call the 'enrichment of everyday life': 'Mundane matters such as casual chat, the perambulation of a tea trolley through a hospital ward, the radio exchange between cab driver and dispatch are to be reviewed as socially awesome events' (p.574). Those authors point to the dangers inherent in such a rhetorical device: if everything is a complex and weighty matter, then notions of 'complexity' or seriousness lose their force altogether. Nevertheless, the exploitation of such differences remains commonplace in ethnographic sociology, and still retains the possibility of extremely effective argumentation. In the text, therefore, the ethnographer retains the right to shift perspective, in order to compare and contrast the 'inside' and 'outside', the esoteric and the exoteric, appearance and reality. Boundaries between social worlds are constructed, only to be breached, while fine gradations and structures are created where none was previously suspected.

It may seem obvious, but it is worth noting that the 'difference' that constructs social worlds may be conveyed through the selection of lexical items. The sociologist will be entirely familiar with the way in which ethnographies are liberally sprinkled with local terms – words and phrases. Sometimes these are embedded in interview fragments and other exemplars; sometimes they are taken over by the voice of the ethnographer and used as descriptive terms in their own right. It is a perfectly standard element of methodological advice that the field-worker should collect the 'folk' terminologies and vocabularies of the culture in question. It is part of the methodological stock-in-trade that the situated vocabularies of the setting are constitutive of its culture. It is, therefore, extremely frequently that one finds the text embedding many examples of such terms and typifications.

The rhetorical functions of such textual elements include the production of 'authenticity' in so far as they vouch for the acquisition of native-like competence in the linguistic registers and dialects. They also function as boundary-markers in demarcating the world of 'the other'. The alien or the exotic speak through strange languages. The preservation of the original lexicon serves to heighten the contrast: in the last analysis 'the other' resists translation. Even the same words are revealed as having both everyday and hermetic significance. We have just seen from *The Racing Game* that horse and 'horse' mean different things (and that 'pigs', 'dogs' and so on have their special meanings too). There is, therefore, a constant play of difference transcribed in the choice of language. Some standard ethnographic treatments are sustained very largely by collections of such esoteric terminologies and their connotations. The text thus inscribes the contrast between the vocabulary and usage of local culture, and those of 'mainstream' or 'cosmopolitan' or 'standard' folkways.

The general area of deviance studies furnishes a large number of studies in which ironic contrasts or paradoxical juxtapositions are used to make the point. The title of one collection edited by Jack Douglas encapsulates this sort of contrast in *Deviance and Respectability* (1970). For, contrary to 'everyday', 'common-sense' or 'official' thought, the 'respectable' person may be shown to be 'really' dishonest or immoral, while the deviant may be shown to have his or her code of conduct, form of rationality, ethical standards and so on.

Weinberg's description of naturists trades on some such resonances. As Weinberg (1970) opens his account: 'In our society the public exposure of human sexual organs is proscribed; at the same time, an organized group exists who breach this moral rule. They call themselves "social nudists"' (p.375). But the point of the analysis is to demonstrate that such nudists, although apparently flouting the rules, do so in a highly respectable way. Weinberg's summary of this is as follows:

> The basis for the construction of a situated morality in the nudist camp is provided by the official interpretations that camps maintain regarding the moral means of public heterosexual nudity. These are (1) that nudity and sexuality are unrelated, (2) that there is nothing shameful about exposing the human body, (3) that the abandonment of clothes leads to a feeling of freedom and natural pleasure, and (4) that nude activities, especially the entire body's exposure to the sun, lead to a feeling of physical, mental, and spiritual well-being.
>
> (Weinberg 1970, p.376)

The moral order of the nudist camp is, then, embodied in a number of maxims, which Weinberg summarizes as: No staring; No sex talk; No body contact; No alcoholic beverages; No accentuation of the body; No unnatural attempts at covering the body. Hence the nudist camp, far from being a place of licence or bawdy behaviour (as in popular associations and stereotypes), actually comes over in an almost puritanical context, in which restraints are the order of the day. Those who act in a way congruent with everyday assumptions about heterosexual nudity, by becoming sexually excited, for instance, are regarded as 'unnatural' or 'sick' by Weinberg's nudists. This care with which the nudists manage their respectability is also contrasted with the fact that they 'envision themselves as being labelled deviant by members of the clothed society. They anticipate that if their nudist participation were "known about" they would be socially typed in the following ways: (1) as sexually available or "promiscuous", (2) as "nuts".' Hence, despite their own belief in the 'naturalness' of nudity, and the extreme 'respectability' of nudist camps, the nudists themselves are forced to be secretive about their activities – as if they 'really were' sexually promiscuous and so on.

The paradox of deviance

It is, of course, the common coin of many deviance studies that deviance and respectability are inextricably, even paradoxically, linked. Douglas (1970), for example, writes;

> Deviance and respectability are necessarily linked together: each necessarily implies the other; each is a necessary condition for the existence of the other.

This is by no means simply a matter of abstract and arbitrary definitions given to the terms of sociologists. Deviance and respectability are necessarily linked together in the social meanings of the terms as used by the members of our society in their everyday lives: when we observe and analyse the moral communications in our everyday lives we find that the social meanings of either deviance (immorality) or respectability (morality) can be adequately understood only if reference, whether implicit or explicit, is made to the other, its opposite.

(Douglas 1970, p.3)

Such a perspective is by no means restricted to ethnographic work – and certainly not to interactionist or phenomenological approaches. It is characteristic of functionalist viewpoints as well. Indeed, of functionalism, Matza (1969) remarks in this context that irony was cultivated in the portrayal of deviant worlds and their relation to the social system in general. The 'labelling' perspective on deviance incorporates at its very centre the ironic contrast between deviance and respectability. So-called 'labelling theory' has enjoyed considerable vogue, only to become in turn the focus of vigorous criticism. Again it must be stressed that no attempt is made here to evaluate labelling as sociological theory. Rather, the point here is to note how the labelling perspective trades on the paradoxical interrelationship between official agencies of law and control on the one hand, and the identities of the criminals and deviants on whom they operate, on the other.

From this viewpoint, then, the analytic focus becomes not the search for causes and correlates of crime (as in 'conventional' criminology), but rather the documentation of how deviant identities are socially produced by the organized activities of the controllers. Here, therefore, the labelling approach is founded upon contrast and paradox. The natural attitude of conventional wisdom is overturned, in that it is the controller rather than the controlled who is subject to enquiry. And whereas the law and the lawbreaker are conventionally portrayed as antithetical, in the labelling perspective their relationship is shown as, paradoxically, mutually interdependent.

A rich ironic vein is tapped by Jock Young in his work on drug-takers, where he contrasts 'official' views of the reality of drug-taking with the reality of an observed drug-using sub-culture in London (Young 1971). Significantly, the 'official' view is labelled 'fantasy', Young arguing that it enshrines mistaken ideas on the nature of drug-users, the effects of drugs and so on. Young's description can be summarized as a series of contrasts, between 'reality' (that is, his interpretations of a Notting Hill social world of marijuana users), and the 'fantasy' stereotype (the way Young glosses the portrayals of drug-users in general in the mass media).

	'Reality'	'Fantasy'
1	Highly organized bohemian community.	Isolated drug-users in socially disorganized groups.
2	Clear-cut values: hedonism, spontaneity, expressivity, disdain for work, etc.	Asocial, lacking in values; *or* ideologically motivated group of corrupters of the young.
3	Drug-taking irregular: not essential prerequisite to group membership; instrumental and symbolic use of drug. Drugs important, but not central.	Backbone of the culture; all other activities subordinate to it.
4	User and seller not fixed roles, at street level.	Sharp contrast between the 'pusher' and the buyer – between the corrupter and the corrupted.
5	Psychologically stable individuals.	Immature, unstable young people, led astray by pushers.
6	Marijuana users disdain heroin addicts.	Heroin addicts and marijuana users often indistinguishable.
7	Large numbers of marijuana users in Notting Hill.	Small numbers (though perceived as too large and increasingly rapidly).
8	Effects of marijuana, when taken in a supportive culture, mildly euphoric; psychotic effects rare and temporary.	Exaggerated ambivalence: drugs plunge the user into misery, and hold promise of unlimited pleasure: from extreme sexuality, though aggressive criminality, to wildly psychotic episodes.

The first irony, then, is the fact that the official views of politicians, police-men, mass media and so on, regard the drug-taker as deluded, disoriented, and disorganized – as living in a world of 'fantasy': indeed it is the hallucinogenic property of psychotropic drugs which occupies a central place in the popular and official view of drug-users. Ironically, then, Young argues that it is the guardians of morality and received wisdom who are living in an unreal world. These latter are portrayed as having unreasonable and unfounded beliefs, whereas the mem-bers of the drug-using sub-culture are pictured as rational, balanced members of a stable social world.

The irony of Young's account is redoubled in the implications of the fantasy/reality contrasts. For, he argues, although the official fantasy is essentially unfounded, it can become reality. It becomes a sort of self-fulfilling prophecy, through the mechanism of 'deviancy amplification'. Briefly, the thesis is that although not *essentially* criminal, disorganized, anti-social, the drug-culture can be made that by the activities of agents of social control. Informed by their 'fantasies' the police will crack down on drug-users. In response, the latter will see themselves as increasingly persecuted, will withdraw from mainstream society and go 'underground', and as 'soft' drugs become more difficult to obtain the distribution of such substances may become more dependent on criminal suppliers. In the original 'reality' there is no distinction between the 'user' and the 'pusher'. In the official, 'absolutist' fantasy, the evil pusher and his innocent victim are sharply differentiated. The activities of law enforcers can finally confirm the fantasy into reality, as the drug-user resorts to organized crime.

This is not the place to dwell on this sociological analysis as such – except to point to the difficulty of recognizing the 'pure' or essential characteristics of such drug sub-cultures prior to or independent of the transformations wrought by official agencies, which generate their own version of reality and bring it into being. What is remarkable is the interplay between reality-fantasy-reality and the ironic play which Young makes with such transformations. The argument Young proposes at this point is thus carried forward entirely by means of his use of irony.

Young's analysis is paralleled by Lejeune and Alex (1973). They focus on responses to mugging – such as the 'rugged individualism' of vigilante patrols and self-defence:

> Mugging sets into motion social psychological forces which contribute to increasing the condition of social disorder in the urban community. The mugger's victim adapts to his misfortune by adopting modes of perception and attitudes congruent with a Hobbesian view of man. As a consequence of being a victim, he sees the city as an urban jungle; as a situation where others, particularly strangers, are not be trusted.
>
> (Lejeune and Alex 1973, pp.259-87)

Hence the 'victim' takes on the presumed attributes of the 'evil doers' they respond to. Thus is the irony of the process of 'amplification' recapitulated.

Irony is drawn on quite explicitly by Adler and Adler (1980). They point to a paradox in the life-style and identity of some drug dealers: that is, a tension between the need for secrecy (in order to avoid arrest) and the desire for 'reputation', excitement, power and prestige – 'characteristics inherent in secrecy often lead to its violation'. Adler and Adler describe competing forces in the impression-management of drug-dealers. They outline their strategies for maintaining secrecy and avoiding detection. Those rational interests compete with 'hedonistic' impulses that result in a 'flamboyant and boastful life-style'.

The ambiguities of morality are explored in Ditton's ethnography of pilfering among bread-delivery roundsmen (Ditton 1977). Ditton is unusually explicit about his own textual strategy, not least because of his desire to display the pilfering worker as a rational being. Indeed, Ditton explicitly invokes the 'reasonable person enthymeme' (cf. Edmondson 1984):

> In producing such a consciously theorised ethnography of salesmen, I have followed the rule of grounding the interpretation of fiddling as an 'Everyman Performance'. That is, I have tried to depict sufficient conditions for a reasonable man to consider fiddling to be, under the circumstances, a rational performance. This specific rule is derived from the general axiom that an analysis which portrays a phenomenon as bizarre or strange has failed to understand that phenomenon.
>
> (Ditton 1977, p.12)

His monograph is therefore devoted to persuading an implied reader of the rationality of the salesman's actions. He shows, for instance, that the practice of 'fiddling' is very similar to the 'legitimate' practice of business. The values of the pilferers and of their employees are thus congruent: 'In this broader sense, fiddling is a subculture of legitimate *commerce* itself, (p.173, emphasis in original).

Ditton thus employs well-established rhetorical and argumentative strategies to reveal the reasonable in the deviant, and the essential similarity between the criminal and the legitimate. For the sociologist reader, the plausibility of Ditton's account may be sustained by the use of classic themes. The monograph is ordered in terms of thematic chapters that evoke a paradigmatic set of references and connotations. The chapter titles themselves are a fine example of the rhetorical work that can be achieved by the invocation of appropriate intertextual connotations. The substantive chapters are: 'Process: Becoming a Fiddler'; 'Interaction: Managing Customers'; 'Structure: "Part-Time" Crimes at Wellbread's'; 'Characters: Public Identity Negotiation and Managerial Reaction'; 'Motives: Private Identity Preservation – Getting Caught and Getting Off'. The coupling of formal sociological categories and a local descriptive extension in each chapter title is a noteworthy rhetorical device in its own right: the precariously 'trivial' and ephemeral phenomenon of petty crime is elevated to a plane of overtly scholarly discourse. This transformation in itself plays upon a series of contrasts: between the specific and the general, the topical and the generic, the specific and the archetypal.

Anderson and Sharrock (1983) also summarize this tradition of 'moral reversal' in the sociology of deviance.

> What earned the moral disfavour of society in the behaviour of industrial saboteurs, vandals and hooligans, etc., we were told, was the ostensibly wanton and purposeless nature of the act (note that such attributions were typically never evidenced). A little ethnography could show that one could 'appreciate' these acts. One could find and erect world views and situations in which they were 'logical' and 'purposeful'.
>
> (Anderson and Sharrock 1983, p.577)

Hence, they continue, 'The mad were made sane, hooligans shown to be purposeful, school failures revealed as bright, pornographers acclaimed as socially functional and so on' (p.578).

It is clear that Anderson and Sharrock take a dim view of the use of irony. They are perfectly reasonable in suggesting that its unprincipled use can be dangerous. Unfortunately, they base their arguments and (highly rhetorical) strictures on a mistaken distinction. They tend to endorse a crude distinction between rhetorical and scientific discourse, and are too ready to dismiss the rhetorical as if it were a box of tricks or sleight of hand. They see the trope as mystificatory. Their paper stands in contrast to that of Brown (1983). (The respective papers are, ironically, juxtaposed in the same number of the same journal.) Brown celebrates the use of dialectical irony as a revelatory device. Whereas Anderson and Sharrock portray moral reversal in deviance theory as a cheap trick, Brown endorses its subversive powers:

> For example, we may wish to look at 'crime' from the perspective of 'sociology'. In this instance we could assume a calculated naïveté. The normative jurisprudence of the focal realm, crime, would be de-realized through ironic bracketing, that is, the laws defining 'criminal behavior' would be made a topic rather than a presupposition of the inquiry. The researcher would pretend that there is no known difference between criminal and noncriminal conduct....By thus ironizing the subject matter, we become able to explore the coming to consciousness of the analytic categories of the conventional approach, and to note the interests that such processes and categories may serve.
>
> (Brown 1983, p.561)

Chapter nine

Conclusion: textual possibilities

By way of conclusion it may be as well to recapitulate some of the justifications and caveats with which this book began. Not least in importance is the need to head off some potential misunderstandings of the enterprise.

Confronted by the recognition that sociology is conducted through rhetorical, textual devices, some critics are likely to respond that the 'scientific' status of the subject has been undermined. It remains commonplace, after all, to regard 'rhetoric' as mere ornamentation, or worse. It is seen, perhaps, as the will-o'-the-wisp counterpart to the solid 'fact', indisputable logic, and correct method. Rhetoric may be seen as the enemy of reason. There may be few unreconstructed positivists among contemporary social scientists, but there are many for whom the contrasts of fact and fiction, of rhetoric and science remain tacit articles of faith. But the Enlightenment's divorce of rhetoric from science should not be taken on board by those whose job it is to understand precisely how categories and contrasts like those are produced, shared and reproduced.

My intention throughout this book has in no sense been to discredit sociological ethnography. On the one hand I have paid some attention to the degree to which all 'factual' or authoritative accounts, whether they derive from natural or cultural disciplines, depend upon conventions of textuality. If they are to be recognized *as* authoritative then they must persuade the reader of their plausibility. Moreover, the very interpretative framework implied by a term such as 'discipline' rests upon certain conventions of 'genre'. The status of any discipline is not enhanced by a flat denial of its conventional features, nor by a purblind reluctance to suspend naïve theories of representation. A readiness to question and to examine those conventions, on the other hand, is not *ipso facto* a threat to the decencies of scholarly enquiry.

This point still requires emphasis. If I seek to explore the conventional modes of representation characteristic of a genre, such as ethnography, then I do not see that as an assault on its epistemological security. Ultimately there will be no escape from conventional forms of some sort. It is entirely obvious to any contemporary scholar that there can be no neutral language of description: and that is especially clear when the social and cultural domains are in question. We do not need to endorse an especially strong Sapir-Whorf view of linguistically-determined relativism to recognize that the resources of natural language are themselves conventionally patterned. Different languages, different linguistic communities, use communicative resources differently. When we use natural language to convey social realities – our own or that of others – then we inevitably draw upon those resources and conventions in our scholarly accounts.

However, the post-Saussurean recognition that the linguistic sign is 'arbitrary' does not condemn us to the view that we have lost everything in a sea of whimsical or random semiosis. It is all too easy to take the lessons of 'the sign' and to apply them in unnecessarily literal ways. The fact that linguistic signs derive their meaning from their relations with other signs – paradigmatic and syntagmatic – does not strip them of referential function. Take Saussure's famous example. He refers to the 8.15 train from Zurich to Geneva, and points out that it remains 'the 8.15 train' even if it departs half an hour late. The identification of the train only makes sense in relation to other identifiers within the same system (timetable, destinations, and so on). Our knowledge that there are conventions at work here, and that the domain of Swiss trains (or whatever) is a system of signification does not prevent us from using the conventions to catch the train or giving adequate directions for how to do so to someone else.

The recognition of the textual conventions of ethnography, then, does not rob it of its referential value, nor does it relegate it to a second division of non-sciences. If we comprehend how our understandings of the world are fashioned and conveyed, then we need not fear that self-understanding. Rather than detracting from our scholarly endeavours, an understanding of our textual practices can only strengthen the critical reflection of a mature discipline. As sociology has developed it has indeed grown more self-conscious of its own language. In a sociological universe that has lost its innocence, then, we can hardly escape scrutiny of sociology's language and texts. Ethnomethodology, structuralism and post-structuralism, feminism – these have all contributed to the 'linguistic turn' in our understanding of the social and of the sociological.

Our growing, sometimes uncomfortable, awareness of language and representation has at times revealed a paradox at the heart of the classic ethnographic genre. On the one hand, its adherents – or many of them at any rate – have endorsed a broadly 'interpretative' view of sociology. Especially since the codification of 'qualitative sociology' within an interactionist-cum-phenomenological framework, the practitioners of sociological ethnography have consistently appealed to a special sensitivity to matters of language and meaning. The classic texts of symbolic interactionism – to which appeal is often made – enshrine a professed reverence for language as the vehicle of meaningful human conduct. George Herbert Mead may be appealed to in such contexts for the justification of such a view, and as the progenitor of an intellectual heritage in which language is accorded a central place.

Seen from such an interpretivist perspective, 'language' is no mere transparent medium of otherwise unproblematic communication. Language is constitutive of social reality (of the 'definition of the situation', of 'typifications' and 'labels'). Ethnographers have exhorted one another in their textbooks and courses to pay close attention to the cultural implications of language use: they recognize and collect 'folk terms' and categories; they regard 'member identified types' as major elements in the cultural shaping of perception and action; language is the repository of socially shared experiences; 'vocabularies of motive' are fundamental to social actors' ways of rendering action rational; 'accounts' are to be understood as social action, rather than taken at face value; and so on. The more seriously we take the epistemological foundations that are claimed for modern qualitative sociology, then the more centrally is language placed, and the more it is treated as a problematic topic in its own right.

And yet, until relatively recent years, sociologists in the tradition have been somewhat insouciant about their own uses of language. The language – the texts – of the sociologist has not received anything like the attention that the linguistic practices of those sociologists' 'subjects' have. The ethnography – in sociology and in anthropology – was born with this paradox, this asymmetry. Ethnographers are conscious of the cultural conventions that are their subject-matter, but have all too often remained blissfully unaware of their own cultural conventions.

As observed elsewhere, ethnography in general has become increasingly codified, and increasingly the topic of methodological writing and precept (Hammersley and Atkinson 1983). It is worth noting where that advice has been focused. The acts of social research have been recognized for what they are, social transactions themselves, and a very great deal of the advice on offer is concerned with the social accomplishment of social research. We learn a great deal about how to enter 'the field', how to establish and maintain productive social relationships, how to conduct oneself tactfully and ethically while collecting data, and so forth. Critical self-appraisal on these matters is required of the modern ethnographer. But if the standard textbooks and courses on ethnography are examined, it is clear that not all aspects of the research process are granted equal treatment. There is a chronological element to it: the early phases of fieldwork, such as 'negotiating access', are dwelt on at length (quite properly), as are the crucial 'first days in the field' (equally properly). But as the research process develops, so the standard sources have less and less to say. The voice of critical reflection falls silent and the collective wisdom of the socio-logical community wears progressively thinner. The novice and the experienced ethnographer alike are likely to find remarkably little advice on how to proceed, and little in the way of shared understanding within the scholarly community. There is even a lack of shared vocabulary in which to discuss the available procedures and models. Understandably, few sociologists take a close interest in rhetoric and textual criticism, and there are few sources of informed criticism and commentary.

A major and recent exception has been provided by Van Maanen (1988), who has attempted the task of formulating some practical advice, as well as more general appreciation, concerning textual formats and styles of ethnographic reportage. It remains to be seen whether Van Maanen's work, together with this book and others, will be translated into self-conscious methodological reflection by ethnographers themselves.

In the absence of any explicit frames of reference for reflexive awareness there has been a tendency, and a danger, for ethnography to be couched in textual forms that are themselves taken-for-granted. From its early years in anthropology and sociology the ethnographic monograph grew out of genres – the realist novel, the travel account, investigative journalism – that treated language relatively unproblematically. The conventions of 'realist' and 'factual' writing are themselves taken for granted. Whereas the interpretative sociologist is committed to a view of language that treats it as constitutive of reality, the ethnographic text too often seems to treat its own language as a transparent medium. There is in that a clear paradox and danger.

Bruyn (1966) has enunciated the dangers of sociological language that escapes the control of critical scrutiny:

> Language, if left unstudied and unsupervised, may even come to control its creators. The social scientist may well become like the sorcerer's apprentice; he can weave a magic and a spell with his words about society which can take the shape of myths having a force on the minds of men not unlike the myths of ancient times. Scientific language, then, must be studied not for its own sake, as in linguistics, but also for other reasons, including the necessity of reducing the magical power that comes with use and misuse of language in social and political life.
>
> (Bruyn 1966, p.125)

It is not only the 'magical' power of words that needs attention: the mundane language of everyday sociological description demands our vigilance. We certainly cannot rely upon the unexamined conventions of a genre through which social phenomena are represented. It is the responsibility of the ethnographer to treat reading and writing seriously in the act of 'interpretation' of cultural forms.

If we recognize – as we must – that our acts of research inevitably implicate us and involve us in the everyday construction of social reality, then we must also recognize that our *accounts* of the social world are equally implicated. Our textual practices themselves constitute the social realities constructed and reconstructed in ethnographic writing. Theory and method are inextricably linked: they are equally closely tied to modes of writing.

It would be wrong, however, to conclude this book with the implicit message that ethnography – and interpretative sociology more generally – has generated no explicit interest in the textual forms of sociological writing. Reference has already been made to the work of Susan Krieger, who, in two monographs, has quite explicitly tried to use 'literary' forms to construct her texts, and who has contributed to the methodological literature in that vein also. I have suggested that her actual efforts have not been an unqualified success, but they are important experiments in sociological writing for all that. In a similar vein one must draw attention to the work of Bluebond-Langer, which embeds dramatic reconstructions within more 'conventional' ethnographic writing to depict the experiences of dying children.

Drawing on rather different sorts of subject-matter (in the sociology of science for the most part), Mulkay has been more active than any other in exploring the textual possibilities for sociological production. Mulkay's empirical subject-matter includes the texts (written and spoken) of scientists' discourse. In exploring the forms of argument and persuasion, and the ritual forms of politeness and modesty, Mulkay has also drawn on alternative conventions of reportage. He has felt free to present his analyses in the form of dialogues, one-act plays and parodies (cf. Mulkay 1985). On the use of parody, for instance, Mulkay offers the following observation, that all sociological analysis is a kind of 'parody'. It starts with texts – 'original' texts such as interview transcripts, field notes or documents – and is then couched in a 'secondary' text.

> One necessary feature of the secondary, analytical text is that it differs from the original text. If the secondary text did not differ from the original text, it would be a mere repetition of that text and would be analytically empty. The secondary text inevitably selects from the original text, summarizes it, ignores part of it, rephrases it, puts it in a new context, identifies its important and unimportant features, simplifies it, and so on. In other words, the analytical text systematically deviates from and, in this sense, distorts the original text as it performs analytical work on that text and re-presents it for analytical purposes. This systematic distortion is captured in the frequently used distinction between raw data (original text) and results or findings. The raw data are manipulated, re-ordered and re-presented in the analytical text to reveal their sociological meaning.
>
> (Mulkay 1985, pp.237-8)

The element of 'parody' captures the nature of secondary, analytical sociology, Mulkay proposes, in that

> a parody is a secondary text which is closely based on (alongside of) an original text, but which differs from the original text in ways which reveal the true nature of the original text (its central features) and at the same time the superiority of the secondary text (undermine the standing of the original text).
>
> (Mulkay 1985, p.238)

Hence parody may be a form of sociological analysis, and sociological analysis has elements of the parodic. Its distance and difference from the original 'texts' give it an ironic tone (cf. Woolgar 1983), and its re-ordering of reality may result in texts of a surrealist character (Clifford 1981).

Mulkay's own textual experiments highlight the artful character of *all* sociological argument, not only his own contrivances and conceits. He helps us to recognize the conventions, and to recognize the availability of alternative conventions. (For although Mulkay's essays are couched in ways that are not conventional for sociology, they still conform to conventions of other, more 'literary' genres.) The use of 'alternative' literary forms is also exemplified in a more recent collection of papers in the sociology of science (Woolgar 1988). Various contributors to that volume employ the 'other voice' device to express ideas in dialogue form (for example, Woolgar and Ashmore 1988; Pinch and Pinch 1988). The latter paper is co-authored by 'the same' author in two voices, for instance. The contributors' collective concern is the exploration of 'reflexivity': of the constitutive work of representations in the natural and social sciences. They successfully point out that a sociology that relativizes the natural–scientific cannot claim exemption for itself. We must recognize the contrivance of our own work too. Their work thus leads to a self-conscious textuality, simultaneously foregrounding the work of producing the text and the observations inscribed therein. The 'alternative' modes of presentation can be revealing, and can help to make the sociological work itself anthropologically strange. Like many such innovations it also runs the risk of descent into 'cleverness' and pretension.

There is no need for sociologists all to flock towards 'alternative' literary modes. The point of the argument is *not* to suggest that suddenly, from now on, sociological ethnography should be represented through pastiche of literary forms. The discipline will not be aided by the unprincipled adoption of any particular textual practices, 'literary' or otherwise. On the other hand, we must always be aware of the fact that there are many available styles, even within the domain of 'factual' reporting. Critics such as Anderson (1987) have alerted us to the stylistic varieties of contemporary non-fiction. Anderson's study of Wolfe, Capote, Mailer and Didion shows clearly that each author – while working within the domain of non-fictional reportage – has a very distinctive voice. The 'new journalism' and the 'non-fiction novel' are, of course, genres where 'literary' values are especially salient (cf. Weber 1980; Hollowell 1977). Contemporary writing readily blurs and undermines the boundaries between 'fact' and 'fiction', and as Anderson's work emphasizes, style itself constitutes the argument of the non-fictional.

The ethnography, then, cannot inhabit a world of texts where conventionality is taken for granted, or where language is treated as unproblematic. The fully mature ethnography requires a reflexive awareness of its own writing, the possibilities and limits of its own language, and a principled exploration of its modes of representation. Not only do we need to cultivate a self-conscious construction of ethnographic texts, but also a readiness to *read* texts from a more 'literary-critical' perspective. Sociologists and their students must cultivate the discipline of reading their own and others' arguments for their stylistic and rhetorical properties.

These are not easy or comforting disciplines to embrace. They certainly do not make the tasks of sociological understanding any easier. But then, any increase in critical self-consciousness is likely to make one's work more demanding. It is the sloppy and the glib that are easy; and a facile reliance on unexamined rhetorical forms is certainly not the way to achieve sociological insights. Let us conclude on a more optimistic note, however. For decades the ethnographer has succeeded in translating hard work 'in the field' into texts of cultural representation and interpretation. The use of the ethnographic genre has contributed to the systematic self-understanding of contemporary society. The ethnographic genre is flourishing in modern sociology, and will continue to do so. It can only develop even more vigorously and productively if its adherents continue to expand their understanding to encompass their own processes and products. A critical awareness in no way undermines the value or need of empirical research. This book will have failed if it seems to render the work of ethnography less important, or even impossible. It will have succeeded if it encourages others to find a new complexity and a new source of fascination in their own writing and the writing of others.

References

Adler, P.A. and Adler P. (1980), 'The Irony of Secrecy in the Drug World'. *Urban Life*, 8 (4): 447–65.

Anderson, C. (1987) *Style as Argument: Contemporary American Nonfiction*. Carbondale and Edwardsville: Southern Illinois University Press.

Anderson, D.C. (1978) 'Some Organizational Features in the Local Production of a Plausible Text'. *The Philosophy of the Social Sciences*, 8: 113–35.

Anderson, D.C. and Sharrock, W.W. (1983) 'Irony as a Methodological Theory: A Sketch of Four Sociological Variations'. *Poetics Today*, 4 (3): 565–79.

Anderson, N. (1923) *The Hobo: The Sociology of Homeless Men*. Chicago: University of Chicago Press.

Ankersmit, F.R. (1983) *Narrative Logic: A Semantic Analysis of the Historian's Language*. The Hague: Nijhoff.

Atkinson, P.A. (1983) 'Writing Ethnography'. In H.J. Helle (ed.), *Kultur und Institution*. Berlin: Duncker und Humblot.

Barthes, R. (1967) *Writing Degree Zero*. London: Cape.

————(1968) 'L'Effet de Réel'. *Communications*, 11: 84–9.

————(1974) *S/Z*. New York: Hill & Wang.

Bazerman, C. (1981) 'What Written Knowledge Does: Three Examples of Academic Discourse'. *Philosophy of the Social Sciences*, 11 (3): 361–87.

————(1987) 'Codifying the Social Scientific Style: The APA *Publication Manual* as a Behaviorist Rhetoric'. In J.S. Nelson, A. Megill and D.N. McCloskey (eds), *The Rhetoric of the Human Sciences*. Madison: University of Wisconsin Press.

Becker, H.S. (1986) *Writing for Social Scientists*. Chicago: University of Chicago Press.

Becker, H.S., Geer, B., Hughes, E.C. and Strauss, A.L. (1961) *Boys in White: Student Culture in Medical School*. Chicago: University of Chicago Press.

Beer, G.P.K. (1983) *Darwin's Plots: Evolutionary Narrative in Darwin, George Eliot, and Nineteenth Century Fiction*. London: Routledge & Kegan Paul.

Benveniste, E. (1970) *Problems in General Linguistics*. Miami: University of Miami Press.

Berger, P. and Luckmann, T. (1966) *The Social Construction of Reality*. London: Allen Lane.

Bigus, O. (1972) 'The Milkman and His Customer: A Cultivated Relationship'. *Urban Life and Culture*, 1: 131–65.

Blau, P. and Duncan, O.D. (1967) *The American Occupational Structure*. New York: John Wiley & Sons.

Bluebond-Langer, M. (1980) *The Private Worlds of Dying Children*. Princeton: Princeton University Press.

Boon, J.A. (1982) *Other Tribes, Other Scribes: Symbolic Anthropology in the Comparative Study of Cultures, Histories, Religions, and Texts.* Cambridge: Cambridge University Press.

————(1983) 'Functionalists Write Too: Frazer/Malinowski and the Semiotics of the Monograph'. *Semiotica*, 46 (2–4): 131–49.

Brown, R.H. (1977) *A Poetic for Sociology*. Cambridge: Cambridge University Press.

————(1983) 'Dialectical Irony, Literary Form and Sociological Theory'. *Poetics Today*, 4 (3): 543–64.

Bruyn, S. (1966) *The Human Perspective: The Methodology of Participant Observation*. Englewood Cliffs, NJ: Prentice-Hall.

Bulmer, M. (1984) *The Chicago School of Sociology: Institutionalization, Diversity and the Rise of Sociological Research*. Chicago: University of Chicago Press.

Burgess, E.W. (1930) 'Discussion'. In C.R. Shaw, *The Jack-Roller*. Chicago: University of Chicago Press.

Cahill, S.E. (1985) 'Meanwhile backstage: public bathrooms and the integration order'. *Urban Life*, 14 (1): 33–58.

Campbell, J.A. (1987) 'Charles Darwin: Rhetorician of Science'. In J.S. Nelson, A. Megill and D.N. McCloskey (eds), *The Rhetoric of the Human Sciences*. Madison: University of Wisconsin Press.

Carey, J.J. (1975) *Sociology and Public Affairs: The Chicago School*. Beverly Hills: Sage.

Castaneda, C. (1968) *The Teachings of Don Juan*. Berkeley: University of California Press.

Clegg, S (1985) 'Feminist Methodology – Fact or Fiction?' *Quality and Quantity*, 19 (1): 83–9.

Clifford, J. (1981) 'On Ethnographic Surrealism'. *Comparative Studies in Society and History*, 23 (4): 539–64.

————(1986) 'On Ethnographic Allegory'. In J. Clifford and G.E. Marcus (eds)., *Writing Culture: The Poetics and Politics of Ethnography*. Berkeley: University of California Press.

————(1988) *The Predicament of Culture*. Cambridge, Mass.: Harvard University Press.

Clifford, J. and Marcus, G.E. (eds) (1986) *Writing Culture: The Poetics and Politics of Ethnography*. Berkeley: University of California Press.

Cowley, M. (1950) 'A Natural History of American Naturalism'. In S. Persons (ed.), *Evolutionary Thought in America*. New Haven, Conn.: Yale University Press.

Crapanzano, V. (1986) 'Hermes' Dilemma: The Masking of Subversion in Ethnographic Description'. In J. Clifford and G.E. Marcus (eds), *Writing Culture: The Poetics and Politics of Ethnography*. Berkeley: University of California Press.

Cressey, P.G. (1971) 'The taxi-dance hall as a social world'. In J.F. Short Jr (ed.), *The Social Fabric of the Metropolis: Contributions of the Chicago School of Urban Sociology*. Chicago: University of Chicago Press.

Culler, J. (1975) *Structuralist Poetics: Structuralism, Linguistics and the Study of Literature*. London: Routledge & Kegan Paul.

————(1983) *Barthes*. London: Fontana.

————(1988) *Framing the Sign*. Oxford: Basil Blackwell.

Danto, A.C. (1985) *Narration and Knowledge*. New York: Columbia University Press.

Davis, F. (1972) *Illness, Interaction and the Self*. Belmont, Ca: Wadsworth.

————(1974) 'Stories and Sociology'. *Urban Life and Culture*, 3 (3): 310–16.

Ditton, J. (1977) *Part-Time Crime: An Ethnography of Fiddling and Pilferage*. London: Macmillan.

Dixon, C. (1972) 'Guided Options as a Pattern of Control in a Headstart Program'. *Urban Life and Culture*, 1 (2): 203–17.

Dore, R. (1973) *British Factory – Japanese Factory*. London: Allen & Unwin.

Douglas, J. (ed.) (1970) *Deviance and Respectability: The Social Construction of Moral Meanings*. New York: Basic Books.

Drake, St C. and Cayton, H.R. (1945) *Black Metropolis: A Study of Negro Life in a Northern City*. New York: Harcourt Brace.

Eco, U. (1983) *The Name of the Rose*. London: Secker & Warburg.

Edgerton, R.B. (1979) *Alone Together: Social Order on an Urban Beach*. Berkeley: University of California Press.

Edmondson, R. (1984) *Rhetoric in Sociology*. London: Macmillan.

Emerson, J. (1970) 'Behavior in Private Places: Sustaining Definitions of Reality in Gynecological Examinations'. In H.P. Dreitzel (ed.), *Recent Sociology No. 2: Patterns of Communicative Behavior*. New York: Macmillan.

Evans-Pritchard, E. (1940) *The Nuer*. Oxford: Clarendon Press.

Fabian, J. (1983) *Time and the Other: How Anthropology Makes its Object*. New York: Columbia University Press.

Faris, R.E.L. (1970) *Chicago Sociology: 1920–1932*. Chicago: University of Chicago Press.

Farrell, J.T. (1954) *Reflections at Fifty and Other Essays*. New York: Vanguard.

Festinger, L., Riecken, W. and Schachter, S. (1964) *When Prophecy Fails*. New York: Harper & Row.

Forster, E.M. (1927) *Aspects of the Novel*. London: Edward Arnold.

————(1959) *A Passage to India*. Harmondsworth: Penguin.

Fowler, A. (1982) *Kinds of Literature: An Introduction to the Theory of Genres and Modes*. London: Oxford University Press.

Fowler, R. (1977) *Linguistics and the Novel*. London: Methuen.

Gans, H. (1962) *The Urban Villagers: Group and Class in the Life of Italian-Americans*. New York: Free Press.

Geertz, C. (1973) *The Interpretation of Cultures*. New York: Basic Books.

————(1983) 'Slide Show: Evans-Pritchard's African Transparencies'. *Raritan*, 3 (Fall): 62–80.

————(1988) *Works and Lives: The Anthropologist as Author*. Cambridge: Polity.

Geis, G. (1982) 'The Jack-Roller: The Appeal, the Person, and the Impact'. In J. Snodgrass, *The Jack-Roller at Seventy: A Fifty-Year Follow-Up*. Lexington, Mass.: Lexington Books.

Genette, G. (1980) *Narrative Discourse*. Ithaca, NY: Cornell University Press.

Gilbert, G.N. (1977) 'Referencing as Persuasion'. *Social Studies of Science*, 7 (1): 113–22.

Gilbert, G.N. and Mulkay, M. (1980) *Opening Pandora's Box: A Sociological Analysis of Scientists' Discourse*. Cambridge: Cambridge University Press.

Gillespie, C.C. (1960) *The Edge of Objectivity*. Princeton: Princeton University Press.

Goffman, E. (1963) *Behavior in Public Places: Notes on the Social Organisation of Gatherings*. Glencoe: Free Press.

————(1967) 'On Face Work' in *Interaction Ritual*. London: Allen Lane.

Goldthorpe, J., Lockwood, D., Bechhofer, F. and Platt, J. (1968a) *The Affluent Worker: Attitudes and Behaviour*. Cambridge: Cambridge University Press.

————(1968b) *The Affluent Worker: Political Attitudes and Behaviour*. Cambridge: Cambridge University Press.

————(1969) *The Affluent Worker in the Class Structure*. Cambridge: Cambridge University Press.

Gouldner, A. (1954) *Patterns of Industrial Bureaucracy*. New York: Free Press.

Greimas, A.J. (1966) *Sémantique Structurale*. Paris: Larousse.

Gusfield, J. (1976) 'The literary rhetoric of science: comedy and pathos in drinking driver research'. *American Sociological Review*, 41: 16–34.

Hamblin, D.H. (1974) 'The Counsellor and Alienated Youth'. *British Journal of Guidance and Counselling*, 2 (Jan): 87–95.

Hammersley, M. and Atkinson, P. (1983) *Ethnography: Principles in Practice*. London: Tavistock.

Hayner, N. (1929) 'Hotel Life and Personality'. In E.W. Burgess (ed.), *Personality and the Social Group*. Chicago: University of Chicago Press.

Heath, S. (1972) *The Nouveau Roman: A Study in the Practice of Writing*. London: Elek.

Herzfeld, M. (1983a) 'Signs in the Field: Prospects and Issues for Semiotic Anthropology'. *Semiotica*, 46 (2–4): 99–106.

————(1983b) 'Looking Both Ways: The Ethnographer in the Text'. *Semiotica*, 46 (2–4): 151–66.

Hexter, J.H. (1968) 'Historiography: The Rhetoric of History'. In D.L. Sills (ed.), *International Encyclopedia of the Social Sciences*. New York: Crowell, Collier Macmillan.

Hey, V. (1986) *Patriarchy and Pub Culture*, London: Tavistock.

Hollowell, J. (1977) *Fact and Fiction: The New Journalism and the Nonfiction Novel*. Chapel Hill: University of North Carolina Press.

Hughes, E.C. (1943) *French Canada in Transition*. London: Kegan Paul.

Humphreys, L. (1970) *Tearoom Trade: A Study of Homosexual Encounters in Public Places*. Chicago: Aldine.

Jacobs, J. (1969) 'Symbolic Bureaucracy: A Case Study of a Social Welfare Agency'. *Social Forces*, 47 (June): 413–22.

————(1974) *Fun City: An Ethnographic Study of a Retirement Community*. New York: Holt, Rinehart & Winston.

Jakobson, R. (1956) 'Two aspects of language'. In R. Jakobson and M. Halle, *Fundamentals of Language*. The Hague: Mouton.

Junker, B. (1960) *Field Work*. Chicago: University of Chicago Press.

Karp, D. (1980) 'Observing Behavior in Public Places: Problems and Strategies'. In W.B. Shaffir, R.A. Stebbins and A. Turowetz (eds), *Fieldwork Experience: Qualitative Approaches to Social Research*. New York: St Martin's Press.

Keiser, R.L. (1970) 'Fieldwork Among the Vice Lords of Chicago'. In G.D. Spindler (ed.), *Being an Anthropologist*. New York: Holt, Rinehart & Winston.

Klamer, A. (1987) 'As If Economists and their Subjects were Rational'. In J.S. Nelson, A. Megill and D.N. McCloskey (eds), *The Rhetoric of the Human Sciences*. Madison: University of Wisconsin Press.

Klockars, C.B. (1974) *The Professional Fence*. New York: Free Press.

Krieger, S. (1979a) *Hip Capitalism*. Beverly Hills: Sage.

————(1979b) 'Research and the Construction of a Text'. In N.K. Denzin (ed.), *Studies in Symbolic Interaction*. Vol. 2, Greenwich, Conn.: JAI Press.

————(1983) *The Mirror Dance: Identity in a Women's Community*. Philadelphia: Temple University Press.

————(1984) 'Fiction and Social Science'. In N.K. Denzin (ed.), *Studies in Symbolic Interaction*. Vol. 5, Greenwich, Conn.: JAI Press.

Ladurie, E. Le R. (1978) *Montaillou: Cathars and Catholics in a French Village*. London: Scolar Press.

Landau, M. (1984) 'Human Evolution as Narrative'. *American Scientist*, 72 (May–June): 262–8.

——————(1987) 'Paradise Lost: The Theme of Terrestriality in Human Evolution'. In J.S. Nelson, A. Megill and D.N. McCloskey (eds), *The Rhetoric of the Human Sciences*. Madison: University of Wisconsin Press.

Latour, B. and Woolgar, S. (1979) *Laboratory Life: The Construction of Scientific Facts*. Beverly Hills: Sage.

Law, J. and Williams, R.J. (1982) 'Putting the Facts Together: A Study of Scientific Persuasion'. *Social Studies of Science*, 12 (4): 535–58.

Leach, E.R. (1970), *Lévi-Strauss*. London: Fontana.

Lejeune, R. and Alex, N. (1973) 'On being mugged: the event and its aftermath'. *Urban Life*, 2 (3): 259–87.

Lepenies, W. (1988) *Between Literature and Science: The Rise of Sociology*. Cambridge: Cambridge University Press.

Lévi-Strauss, C. (1972) *Structural Anthropology*, Harmondsworth: Penguin.

Lewis, O. (1959) *Five Families: Mexican Case Studies in the Culture of Poverty*. New York: Basic Books.

Liebow, E. (1967) *Tally's Corner, Washington D.C.: A Study of Negro Streetcorner Men*. London: Routledge & Kegan Paul.

Lodge, D. (1977) *The Modes of Modern Writing*. London: Edward Arnold.

Lofland, J. (1971) *Analyzing Social Settings: A Guide to Qualitative Observation and Analysis*. Belmont, Ca: Wadsworth.

——————(1974) 'Styles of Reporting Qualitative Field Research'. *American Sociologist*, 9 (Aug): 101–11.

——————(1977) *Doomsday Cult* (enlarged edn). New York: Irvington. First edn 1966, Englewood Cliffs, NJ: Prentice-Hall.

Lofland, J. and Lofland, L. (1984) *Analyzing Social Settings* (2nd edn). Belmont, Ca: Wadsworth.

Lofland, L.H. (1974) 'The "Thereness" of Women: A Selective Review of Urban Sociology'. In M. Millman and R.M. Kanter (eds), *Another Voice: Feminist Perspectives on Social Life and Social Science*. New York: Anchor Books.

Macauley, R. and Lanning, G. (1964) *Technique in Fiction*. New York: Harper & Row.

McCloskey, D.N. (1983) 'The Rhetoric of Economics'. *Journal of Economic Literature*, 21 (June): 481–517.

——————(1985) *The Rhetoric of Economics*. Madison: University of Wisconsin Press.

McHale, B. (1978) 'Free Indirect Discourse: A Survey of Recent Accounts'. *Poetics and Theory of Literature*, 3: 249–87.

Maisel, R. (1974) 'The flea market as an action scene'. *Urban Life*, 2 (4): 488–505.

March, J. (1979) 'Introduction'. In S. Krieger, *Hip Capitalism*. Beverly Hills: Sage.

Marcus, G.E. (1986) 'Contemporary Problems of Ethnography in the Modern World System'. In J. Clifford and G.E. Marcus (eds), *Writing Culture: The Poetics and Politics of Ethnography*. Berkeley: University of California Press.

Matza, D. (1969) *Becoming Deviant*. Englewood Cliffs, NJ: Prentice Hall.

Megill, A. and McCloskey, D.N. (1987) 'The Rhetoric of History'. In J.S. Nelson, A. Megill and D.N. McCloskey (eds), *The Rhetoric of the Human Sciences*. Madison: University of Wisconsin Press.

Merton, R.K., Reaer, G.G. and Kendall, P.L. (1957) *The Student Physician*. Cambridge, Mass.: Harvard University Press.

Miller, S.M. (1952) 'The Participant Observer and "Over-Rapport"'. *American Sociological Review*, 17 (1): 97–9.

Mills, C.W. (1959) *The Sociological Imagination*. London: Oxford University Press.

Moi, T. (1985) *Sexual/Textual Politics*. London: Methuen.

Mulkay, M.J. (1985) *The Word and the World: Explorations in the Form of Sociological Analysis*. London: George Allen & Unwin.

Nash, J. (1975) 'Bus Riding: Community on Wheels'. *Urban Life*, 4 (1): 99–124.

Nelson, J.S., Megill, A. and McCloskey, D.N. (eds) (1987) *The Rhetoric of the Human Sciences*. Madison: University of Wisconsin Press.

Peirce, C.S. (1931-58) *Collected Papers*. Cambridge, Mass.: Harvard University Press.

Pinch, T. and Pinch, T. (1988) 'Reservations About Reflexivity and New Literary Forms, or Why Let the Devil Have All the Good Tunes?' In S. Woolgar (ed.), *Knowledge and Reflexivity: New Frontiers in the Sociology of Knowledge*. London: Sage.

Plummer, K. (1983) *Documents of Life*. London: George Allen & Unwin.

Pratt, M.L. (1986a) 'Fieldwork in Common Places'. In J. Clifford and G.E. Marcus (eds), *Writing Culture: The Poetics and Politics of Ethnography*. Berkeley: University of California Press.

————(1986b) 'Scratches on the Face of the Country: Or, What Mr Barrow Saw in the Land of the Bushmen'. In L. Gates Jr (ed.), *'Race', Writing, and Difference*. Chicago: University of Chicago Press.

Propp, V. (1958) *Morphology of the Folktale*. Bloomington: Indiana Research Center in Anthropology.

Rex, J. and Moore, R. (1967) *Race, Community and Conflict*. London: Oxford University Press.

Rimmon-Kenan, S. (1983) *Narrative Fiction: Contemporary Poetics*. London: Methuen.

Rock, P. (1979) *The Making of Symbolic Interactionism*. London: Macmillan.

Rosaldo, R. (1986) 'From the Door of His Tent'. In J. Clifford and G.E. Marcus (eds), *Writing Culture: The Poetics and Politics of Ethnography*. Berkeley: University of California Press.

Schön, D.A. (1963) *The Displacement of Concepts*. London: Tavistock.

Scott, M. (1968) *The Racing Game*. Chicago: Aldine.

Shaw, C. (1930) *The Jack-Roller*. Chicago: University of Chicago Press.

Shuval, J. (1975) 'From "Boy" to "Colleague": Processes of Role Transformation in Professional Socialization'. *Social Science and Medicine*, 9: 413–20.

Silverman, D. (1975) *Reading Castaneda*. London: Routledge & Kegan Paul.

Small, H.G. (1978) 'Cited Documents as Concept Symbols'. *Social Studies of Science*, 8 (3): 327–40.

Snodgrass, J. (1982) *The Jack-Roller at Seventy: A Fifty-Year Follow-Up*. Lexington, Mass.: Lexington Books.

Spencer, J. (1989) 'Anthropology as a kind of writing'. *Man*, 24 (1): 145–64.

Spradley, J.P. and Mann, B.J. (1975) *The Cocktail Waitress*. New York: John Wiley & Sons.

Stanley, L. and Wise, S. (1983) *Breaking Out: Feminist Consciousness and Feminist Research*. London: Routledge & Kegan Paul.

Strathern, M. (1987) 'The Limits of Auto-Anthropology', in A. Jackson (ed.), *Anthropology at Home*. London: Tavistock.

Sutherland, E.H. (1937) *The Professional Thief*. Chicago: University of Chicago Press.

Suttles, G.D. (1968) *The Social Order of the Slum*. Chicago: University of Chicago Press.

Thomas, W.I. (1923) *The Unadjusted Girl*. Boston: Little, Brown & Co.

Thrasher, F. (1927) *The Gang*. Chicago: University of Chicago Press.

Todorov, T. (1968) 'Introduction, Le Vraisemblable'. *Communications*, 11: 1–4.

————(1972) 'Language and Literature'. In R. Macksey and E. Donato (eds), *The Structuralist Controversy*. Baltimore: Johns Hopkins University Press.

————(1977) *The Poetics of Prose*. Oxford: Basil Blackwell.

Tomashevski, B. (1965) 'Thematics'. In L.T. Lemon and M.J. Reis (eds), *Russian Formalist Criticism*. Lincoln: University of Nebraska Press.

Van Maanen, J. (1988) *Tales of the Field: On Writing Ethnography*. Chicago: University of Chicago Press.

Weber, R. (1980) *The Literature of Fact: Literary Nonfiction in American Writing*. Athens: Ohio University Press.

Weedon, C. (1987) *Feminist Practice and Poststructuralist Theory*. Oxford: Basil Blackwell.

Weinberg, M.S. (1970) 'The Nudist Management of Respectability: Strategy for, and Consequences of, the Construction of a Situated Morality'. In J. Douglas (ed.), *Deviance and Respectability: The Social Construction of Moral Meanings*. New York: Basic Books.

White, H. (1973) *Metahistory: The Historical Imagination in Nineteenth Century Europe*. Baltimore: Johns Hopkins University Press.

Whyte, W.F. (1981) *Street Corner Society: The Social Structure of an Italian Slum*. Third edn Chicago: University of Chicago Press. First edn 1955.

Williams, M.D. (1981) *On the Street Where I Lived*. New York: Holt, Rinehart & Winston.

Willis, P. (1977) *Learning to Labour: How Working Class Kids Get Working Class Jobs*. Farnborough: Saxon House.

Wiseman, J.P. (1979) 'Close encounters of the quasi-primary kind; sociability in urban second-hand clothing stores'. *Urban Life*, 8 (1): 23–51.

Woodward, J. (1965) *Industrial Organization: Theory and Practice*. London: Oxford University Press.

Woolgar, S. (1983) 'Irony in the Social Study of Science'. In K.D. Knorr-Cetina and M.J. Mulkay (eds), *Science Observed: Perspectives on the Social Study of Science*. Beverly Hills: Sage.

————(ed.) (1988) *Knowledge and Reflexivity: New Frontiers in the Sociology of Knowledge*. London: Sage.

Woolgar, S. and Ashmore, M. (1988) 'The Next Step: An Introduction to the Reflexive Project'. In S. Woolgar (ed.), *Knowledge and Reflexivity*. London: Sage.

Yearley, S. (1981) 'Textual Persuasion: The Role of Social Accounting in the Construction of Scientific Arguments'. *Philosophy of Social Science*, 11: 409–35.

Young, J. (1971) *The Drugtakers: The Social Meaning of Drug Use*. London: Paladin.

Young, R.M. (1985) *Darwin's Metaphor*. Cambridge: Cambridge University Press.

Zorbaugh, H.W. (1929) *The Gold Coast and the Slum*. Chicago: University of Chicago Press.

Index